ROUTLEDGE LIBRA
ECONOMICS AN

Volume

INTERVEN
THE MIXED I

INTERVENTION IN THE MIXED ECONOMY

The Evolution of British Industrial Policy 1964–72

STEPHEN YOUNG
WITH
A. V. LOWE

Routledge
Taylor & Francis Group
LONDON AND NEW YORK

First published in 1974 by Croom Helm Ltd.

This edition first published in 2026
by Routledge
4 Park Square, Milton Park, Abingdon, Oxon OX14 4RN

and by Routledge
605 Third Avenue, New York, NY 10158

Routledge is an imprint of the Taylor & Francis Group, an informa business

British Library Cataloguing in Publication Data
A catalogue record for this book is available from the British Library

ISBN: 978-1-032-97576-4 (Set)
ISBN: 978-1-041-12965-3 (Volume 19) (hbk)
ISBN: 978-1-041-12970-7 (Volume 19) (pbk)
ISBN: 978-1-003-66744-5 (Volume 19) (ebk)

DOI: 10.4324/9781003667445

Publisher's Note
The publisher has gone to great lengths to ensure the quality of this reprint but points out that some imperfections in the original copies may be apparent.

Disclaimer
The publisher has made every effort to trace copyright holders and would welcome correspondence from those they have been unable to trace.

Intervention in the Mixed Economy

THE EVOLUTION OF BRITISH INDUSTRIAL POLICY 1964-72

STEPHEN YOUNG with A.V. LOWE

CROOM HELM, LONDON

First published 1974
Reprinted 1975

Croom Helm Ltd
2–10 St. John's Road London SW11

ISBN 0-85664-098-0

Printed in Great Britain
by Biddles of Guildford

CONTENTS

To the memory of Benedict Lundy

PREFACE

The broad object of this book is to discuss the problem of intervention in the mixed economy by analysing some of the most important aspects of British industrial policy between 1964 and 1972. It was in 1964 that what turned out to be an interventionist Labour Government came to power. The importance of 1972 was that it witnessed, with the passage of the 1972 Industry Act, the Conservative Government's retreat from its attempt to 'disengage' from the affairs of private industry. These are not hard and fast dates though, as the periods before 1964, and between 1972 and the election of February 1974 are discussed in some respects. Although the subject of the nationalised industries does arise, the analysis concentrates on the private sector, and despite the recent growth of the service sector, on manufacturing industry. Most government intervention in the private sector has been directed towards the latter, which accounts for about a third of Britain's Gross National Product, provides employment for about a third of the working population, and contributes two-thirds of Britain's foreign trade earnings. It is impossible in such a short space to provide a fully comprehensive account of the phenomenon of intervention in a mixed economy like Britain's. The discussion focuses mainly on the increase in intervention during the period, and on the process of implementing these policies. A case study approach is used to provide detailed examples to illustrate the nature of the changes that have been taking place.

The validity of the aims of economic and industrial policies and the process of assessing their results are mainly the province of the economist. However, the economist is ill-fitted, compared with the political scientist, to investigate the area between the statement of the aim and the measurement of the impact of the policy; that is the on-going means by which policies are formulated and the processes by which they are implemented. The outcome of industrial policy measures is largely dependent on this area between the statement of the aim and the point where the result can be assessed. As a result this book is not concerned with questioning the aims of industrial policy – whether, for example, economic growth is desirable. These are taken as given, and the discussion concentrates instead on analysing the situation as governments have seen it. Similarly the analysis ignores for the most part the results of policies. Thus, although there is descriptive analysis of a general nature, the discussion concentrates, especially in the case studies and in the conclusions, on the implementation of industrial policy. The object is to present the changing situation as it has confronted governments.

Every book has its purpose and its limits. This book analyses the most important aspects of recent British industrial policy, and discusses more generally the problems confronting governments that intervene in private industry in a developed mixed economy. The object is thus to interpret the *existing* situation. The book does not attempt to be prescriptive: indeed there are no easy solutions to these problems. The detail needed to illustrate the changes that have taken place means that there is no space to deal properly with some important issues that have arisen during the period – industrial democracy and the social responsibilities of the private sector firm; the growing concentration of industry, and separation of ownership from control, for example. The discussion also raises big questions about the changing nature of the 'corporate state'. Again there is no space to relate the analysis to the on-going debate on this subject. However, the detailed case studies in themselves may make a useful contribution to that debate.

Chapter 1 outlines the growth of intervention up to 1964. Chapter 2 describes the range of Labour's economic and industrial policies. In the following chapter attention is focused on some of the outstanding features of intervention in the late 1960s. Attention is then concentrated on the highly novel Industrial Reorganisation Corporation (IRC).

The IRC emerged as much the most flexible of all Labour's innovations. Thus a detailed study of the Corporation has the great advantage of providing an opportunity to analyse many different but important aspects of the processes of making and implementing interventionist industrial policies. The IRC's experience raised, sometimes in acute form, many of the issues that have been at the heart of the evolution of industrial policy in Britain during the period being discussed. Chapter 4 provides a factual background against which discussion is focused, in Chapters 5–10, on the most important problems associated with detailed interventionist industrial policies, especially when public funds are involved. It is only by going into such detail that it is possible to understand the real nature of the problems facing the intervening government on the one hand, and the difficulties that arise from the firm's point of view on the other. The report of the Trade and Industry Sub-Committee of the Expenditure Committee on *Public Money in the Private Sector* was, as its members acknowledged in their report, 'wide rather than deep'*. Thus detailed

*Sixth report from the Expenditure Committee, HC 347 of 1971-72, para. 266.

analysis of the IRC provides some empirical evidence with regard to all the problems of injecting and monitoring the use of public funds in the private sector. When it was established the IRC was unique, and since its demise in 1971, the need to study it has become more important as governments responsible for developing mixed economies similar to Britain's in countries as wide apart as Canada, Australia and France have established similar organisations.

Part 3 describes and analyses the 'disengagement' experiment of the early 1970s whereby an attempt was made to reduce the government's involvement with the private sector by providing support on a more limited scale. The impact of the 'disengagement' experiment is analysed through an examination of the restructuring of central government; the public sector, including the nationalised industries; and, more especially, the private sector. The case study approach is again adopted as discussion concentrates on the impact of the policy on two individual firms. Chapters 11, 12 and 13 have been written by Mrs. A.V. Lowe, and I am extremely grateful to her for her contribution. The last four chapters draw together threads that have emerged at various stages of the analysis, particularly from the case studies. Particular emphasis is laid on the problems that confront the government that has decided to intervene.

The writing of this book owes a good deal to the contributions of others. First I am extremely grateful to those twenty people who spared me some of their valuable time to answer various questions in confidence. As a result they must remain anonymous, but it can be said that they included politicians, including ministers, temporary and permanent civil servants and others. With regard to the IRC, interviewing included some who worked inside it and others who have viewed its operations from different parts of Whitehall, and from various parts of industry. Others discussed quite separate but nevertheless often detailed aspects of industrial policy in the late 1960s, and after the 1972 Industry Act. These interviews made a valuable contribution in terms of assessing conflicting published evidence, and in providing insights into matters about which little or nothing had been written. Of even greater importance, however, was the fact that I was able to discuss my developing ideas about broader issues, of the kind dealt with in Chapter 3 and in Part 4, with people who had been involved with the problems at first hand. I have also been very glad of the opportunities I have had over the last few years to discuss many aspects of what follows with under- and post-graduate students and members of the Government Department at Manchester, and others both in different parts of that university, and in other universities. In this connection I would especially like to thank Mrs. Lowe, Dr. Maurice Wright and Roger Williams, all of whom read early drafts and offered much helpful criticism. I am especially grateful to Maurice Wright in whose company I have spent many an hour discussing facts, developing ideas, and searching for weaknesses in my own and other people's arguments.

The whole process of assimilating ideas and facts before thinking them through and developing them further is so complex that it is often extremely difficult to separate what one has read or discussed from what emerges from several years of thinking, talking and writing. Thus I am indebted not just to those to whom acknowledgement has been made, but also to those whose ideas I have unconsciously assimilated over the years. However, despite all the help I have received I am of course responsible for any remaining mistakes or misjudgements.

Finally I must thank my publishers for their encouragement; Mrs. Illingworth, Mrs. Quinn and Mrs. Hainsworth for typing various drafts and being prepared to disrupt their families' lives; and those librarians who have helped me search for obscure documents. My greatest debt though is to my wife Judy, not just for her creative criticism but for her unending patience and constant support.

For the paperback edition a few minor alterations have been made. The main addition has been the updating of the bibliography. The Conservative Government implemented its 1972 Industry Act in a low-key fashion between the summer of 1972 and the election of February 1974. However, the success of the Labour Party at the polls in February and October 1974 thrust the whole subject of intervention into the centre of the political stage. The ensuing debate up to the Third Reading of Labour's Industry Bill in July 1975 related developments, after the completion of this book, to the issues discussed in it, especially in the last three chapters.

CHAPTER 1 THE GROWTH OF INTERVENTION TO 1964

The roots of government intervention in a modern mixed economy like Britain's in the 1970s run very deep. Centuries ago the economy began to evolve from a 'natural economy' in which money did not exist to a 'money economy' in which it did. Once that happened the *de facto* governments began to interfere with the prevailing market conditions by levying taxes and regulating trading conditions.[1] As the centuries went by the state became progressively more involved with the running of the economy, particularly as a result of fighting wars, because money had to be raised, ships had to be built, and armies had to be equipped. Despite an initial reluctance to intervene as the Industrial Revolution developed from the eighteenth century onwards, the first real stirrings on intervention in the sense of government measures to alter the existing situation had been felt by 1870.

> Although there was a great liberalising of economic activity, especially internationally as the result of the acceptance of the doctrine of *laissez-faire,* it has been shown that the state continued to intervene in order to protect the individual, encourage some collective action and even provide services itself.[2]

Another writer has argued that

> Far from being triumphant by the 1850s, the *laissez-faire* movement had been finally routed by techniques of government control of the economy which had their own built-in tendency to develop, grow and multiply.[3]

The period up to the First World War saw the development of even more positive interventionist steps. In 1861 the first stirrings of public enterprise were felt as the National Savings Bank was established, and eight years later the inland telegraphs were nationalised, and the railway and telegraph companies were compensated. In 1900 the National Physical Laboratory was established to counter the "technological advance and military pretentions of Germany".[4] £2½ million, a massive sum at that time, was provided as a loan to the Cunard Company to help build the liners *Lusitania* and *Mauritania.* "By 1914 the *laissez-faire* philosophy was no longer considered efficient in theory nor necessary in practice."[5]

By the time the Second World War broke out, the situation had been further transformed.[6] In the latter half of the First World War Lloyd George's Government intervened extensively, fixing wages, introducing detailed controls, acquiring industries like coal and requisitioning factories to make arms. These controls were subsequently dismantled after the war. However, the depression in the inter-war years and high levels of unemployment which never fell below 10 per cent of the working population, led to further intervention. A protective policy was adopted and support was provided for such sectors as cotton, coal, railways, steel and shipbuilding. By 1939 it had become increasingly clear that "market forces and free competition both at home and in world markets were not enough to ensure the full use of the country's existing capacity."[7]

Close controls were introduced when the Second World War broke out. Its overall effect "permanently altered the relations between the state and industry in three major respects."[8] First it gave experience of the benefits of close co-operation between industry and government. Secondly it led to the government accepting for the first time positive responsibility for guiding the development of the economy and maintaining a low level of unemployment. Thirdly the system whereby government departments 'sponsor' different industries was established. A further significant change that emerged was the clear importance of fostering science. The relationship between universities, industry and government had been close during the First World War, but as a result of such developing problems as radar and atomic energy, these links became even closer during the Second World War.[9] The Labour administrations of 1945 to 1951 removed such basic industries as electricity, coal, gas, railways, road haulage, and civil aviation into public ownership. The Bank of England was also nationalised, and extensive controls were brought to bear on the private sector in an attempt to introduce a system of indicative economic planning.

By contrast, Conservative governments in the 1950s played a much less active role in economic and industrial development. Although the majority of the nationalised industries stayed under state ownership, the controls established in the post-war period were progressively dismantled, and the emphasis of economic and industrial policy was on the broad management of the economy and on 'holding the ring'. The aim was to set the rules but not to become involved in a positive, creative, ongoing sense with playing the game. The Board of Trade symbolised this approach seeing its job as being a referee rather than a player. It was strongly supported by the Treasury. It was left to industry to operate on its own within the framework provided by government.[10] The 1956 Restrictive Trade Practices Act was an example of this approach. At this stage, government was involved financially on a very limited basis, as for example over the promotion of research, the provision through the Export Credit Guarantees Department of insurance for exports, and the Distribution of Industry

Acts of 1945 and 1950.[11] However by the end of the 1950s Whitehall was beginning to become more actively involved again. The main examples are the use of public purchasing power to reduce the number of aircraft companies, and the introduction of the 1959 Cotton Act. Incentives were offered in this case for modernisation, and the orderly elimination of excess capacity.[12] There are many other examples in the later 1950s and early 1960s of the provision of finance for industry and commerce, and of government sponsored reorganisation and reconstruction. Although the Government had become more prepared to be more involved in the affairs of industry in peace time by the end of the 1950s, this was still very much the exception to its basic overall approach.

The watershed to a major extension of intervention was really crossed in 1962. This was the date of the establishment of the National Economic Development Council (NEDC), and the National Economic Development Office (NEDO) to lead the 'dash for planning'.[13] The implication of indicative planning was that in addition to its continuing role as referee, the government should also play a more active part, because if the planning targets were to be met, it had to promote industrial research and efficiency, to identify bottlenecks, and to act to correct inbalances. The period before the Conservatives left office in October 1964 saw for example the creation of the first Economic Development Committees (EDCs), and Industrial Training Boards (ITBs). Assistance was provided for shipbuilding and aerospace and nuclear power. The initial moves towards regional planning were made at this time with the publication of documents on the North-East, Central Scotland, and the South-East.[14] The Government also began to become involved with the development of expanding, as opposed to contracting, sectors. On 28 July 1964, Heath, then President of the Board of Trade, announced his intention to the Commons to introduce legislation to extend the scope and scale of the work of the National Research Development Corporation (NRDC), even though it was at that time a loss-making organisation. The Department of Scientific and Industrial Research (DSIR) and the NRDC both became more active and began to spend increasing amounts of money on stimulating industrial research.[15] The DSIR for example supported research in computers, initiated an Advanced Computer Techniques Project, and amongst others placed a contract with Birmingham University to develop a new kind of forging machine, known as Petroforge. The Warren Spring Laboratory was co-operating with NRDC and various firms in the process control field. Samuel Brittan, with his personal experience of working in Whitehall after the 1964 election, seems to have been perfectly justified to conclude that:

> Much of the small print of the 1965 National Plan, and Mr. Wilson's own 'purposive physical intervention' had already been enacted before Labour came to office.[16]

The difference between the 1962-4 Conservative administration and the Labour one that followed, was one of emphasis and scale, rather than one of principles. As the next chapter shows Labour extended many of the policies they inherited and initiated many of their own, but the fact remains that much of what they implemented was the result of Conservative innovation. On the other hand there was an important underlying difference. Labour were more prepared to discriminate through the Ministry of Technology, which was established in 1964. Despite the exceptions that have been mentioned, the Conservatives had relied much more on the basically neutral approach of 'holding the ring' that the Board of Trade had been responsible for in the 1950s. This is clearly illustrated by the case of the machine tool industry. In 1964 Heath argued that it was the industry's job and not the Government's to react to the Mitchell Report on the industry.[17] By contrast the Ministry of Technology was to actively seek out ways of promoting the development of that industry after 1964.

PART I

INDUSTRIAL POLICY TOWARDS THE PRIVATE SECTOR 1964–70

CHAPTER 2 THE RANGE OF POLICIES

Between 1964 and 1970, the two Labour Governments implemented a variety of economic and industrial policies which were directed at the private sector of industry. The overriding aim[1] was to carry out measures designed to make firms pursue lines of action which enable their record, on such economic indicators as R&D, productivity, profits and exports, to match those of companies in other mixed economy, western industrial democracies. These industrial policies were designed to hasten the process of change, thus promoting the modernisation of British industry. It was argued on the one hand, that real wages and thus living standards would rise, while on the other, that Britain's steadily declining share of world trade would be brought under control, thus creating a stable payments surplus to help pay for wide-ranging social programmes. Labour came to power with a lot of ideas but few detailed plans. Many policy measures were adaptations, sometimes extensive ones, of the pre-1964 policies. Most new initiatives emerged in the light of experience of office. This chapter reviews the whole range of industrial policies employed by Labour between 1964 and 1970. Against this background Chapter 3 analyses the more 'interventionist' features of industrial policy in the period. Many of the themes that arise are subsequently discussed further in Part IV.

A simple typology of the Government's means of controlling economic development, and strengthening the performance of British industry is developed, as a means of outlining the whole range of policies towards the private sector. It is a descriptive and analytical model not a prescriptive one, designed to throw light on the nature of the relationship between central government on the one hand, and the firm on the other. It is used in Chapter 3 to help identify with regard to the mid and late 1960s, some of the main characteristics of that widely used term 'intervention'.

Individual firms are taken as the operational unit of the typology because they and not industries are the decision-makers.[2] The private sector is defined as all the industries outside the nationalised industries in October 1964. Policies here are taken to mean pre-existing and newly devised measures that ministers used to control or stimulate the development of the economy, and not those which acted more indirectly, like health or education.

The basic aim of this typology is to assess the extent to which individual firms in various parts of the private sector were affected by different measures. The typology focuses on the means and the process of implementing these measures. The criterion applied to each policy is the extent to which implementation affected the firm's operational freedom of action. This has been taken as the main yardstick because 'intervention' implies interference, or restriction of a firm's ability to choose freely among alternative courses of action. It is important when analysing industrial policy in this period to determine how far, or in what senses, this hypothesis is true.

The concept of a policy 'discriminating' in favour of, or against industries or firms, is used in the typology to assess whether a policy is one which favours one industry or firm as against another. Discrimination between firms, and not for example between regions, is stressed here, again because the firm is the decision-making unit. Non-discriminatory or neutral policies are taken to be those which apply to all firms whether in the primary, manufacturing, or service sectors. Where a policy is said to discriminate for or against a whole industry, this means all firms within that sector.

In practice, one is forced to modify the approach of concentrating on the actual precise effect of a policy on a firm's operational freedom of action. This is mainly because different industries, and even firms within the same industry, can be affected quite differently by the same measures. A credit squeeze for example can hit a smaller firm much harder than a big one. In addition the time within which measures take effect varies considerably. Deflation for instance will affect firms selling consumer goods more quickly that it will those making capital goods like machine tools to sell to manufacturers installing new equipment. Thus if policies were to be examined strictly from the angle of the firm, the same policy would have different, and sometimes unexpected effects on firms of different sizes, even within the same industry.

This means that ideally a different typology should be developed for each industry, and in some cases even for different sized firms in that industry. However, taking a very broad view enables the analysis to include as wide a variety of measures as possible, and to relate these to subsequent discussion of the main features of industrial policy in the mid and late 1960s. Thus a broad overview is outlined in this chapter even though in some respects it is oversimplified. The basis of the typology in fact rests on assessing and classifying individual measures in terms of central government's intention as to how individual firms and industries would be affected. Similarly, the use of the concept of discrimination refers to the Government's intention, and not to actual practical results.

Table 1 divides into two parts the means by which the 1964-70 Labour Government sought to control economic development and strengthen the performance of British industry. On the left are the

Table 1 The Range of Government Policies Towards the Private Sector 1964-70

	(i)	(ii)	(iii)	(iv)
	Economic and Legal Framework		Non-Regulatory Meas	
	Economic & Fiscal Controls	Legal Regulation	Encouragement & Exhortation	Provision of Advice & Service
ies that eutral een primary ıfacturing & :e industries				
ies that minate een industries				
ies that minate een firms n industries				

regulatory controls. These are the financial and legal controls and regulations that collectively defined the shape of the economic and legal framework or environment in which firms had to operate. The first of these were economic and fiscal measures, which in turn subdivided into those which were broadly neutral, and those which were discriminating between industries. Second was the use of legal regulations. This section includes measures which were neutral, others which discriminated between industries and others again which discriminated between firms.

On the right hand side of Table 1 are the non-regulatory measures. These were developed as ways of encouraging and stimulating firms into acting as they might well not otherwise have done in an attempt to strengthen economic and export performance, and technological strength. First in this category were measures of encouragement and exhortation, and second was the provision of advice and services. Some measures in each of these categories were essentially neutral, while others discriminated between industries. The third non-regulatory measure was a series of financial inducements. There were no neutral policies here, as the purpose behind them as to discriminate between industries, and between firms within an industry.

The Economic and Legal Framework

The Labour Government set out to use financial controls and legal regulations to reshape the economic and legal framework in which firms operated.

(i) It relied on using traditional macro-economic measures. Fiscal, bank rate and credit policies were used to alter the level of demand in the economy and the availability of labour according to whether reflationary or deflationary policies were being pursued. The Government also tried to direct the development of the economy by using new economic controls. These included changing the approach to company taxation with the introduction of Corporation Tax; compulsory prices and incomes policies; and measures such as the Redundancy Payments Act, under which employers paid contributions to the Redundancy Fund via the mechanism of the National Insurance Stamp. The shape of the framework in which firms operated was also affected by the Government's ability, which it used in both traditional and new ways, to control the rise in prices introduced by the nationalised industries. These included such services as post, telephones, railways and freight, and such sources of energy as electricity, gas and coal.[3]

In addition the Labour Government used more discriminatory fiscal measures. Import surcharges are an example of one such that had been used before. These were introduced in November 1964 and August 1968 and operated in favour respectively of manufacturing industry and of firms producing refrigerators. New discriminatory measures were also devised. As a result of the refunds to manufacturing industry and to transport in the public sector, the Selective Employment Tax (SET) became effectively a tax on the construction, distribution and service industries. In practice this helped to make labour cheaper for manufacturing industry. A second innovation was the Regional Employment Premium (REP) which, as a payroll subsidy based on numbers employed by firms in Development Areas, discriminated in favour of manufacturing firms located in those areas.

(ii) The second broad means of shaping the framework in which private sector firms operated was through the use of legal regulation. Some of the non-discriminatory laws were inherited and broadly applied as they had been before 1964. Examples include the 1948 Companies Act, copyright, trademarks, and weights and measures. Other regulations were substantially altered. The 1967 Companies Act amended some aspects of previous company legislation, abolishing the exempt private company and requiring more detailed disclosure of previously withheld information. The 1965 Monopolies and Mergers Act extended previous monopolies legislation, and the 1968 Restrictive Trade Practices Act amended in 1956 Act of the same name. The 1968 Trade Descriptions Act was one of the few innovations.

There was a strong element of discrimination in some of these legal regulations and the ways in which they were used. Amongst those which were inherited were some that effectively discriminated between industries. This was the case with references to the Monopolies Commission (MC) and to the Restrictive Trade Practices Court and the use of the system of Industrial Development Certificates to encourage investment in the more deprived regions. Amongst the measures that discriminated between industries which were introduced after 1964 was the decision to introduce metrication which affected such sectors as the construction industries and their suppliers, and many parts of engineering and aerospace.[4] Important work was done within the Ministry of Technology (MinTech) on standards and quality assurance:

> There is probably no central action which can contribute more to the general improvement of technology than the establishement of standards, and the reduction of variety and introduction of proper arrangements for quality assurance; for where performance standards exist, manufacturers must get the technology to enable them to meet them.[5]

A prominent example was the BS9000 scheme for quality assurance whereby electronic components were made to common civil and military specifications. The use of references to the Monopolies

Commission, Restrictive Trade Practices Court and the National Board for Prices and Incomes (NBPI) between 1964 and 1970 sometimes discriminated between industries, but often between firms. The important feature here was the increased scale on which such references were made by comparison with the pre-1964 situation.

Non-Regulatory Measures

Within the limits to firms' activities imposed by the economic and legal regulations there were three basic non-regulatory means by which the Government attempted to stimulate and encourage firms to strengthen their economic and export performances and technological strength. These are outlined in ascending order, according to the degree to which individual firms were free if they wished to ignore them.

(iii) The first of these means was by the simple expression of encouragement and by exhortation. This was frequently done in a non-discriminatory fashion, ministers continually referring to the need to exercise wage restraint and increase productivity, exports and capital investment. In doing this they were obviously hoping that the mass media would give so much attention to these problems that the industrial climate would be influenced, so that private decisions might better reflect Government aims. The pursuit of voluntary wages policies and the frequent ministerial speeches aimed at encouraging industry to step up its capital investment were good examples of this approach.

Exhortation was also used in a more discriminatory manner. Many government institutions, particularly the NED Office, were involved with organising a great many conferences and seminars on a variety of subjects. Business executives were invited to these in the hope that on their return to their firms their subsequent decision-making would reflect what they had learned at the conferences, thus furthering the end of strengthening industry. A typical example was a big conference on the machine tool industry in 1969.[6] More technical conferences were organised by government research establishments. The National Engineering Laboratory (NEL) for example held several conferences in 1967 and 1968 for industrialists to promote wider understanding of the programme languages needed to use numerically-controlled (NC) machine tools.[7]

A great deal of the work of the EDCs falls into this category of measures of encouragement. The EDCs had two basic functions – to help draw up and implement indicative plans, and to help improve industrial efficiency. They concentrated mostly on the latter after July 1966. There were numerous reports by the 23 different EDCs that had been established by 1967.[8] They covered many aspects of commercial practice including such subjects as, R&D, training, product and firm rationalisation, marketing, exports, import substitution, and so on. Many of these were designed to stimulate new courses of action in industry. The Mechanical Engineering EDC for example published a study of exporting which analysed the factors that seemed to be of crucial importance to success.[9] One of the most successful publications of this type was *Gold in Your Hands.* This was a guide to profitable stock control in retailing, and sold more than 40,000 copies in its first four years.[10] Other reports on subjects of concern to an industry contained recommendations or 'action programmes' for the Government, firms, trade associations and unions. A typical example was the report on *The Placing and Management of Contracts for Building and Civil Engineering Work.* This was commonly called the Banwell Report and was published in 1964. Both the Building and Civil Engineering EDCs subsequently published reports examining how far the 'action programme' had been implemented and a conference was later organised on the subject.[12] The fact that these were necessary went a long way to illustrate that individual firms were quite free to ignore all EDC activity. With these and other measures of encouragement they did not have to react to the stream of reports and circulars that emanated from Whitehall, NEDO, government research establishments and trade associations.

There was certainly nothing fundamentally novel in Labour's use of encouragement. What was new was the scale on which it was developed. More importance was attached to voluntary wages policies than had been the case before 1964, and because after 1964 there were more EDCs and other committees and para-government agencies, there were correspondingly many more reports with recommendations for action by industry.

(iv) The second category of non-regulatory measures was the provision of advice and services.[13] While these were more deliberately directed at specifically chosen industries than the encouragement measures, there was still no element of compulsion. It was left to the individual firm to decide whether to ignore or take advantage of these facilities. The whole range of export services are an example of non-discriminatory measures in this category: these included the holding of British Weeks and trade fairs in foreign cities, the dissemination to companies at home of commercial intelligence about overseas markets, the provision of insurance against defaults by overseas buyers, and the Technical Help to Exporters Service, which provided details of foreign technical regulations for a wide variety of industries. A second important example was the Ministry of Labour/Department of Employment and Productivity (DEP) figures on the breakdown of the availability of different types of labour in different geographical areas. This service was evolved to help persuade firms to move or to expand elsewhere. It was argued that a company would be more likely to move if it could be clearly shown the areas where there would be labour to meet its needs.

The provision of advice and services contained a steadily increasing element of discrimination. The dissemination of information after background research is a clear example. This was an important function of government research establishments. The Torry Research Station, for example, dealt with fishing and fish processing and the National Physical Laboratory (NPL) covered measurement and other fields like ship design.[14] The NEL was engaged in research covering various parts of mechanical engineering. There is evidence to suggest that for example circularising the results of its research into the performance of mixed-flow fans led directly to production breakthroughs.[15] The dissemination of information was also an important function of the forty-two Research Associations (RAs), many of which received government grants-in-aid. The Machine Tool Industry RA, for example, maintained a register of R&D in that sector and circulated the firms concerned. MinTech made an important contribution in this field by establishing a Technical Information and Library Services Reports Centre. The object was to coordinate the substantial flow of technical reports published by organisations all over the world, and then to seek to make the information as widely available as possible to those who would be likely to be able to take advantage of it.[16]

A second main type of discriminatory advisory service was the wide range of productivity, consultancy, educational and training services that were established to help stimulate new practices throughout industry. Many organisations went beyond distributing research findings to offer a variety of services. The Hydraulics Research Station for example investigated the problems associated with the design and installation of off-shore drilling rigs for oil companies.[17] In June 1966 the National Computing Centre (NCC) was established to give advice to computer users on various applications of computers, to provide training facilities, and to do research into programming. The object was to encourage more industrialists to use computers.[18] This was also the aim behind the Atlas Centre for Computer Aided Design which was later established at Cambridge. Here industrialists could use the facilities and take advantage of trained staff to help solve problems arising from the design of a new product.[19]

Among the organisations providing advice and services on a discriminatory basis, there are many examples of Labour's attempt to reorientate military research towards industry, which was then able to benefit from what had been defence-orientated work. This was particularly the case with regard to the Atomic Energy Authority (AEA) which was allowed to undertake non-nuclear research if so instructed by the Minister of Technology under Section 4 of the 1965 Science and Technology Act. An important example was the establishment of the Non-Destructive Testing Centre by the AEA. Much of the work of the new Centre was concerned with the development of non-destructive testing techniques. In this connection contract work was performed for industry. The Centre was also concerned with background research and providing advice for industry.[20] In a similar way AEA's Ceramics Centre disseminated to industry knowledge gained in the process of making and testing ceramic materials in the nuclear energy programme. Work of the Royal Radar Establishment was also reorientated so it would be of greater assistance to industry.[21] The Industrial Systems Unit was able to give advice to makers and users of electronic equipment with industrial process control problems. The Royal Aircraft Establishment came to play an important role in MinTech's Numerical Control Advisory and Demonstration Service.[22] This was a versatile scheme involving such things as courses to teach how to handle NC equipment; free assessment of the potential of NC in operation. The Production Engineering Research Association (PERA) was also closely involved.

As with the other categories of both regulatory and non-regulatory means by which the Government sought to direct the development of the economy, the range of advice and services represented a mixture of initiated and inherited measures. Some of the new ones, including for example the promotional work in industries like computers, have been mentioned. On the other hand most export policies and many of the government research stations like NPL, NEL, and the AEA, were well established by 1964. In the next six years few of the inherited advisory and promotional services remained unaltered: they were usually re-examined and subsequently developed, often with increased financial support. The provision of advice and services received a great deal of attention from industrial policy-makers in the late 1960s. There are several reasons for this: schemes could be tailored to meet the broad requirements of industrialists, a little money could be made to go a long way, and often, as with the NCC, bodies could, once they were established, earn money to cover their expenditure. In addition such measures were readily acceptable to managers and trade associations. Not only could they make what use of them they liked, but they were not offended by the provision of finance implying that their industry was in some sort of a crisis. This whole area is a tremendously important part of industrial policy and one which is often overlooked.[23] What has been described here is only the tip of a huge iceberg. The variety of these services was underlined by the progressive expansion of the Industrial Liaison Scheme. One of the main functions of the Industrial Liaison Centres was to help put local firms facing technical difficulties in touch with organisations with the expertise to help solve the problem.[24] They thus advised as to what sources of assistance were available throughout the country.

(v) The third non-regulatory means of stimulating firms was the development of a system of financial inducements each of which attempted to make firms behave in ways in which they might well not otherwise have done. None of the measures under this heading can be described as non-discriminatory. The main feature of financial inducements was that they discriminated between industries and between firms. This in fact amounted to the same thing in a very few cases like computers or aluminium smelters where there were only a few firms or consortia.

Many regional policies provide examples of financial inducements that discriminated between industries. Some, like advance factories, were inherited and continued, and some, like mobility of labour schemes and the 1960 Local Employment Act, were inherited and extended. Thus the Nucleus Labour Force Scheme was added to the Key Workers Scheme, and the provision of removals, operational and building grants under the Act was increased. Use was also made of new measures, for instance the investments grants system introduced under the 1966 Industrial Development Act. In the 1964-70 period these measures applied to industries within the manufacturing sector and discriminated in their favour. The progressive geographic extension of the assisted areas meant that most regional policies increasingly discriminated in favour of manufacturing industry as a whole, because as the areas grew in size more of the relevant firms found themselves situated within the area, and those outside had more choice of relocation within them. In the service sector there was also discrimination in favour of the hotel industry through the 1969 Development of Tourism Act, part of which provided for grants and loans for improvements and for extensions to existing hotels in the UK, under the Hotel Improvement Scheme.

The highly discriminatory allocations of finance by government or its agents to individual firms within industries took two main forms. Both these had been applied to a limited extent before 1964. What was new was the scale on which public funds were made available to industry. First, a whole industry was singled out by government for special attention, as was the case with computers. In 1968 the aim of merging the main companies was achieved with the establishment of International Computers Limited (ICL). Through the Industrial Expansion Act the Government purchased £3½ million worth of shares and agreed to provide £13½ million in grants over four years to assist with R&D costs. The Ministry placed development contracts with the industry on a cost-sharing basis through the Advance Computers Technology Project, and the Science Research Council and the NRDC also provided assistance. Through the work of the Computer Advisory Service advantage was taken of public sector purchasing power.[25] In aerospace the basic aim was to implement the recommendations of the Plowden Committee which reported in 1965.[26] Money was provided for both the civil and military parts of the industry. It covered such aspects as multilateral space programmes, like the Black Arrow; background research in such fields as noise, fabrication methods and avionics; and launching costs as with the RB211, Concorde, and various military projects. Public funds were also used in an abortive attempt to rescue the light aircraft company from bankruptcy. Public sector purchasing, even with non-competitive contracts, gave Whitehall great influence in this particular industry. Finance was provided for the construction of three aluminium smelters, and arrangements were made to provide them with cheap electricity. Also in this category was the nationalisation of the fourteen largest companies in the steel industry which led to establishment of the British Steel Corporation (BSC) in July 1967. Support was also given to the shipbuilding industry. This was done directly by the Minister as with the guarantees in respect of orders for ships placed by British shipowners in British yards, and indirectly by the Shipbuilding Industry Board (SIB) which was established in 1967 to help implement the Geddes Report on the industry.[27] This had called for amalgamations between yards. Although it was allowed to borrow over £50 million from public funds its commitments only reached about half of that. In some of these industries part of the object of providing finance was to change the firm-structure of the industry: shipbuilding and computers are good examples.

However there were cases where although individual industries were singled out for special attention and financial inducements were provided, in practice only a small number of firms were much affected. This was because few chose to take part and fewer still passed the various vetting procedures. A typical example was the Textile Re-equipment Scheme. The object of this was to provide financial incentives for small and medium-sized firms in cotton and allied textiles to install new equipment. This was administered by the Industrial Reorganisation Corporation (IRC) which made only four loans despite applications from dozens of companies.

The second form of highly discriminatory allocation of finance involved the Government or its agents in selecting individual firms for special treatment not extended to others in the same industry. A first example here was the provision, by means of loan, grant or contract, of funds for R&D in advanced industries such as machine tools, electronics, scientific instruments, and micro-circuits. This assistance came from both MinTech directly and from NRDC. Under the 1965 Science and Technology Act the limit of public funds which the latter was allowed to borrow was raised to £25 million. Under the 1968 Industrial Expansion Act this was again raised to £50 million. NRDC supported schemes at all stages from research that might lead to an invention, through to the exploitation of a proven invention. An important example of the latter was the £5 million made available for research purposes to the three leading micro-circuit manufacturers in 1969. There were also joint development projects between other government agencies and individual firms. Churchill Machine Tools worked closely with NEL to develop air-bearing wheel heads to go with Churchill's grinding machines.[28] This was one of many such examples.

A second prominent way in which individual companies were picked out for special attention concerns the Pre-production Order Schemes. This applied initially to machine tools, but by 1970 had been extended on a small scale to machinery for textiles, plastics, printing, fish processing; mechanical handling, construction, scientific equipment, and scientific instruments. The procedure here was that MinTech would purchase from selected manufacturers specially chosen pieces of advanced machinery not yet in full production. It then placed them on free loan with selected users, who were required to report on their working performance to the Ministry and to the maker. At the end of the evaluation period the machine was sold, rented or otherwise disposed of. Most in fact were sold, and over £8 million was spent in this way.[29]

This typology illustrates the increasing emphasis in Whitehall in the late 1960s on incorporating the principle of discrimination into industrial policy-making. This was, as Chapter 1 showed, in marked contrast with the pre-1964 attitude of the Treasury and the Board of Trade which had traditionally sought to operate industrial policies *neutrally*, giving firms and industries as little special treatment as possible.

It is against this background that the radical change in size of the Ministry of Technology between October 1964 and October 1969 assumes great importance.[30] When it was established by the incoming Labour Government in 1964 it was given responsibility for the NRDC, AEA, and the government research establishments, and sponsorship of the four so-called 'bridgehead' industries – computers, electronics, telecommunications, and machine tools. It was given responsibility for the rest of the engineering industry in February 1966, and for shipbuilding in November 1966. In February 1967 it acquired all the functions of the Ministry of Aviation (apart from the civil aviation responsibilities which had been transferred to the Board of Trade in July 1966). This merging of Departments led to profound changes

an attempt to avoid devaluation of the pound by relying on conventional deflationary policies. Although the economic and legal framework was altered during this period and use made of controls, the main emphasis was on non-regulatory measures particularly those designed to restructure industry and strengthen export performance. Measures intended to implement the National Plan were brought forward and amended in the face of the Government's changing needs. Finally there was the period after devaluation when "the main concern was to make devaluation work". The role of policies and para-government bodies bearing on exports now became more important. At the same time Ministers were reluctant to allow too many new measures before the balance of payments crisis was resolved in 1969, fearing unpredictable effects which might have upset the devaluation strategy itself. New measures during this period were only approved when they had a tangible connection with exports either directly, or indirectly if they promised to be of long-term benefit to technological strength. By the time the balance of payments situation had improved new initiatives were for the most part constrained by the election. What the three periods thus had in common was the need to increase exports. From 1964 until 1969-70 when the balance of payments surplus emerged this was the Government's main preoccupation. Soon after taking office Wilson stressed "In the last month the Government have announced a whole range of measures to help the exporter."[3] One of the reasons for reducing the size of the Board of Trade in 1969 was to leave it "free to concentrate much more on exports".[4]

In the face of the need to get tangible results in terms of productivity, capital investment, and the balance of payments, ministers increasingly began to realise that most non-regulatory measures were having a very limited impact, because firms were *completely able to disregard them.* To a large extent the EDCs were a symbol of this situation in that their activities ranged widely across the exhortation and advice and services categories described previously, and because their numbers had been increased by Labour from five to twenty-three. If representatives from the trade associations and the largest firms were not really interested in what central government was trying to get them to do, then it was all too easy to conduct a holding operation and not react in any positive sense. Some Chairmen and individual members became so frustrated that they resigned or left when their contracts could have been renewed. This is not to say that all EDC activity led nowhere: if the trade associations or some of the big firms were determined collectively to have a dialogue with Government they could sometimes get existing policies amended or persuade Government to embark on initiatives. Thus the EDCs for Machine Tools, Distribution, Hotel and Catering, and Civil Engineering all helped to push Government into initiatives or amendments respectively on pre-production orders, SET exemptions, SET exemptions and finance for hotel expansion, and motorway contracts. However these examples cover only some of their activities and seem to have been the exception to the overall pattern whereby the individual firm was hardly affected if it chose not to be.

The way in which most non-regulatory measures had, in practice, little impact in the mid 1960s on the firm is illustrated in Figure 1. The "industrial departments" at the top of the diagram are those responsible for the exhortation and advisory services categories of industrial policy outlined in the preceeding chapter. This principally means the DEA, the DEP, MinTech and the Board of Trade. The phrase "executive agencies" refers to those, like the IRC, SIB and NRDC, which had financial resources and executive responsibilities to help implement industrial policy. Below this are "the other government agents" which basically covers the organisations responsible for implementing policies of exhortation and the advisory services described in the preceeding chapter. Respective examples include the EDCs; and organisations like the industrial research establishments and NCC. "Other government agents" also refers to some independent organisations like the research associations and the trade associations, which were also involved with implementation of Government policy. At the bottom of the diagram comes the individual firm. This was

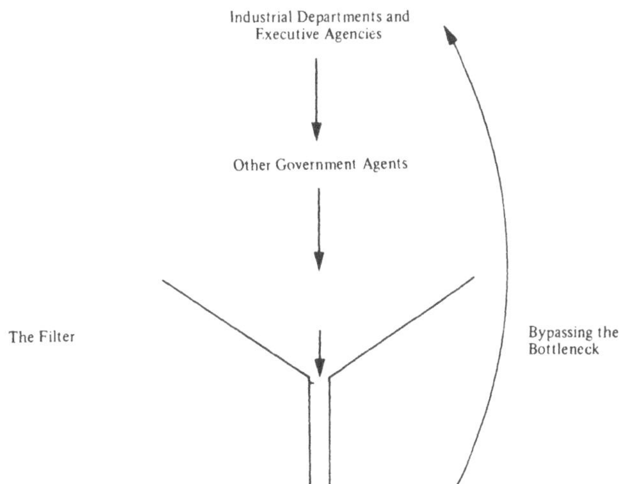

Figure 1: The Impact of Non-Regulatory Measures

taken as the operational unit in the typology in Chapter 2 because, it was argued, it was the firm and not an industry that was the basic decision-making unit with which industrial policymakers were concerned.

The exhortation and advice and services categories of non-regulatory policies emanated from the main industrial departments. Although they were sometimes implemented directly, usually they were implemented via "other government agents". It must be stressed that with both these types of policy the individual firm was *completely free and able to ignore all government measures* in these fields. The Government was aware of this but hoped that because its policies in these two spheres had been designed for the firm's benefit, more and more firms would in time realise this and react positively. The link between the two different tiers of government organisation at the top and the firm at the bottom is shown as a 'filter' because the intention behind these two sets of policies was that they would 'filter' through to the firm which would, in time, respond positively.

However, what appears to have happened in the mid-1960s is that a 'bottleneck' developed in the 'filtering' process between central government and its agents on the one hand, and the decision-making unit within the firm on the other. This was a common occurrence with much of the Government's exhortation, and with many of the ways in which it provided advice and services. Individual firms simply had no need to react to letters and circulars about improving marketing or on the usefulness of research from Government bodies or the Chairman of the relevant EDC. Suggestions for action at the firm level often came via a trade association or the head office of the firm. By the time it reached the point where a decision could be made a lot of the impetus had gone from behind the suggestion. Similarly a company did not have to send executives to conferences or on courses. Even if they went there was no guarantee that the proceedings would have any impact on decision-making at the firm level. It was the same with the facilities provided to make exporting easier, or the advice offered on what kinds of equipment to instal. The impact of policies of exhortation and of advisory services depended not on the Government, or on the policy 'filtering' through, but on *the will of the business executive* at the level of the individual firm to respond positively by taking specific action that reflected the Government's aims.

As a result of the emergence of this 'bottleneck' the Government found during the second and third of Graham's time periods that it was increasingly in a cleft stick, because a lot of Whitehall-inspired energy seemed to be having a very limited impact as a result of the 'filtering' process it had to go through to reach the firm. In addition while the lack of results was becoming apparent in terms of productivity, capital investment and the balance of payments, the need to get results increased for three reasons: first the on-going payments crisis: second the need to cure the continuing lack of expansion in order to end deflation and remove its politically unpopular results of continuing wage restraint and high levels of unemployment; and thirdly the adoption of improving the structure of and strengthening and modernising industry as the new overall policy aim in July 1966, when deflation ended the indicative planning experiment.

The overall result of the disappointing impact of the Government's policies was that by 1966-7 and beyond, Ministers increasingly decided to concentrate industrial policy-making on two strategic fronts. The impetus behind this came mainly from MinTech.[5] First, the provision of advice and services were made more and more specialised in order to be of more direct use and to have more appeal and relevance to the needs of industrialists. The NCC for example developed a variety of means of encouraging more widespread use of computers in industry as a result of its experience after its establishment in June 1966.[6] Similarly, government concern about the slow speed with which continuous process industries were adopting some measure of computer control for their plant led the Warren Spring Laboratory (WSL) to try and fill the gap in a new way. In 1967, since exhortation was having little effect in this area, WSL began to hold courses for firms interested in the possibility of installing process control computers to help run their plant. A pilot-scale computer-controlled acetone plant was built. Industrialists were thus able to work out a computer programme which related to their own circumstances and try it on the plant.[7] These were typical of the way in which various services were extended and others established. This represented a collection of tailor-made attempts to provide firms with what Whitehall thought would be useful facilities.

Ministers' other main concern during and beyond the winter of 1966-7 was to devise means of bypassing the 'bottleneck' that had emerged between the Government and its agents on the one hand, and the individual firm on the other. The need for this had been evident before Labour in fact came to power. Samuel Brittan has commented:

> It seemed at the time (1962-4) that the Conservative Government was carrying out a good deal of the prodding action required to improve the working of an imperfectly competitive and excessively sluggish economy. But too many ministers relied too much on consultation with trade associations and other established channels. There were too many conferences and not enough action.[8]

By the winter of 1966-7 Labour Ministers had learnt to appreciate,

PART II

THE INDUSTRIAL REORGANISATION CORPORATION

CHAPTER 4 THE SCOPE OF IRC ACTIVITY

The IRC formally came into existence after the IRC Act received the Royal Assent on 21 December 1966. The Corporation's functions were outlined in Clause 2. In order to promote "industrial efficiency and profitability" and to assist "the economy of the United Kingdom", the IRC was to "promote or assist the reorganisation or development of any industry".[1] The case for the IRC rested on the premise that production units in British industry were all too often too small. It was argued that although size and efficiency did not necessarily go together British industry needed "a structure which will enable us to make the most effective use in years ahead of our resources of skill, management and capital".[2] The Government argued that the pace at which market forces and the institutions in the field were concentrating industry into bigger units did "not yet match the needs of the national economy".[3] It was left to the IRC Board "to consider which industries it would be expedient"[4] to concentrate on. In addition Clause 2 (1)(b) stated that the Corporation could act at the direct request of the Secretary of State and "establish or develop, or promote or assist the establishement or development of any industrial enterprise". Under Section 2 (5) there was scope for the Minister responsible for the IRC to give it a managerial directive. It has been pointed out that a similar situation with regard to ministerial directive exists with regard to the nationalised industries.[5] The Corporation was endowed with £150 million to fulfil these broad functions.

The most important feature of the IRC Act was the immensely wide powers given to the Corporation. It was actually stated that the IRC should "have the power to do anything . . . . which is calculated to facilitate the discharge of its functions".[6] British governments often phrase Parliamentary bills so that when they reach the statute book wide-ranging powers have been taken. Apart from this case other typical examples include the 1972 Industry Act referred to in Chapter 13, and the 1968 Medicines Act which gave the government of the day far-reaching powers over almost all aspects of the manufacture, distribution and sale of pharmaceutical products. The object is often to take powers that can be used to cope with any contingency. In the case of the IRC Act the wide powers also reflected a certain amount of confusion in Whitehall as to what in practice the IRC's precise role would turn out to be.[7] This is the explanation for the Corporation's imprecisely defined functions. The way was thus cleared for the IRC

Board to interpret the Act broadly. It saw its task as involving "action in concert with industrial companies to restore the international competitiveness of many of our manufacturing and processing industries".[8] This chapter outlines the variety of ways in which the IRC operated.[9] The rest of Part II examines some of the major themes and issues that arise from the IRC's work.

The Corporation was in fact informally established in the summer of 1966, this haste reflected "the importance attached by the Government"[10] to the task of industrial restructuring, especially after the deflationary policies adopted in July 1966. Staff were recruited and research quietly began, so that when the Corporation came into existence it was able immediately to tackle its twin tasks of winning the confidence of businessmen and establishing an order of priorities, by opening an "intensive dialogue with industry".[11] However, despite a great deal of hard work in a wide range of industries there were no obvious results after nearly six months of formal existence.

There were two main reasons why the IRC began so quietly. The first was that the Board could not agree to act decisively before the Corporation had fully gained the confidence of industrialists. This was underlined by a second factor, namely that Grierson, the first Managing Director, was always sceptical about the IRC actually using its powers. His concept of the Corporation was probably best summed up by William Davis, who claimed that Grierson sought to make the IRC "a forum where directors of large companies could discuss their ideas for mergers and reorganisations without feeling that they were talking to the Government but knowing that public money could be forthcoming".[12] At this stage ministers were anxious for action from the IRC. They would have been very disappointed to have learned that the IRC Board, supported by Grierson, dropped a proposal for an amalgamation between the General Electric Company (GEC) and Associated Electrical Industries (AEI) when the companies were sounded out at an informal dinner on 12 June 1967.[13] On the other hand a good example of Grierson's approach seems to have been the English Electric/Elliott Automation (EE/EA) merger which was the IRC's only success in its first six months of existence. In this case the two firms were apparently well advanced with detailed negotiations before they agreed, as a result of their liquidity problems, to approach the IRC for medium-term financial assistance.[14]

The main reason why the IRC changed from the passive organisation it was initially into the active interventionist agency it later became was that the Board changed its consensus view as to what IRC's role should be. The gestation period that Members evidently felt was needed for the Corporation to find its feet, determine priorities, do basic research and establish a relationship with industry had sometime to come to an end if the IRC were to develop in the direction that the Government broadly had intended. At this stage a certain amount of confusion existed as to what the Corporation's precise role should be, but Ministers certainly wanted it to be more active.[15]

The situation was finally altered by GEC s strong concern in September 1967 that the IRC should publicly support their bid for AEI. From Grierson's point of view this put the IRC in a dilemma because it meant overtly supporting one side in what was likely to be a controversial and contested takeover battle. On the other hand it would have been inconsistent for the Board to have withheld support for a merger when it had previously favoured a link between the two firms. Grierson's view of the IRC appears to have been overtaken by events. The Government's attempts to pressurise the IRC were of little consequence when compared to the change that time had wrought within the Corporation itself: it was the GEC bid that produced the change of gear.

The GEC takeover of AEI was to prove a watershed not only in the IRC's relationship with the Government, but in its own evolution. The Corporation had shown that it could produce results by its own methods, without frightening industrialists away. Furthermore Grierson resigned during the battle. The underlying cause appears to have been the confusion that existed in Whitehall as to what the IRC's precise role should be. Grierson was "at no point even remotely"[16] involved in the process of thinking through the concept of the IRC before the White Paper was published. He basically lacked sympathy for what emerged in practice as the Government's view as to what the IRC's role should be. He objected to the Corporation acting "almost like a tribunal without any of the normal judicial safeguards", and "making judgements as to whether certain types of industrial restructuring are better than other types".[17] The importance of Grierson's resignation in the context of the evolution of the IRC was that it opened the way for new leadership.

Grierson's contribution should not however be lightly dismissed. Under his direction the Corporation had begun its research and had also attempted to strengthen British industry in three of the four main ways it was to use. First, it produced mergers in situations where it could limit itself to acting as a catalyst by bringing together willing parties: here it both initiated negotiations and assisted companies that approached it, as was respectively the case with Dunford and Elliott/ Hadfields, and EE/EA. Second, by conducting inquiries it began to play the role of being the Government's merchant bank.[18] Third, it assisted in a rescue operation at Rootes, handling the consequences of a near bankruptcy situation. But Grierson's most important contribution was more intangible. As the only full-time Board Member, he appears to have helped more than most both to calm the fears of suspicious industrialists, and to persuade them that the IRC was there for their benefit. Indeed the IRC was able to move successfully into its active phase in part because of Grierson's skill in handling the passive stage in its development.

Kearton appears to have accepted that Grierson's techniques could achieve valuable results, and under his direction the IRC continued to be the Government's merchant bank and to promote mergers by acting as a catalyst.[19] However, the essential difference between Grierson and Kearton was that the latter was prepared to seize opportunities and be controversial. For example, in both the GEC/AEI and BLMC mergers he was prepared to use the IRC as an "accelerator",[20] putting its influence behind a proposal even when one party was initially opposed to it. It is unlikely that before the voting on GEC's offer Grierson would have followed Kearton's approach and held a meeting with the AEI institutional shareholders to explain why IRC supported GEC's bid.[21] In addition Kearton began to remodel the IRC. The research side was reorganised and with the Reed de-inking plant the Corporation embarked for the first time on its fourth role of providing funds to individual firms for selective investment schemes quite outside a merger situation.

Shortly after the end of Kearton's four months as temporary Managing Director the IRC report noted that "whereas in the early months the emphasis was mainly on establishing contact with companies and hearing their suggestions for possible IRC action, the IRC itself is now more ready to take the initiative in proposing and encouraging action within industry".[22] It was Kearton who presided over the crucial period in this change: Grierson's resignation and the GEC/AEI affair had marked a change of gear, but it was only the Board's subsequent action that made this change permanent. Possibly the most important part of Kearton's entire contribution to the IRC was his forceful leadership at this point which ensured that the Corporation became an active and not merely a passive organisation.

Under Villiers, the new Managing Director, the IRC spent most of its time fulfilling the previously established function of promoting mergers. In the majority of cases it continued to act as a catalyst helping together willing partners. On several occasions the merger came as a result of the IRC initiative,[23] but more usually the Corporation assisted those that approached it for help. Some of the latter were approaching the Corporation for the first time, while others had been approached by the IRC on earlier occasions when it had tried to persuade them to merge.[24] On two occasions it supported takeover offers by multinationals for British firms, and in at least one instance acted as an accelerator again.[25] A new development was supporting British firms in transnational links: Dunlop/Pirelli was one of five examples.

After Villiers' arrival the Corporation continued to act as the Government's merchant bank by undertaking further enquiries for Ministers and by acting as the Government's intermediary with respect to individual firms. This involved being asked to deal with UK companies like Rolls Royce and Cammell Laird that were in difficulties and handling some of the consequences of attempts by multinationals like SKF and Phillips to expand in Britain. The IRC acted as the Government's merchant bank on a steadily widening range of issues, a typical example being the way in which the Corporation was asked to implement reports that it had completed for Ministers.[26] The IRC also continued to fulfil its selective investment function by making capital available to individual well-managed companies.[27]

The Corporation expanded its attempts to strengthen British industry by acting as a rescue operator. Whereas in its merger and selective investment functions the Corporation was dealing with viable firms, in the case of a rescue operation it was dealing with companies which had run into various types of trouble, usually potential bankruptcy or liquidity problems and which therefore needed to be reconstructed. The Corporation found that by 1969 it had "put itself in a position . . . to bring substantial pressure to bear on the top management of ill-run companies."[28] In those sectors where the IRC believed that poor performance was not due to the fragmented state of the industry, it concluded that it must therefore be due to poor management. The result was that the IRC took advantage of its financial resources and used its influence "to stimulate British industrial companies to effective and profitable reform where appropriate without recourse to merger or takeover by others."[29] In some cases it attempted, apparently often going via a firm's institutional shareholders or bankers, to promote internal reorganisation, and in others it proceeded on the assumption that "the existing managements have no prescriptive rights and if they fail to deliver the goods they should make way for those who can." The result was that it "secured management changes which are having beneficial effects. Often these changes have involved the introduction of men from outside the group concerned".[30] A typical example was the provision of short-term finance to Davy Ashmore, a major process plant firm. The company was in danger of being "smashed to pieces because of a catastrophic series of mistakes by top management",[31] but it appeared viable in the long term. Although the IRC had been involved with rescues before, this was a substantial expansion of that role, and emerged as a tremendously important part of IRC's work by 1969. It has been called its stimulation function.[32]

Under Villiers there was one fundamentally new departure. In a very small number of cases, the Corporation played its merger role in much more controversial style, acting as a "steersman"[33] in contested situations by pushing two or more parties to what it judged to be the solution most in the national interest. Thus when Plessey bid for English Electric in August 1968, the IRC helped to steer through an alternative link between GEC and EE. In the case of ball and roller bearings the Corporation devised means of opposing SKF's bids for Ransome and Marles and later for Pollard, arranging instead the creation of Ransome/Hoffmann/Pollard (RHP) in May 1969. When Rank and Kent both put in takeover bids for Cambridge Instruments in June 1968 this steering function involved the IRC in open intervention in the market to buy Kent and Cambridge equity stock, thereby discriminating against Rank and enabling Kent's bid to go through. In the case of Brown Bayley, IRC played its merger broking role by taking over the company in January 1969, afterwards splitting up the two constituent parts in a demerging operation.

Finally under its three different Managing Directors, the Corporation acted in a number of more miscellaneous, often confidential, ways. Examples that have come to light include settling commercial disputes;[34] attempting to promote export standardisation as in pumps;[35] promoting product standardisation as in machine tools through a revolving loan to BLMC to persuade the machine tool makers to manufacture certain advanced tools; and trying, apparently both directly and via the CBI to get institutional investors and bankers to be more actively involved with the management of the companies with which they were involved. Most of these sorts of ventures took place under Villiers, and represented an attempt to complement IRC's more direct attempts to promote change within industry.

It is difficult to assess the contribution of Villiers separately from that of Lockwood, Kearton's successor as Chairman. In their different ways the contributions of Lockwood and Villiers were as vital to the IRC's development as those of Grierson and Kearton. Villiers arrived when the IRC was more than half-way through the process of evolving from a passive into an active initiating body, and Lockwood took over at the start of 1969: although big developments were still to come the latter played mainly a more consolidating role. Villiers was in charge of the day-to-day running of the organisation and, by contrast with Grierson, showed in his handling of the Kent, Brown Bayley and RHP cases that he was prepared to be as controversial as was necessary to achieve the IRC's ends. Between them Villiers and Lockwood seemed to have adopted Kearton's principle of making the IRC as flexible an organisation as possible, so that different problems could be tackled in the most appropriate of a number of different ways. The characters of these four individuals strongly influenced the development of their offices, and the pace at which IRC evolved.

Villiers presided over an increasing amount, and a wide range, of IRC activity. The Board found both totally new methods and new means of using previously established methods, to promote, as they saw it, the international competitiveness of British industry. Apart from RHP, which was by then under way, the age of really big mergers in motors and electricals was finished by September 1968 when the GEC/EE link-up took place. Thereafter the Corporation began to concentrate on smaller rationalisation schemes, many of which involved no finance. It must be stressed that the commonest way by which it promoted mergers was still to act as a catalyst where both firms were agreeable to the merger. Increasingly it found that its original restructuring role was finished.[36] Consequently there were fewer mergers, and more and more time was spent on acting as the Government's merchant banker, on following up the progress being made by firms which had been supported, on extending the rescue function and on providing finance for selective investment. Eleven of the fifteen occasions on which the IRC lent money to individual companies in non-merger situations came after February 1970.[37] The Corporation also spent time studying various problems which it had come across during the course of its earlier work,[38] and on promoting international links and the concept of a "European IRC".[39]

The IRC was thus not a monolithic structure. At different times, under the leadership of very different men facing changing industrial and financial market conditions, and fulfilling different roles, the IRC could adopt varying identities. As a whole, it underwent a fairly rapid process of evolution, from being "so mouselike as to be almost invisible"[40] to becoming so controversial an organisation that in October 1970 the incoming Conservative Government abolished it. Alistair Morton, a senior IRC executive has identified four main eras in the development of the Corporation. The initial groundwork was followed by a merger boom. This gave way to a period of consolidation before at the end of its life the Corporation began to concentrate more on its rescue function.[41] Yet it is important to remember that within each era the IRC was involved with a steadily widening variety of work. This constant evolution must be borne in mind if the Corporation is to be understood.

CHAPTER 5 INTERNAL ORGANISATION

Formal Organisation

The first Chairman of the IRC was Sir Frank (later Lord) Kearton. He had been intimately involved with the thinking through of the concept of IRC, and his appointment was announced when the IRC White Paper was published in January 1966.[1] The rest of the Board was named on 4 May 1966 by George Brown,[2] then Secretary of State for Economic Affairs and himself a strong force behind the creation of IRC. R. Grierson, then an executive director of S.G. Warburg, the merchant bankers, was made Deputy Chairman and Managing Director. He began work almost at once on the job of recruiting the executive staff and creating the IRC out of nothing.

The remaining Members of the Board were J.P. Berkin, at that time Managing Director of Shell Transport and Trading Company; B. Boxall, a Director of Lindustries; L. Cannon, General President of the Electrical Trades Union; B.R. Cant, Managing Director of Hanworthy Engineering; Sir Joseph Lockwood, Chairman of Electrical & Musical Industries (EMI); Professor W.G. McClelland, Director of the Manchester Business School; F. (later Sir Frank) Schon, Chairman and Managing Director of Marchan Products; Sir Donald (later Lord) Stokes, Managing Director of Leyland Motors; and C.R. Wheeler, Chairman of AEI. Even leaving aside what Board Members had learned from previous jobs, their collective industrial experience at the time of their appointments covered a wide range of industries, including mechanical engineering, motor vehicles, electricals, electronics, distribution, rubber, textiles and oil with its associated fuels and synthetic products. This experience was supplemented by some Board members being appointed to other directorships during the IRC's life. Sir Frank Schon for example became a Director of Albright and Wilson. In addition there was also direct experience of management at all levels from small business, through self-contained subsidiaires of larger companies and holding companies to giant corporations. The Board contained a mixture of graduates and relatively self-made men.

The composition of the Board gave some indication of the Government's broad intentions and ensured the existence of elements on the Board that were decisively to affect the way IRC developed. Apart from management experience from a wide range of the manufacturing sector, there was the more theoretical approach of a "small businessman turned academic",[3] practical knowledge of the merger world from the City, and in a situation where the problem of rationalisation was bound to arise, the injection of the worker's view from a man widely regarded as one of the most far-sighted of union leaders. An outstanding feature was the lack of economists. This indicated that the Government wanted the IRC to avoid, for example, complex analyses of the optimum capacity for an industry in 1980, in favour of producing practical ideas and, if necessary, backing them financially. It is important to note here that the Board was composed of men with a belief in the virtues of private enterprise. At their head was Kearton, described by *The Economist* at the time as a man who "makes no secret of his dislike of nationalisation . . . and his belief in efficiency and profit".[4] There was also a complete absence of Government representatives: this had two important effects. It meant that the Members could independently exercise their own commercial judgement. Secondly, taken with the presence on the Board of men who were anyway unlikely to allow themselves to be made into Government pawns, it enabled the Board from the start to make a reality of its independence. George Brown can be credited with using his reputation for twisting people's arms to good effect; he himself was delighted with this list. It seems an excellent example of his desire when making appointments to pick active men, and avoid what he has termed the "extinct or at best rather weary volcanos" on the Treasury and Cabinet Office lists of people thought capable of serving on various committees of inquiry.[5]

Grierson's replacement as Managing Director was Charles Villiers – "a tough, self-confident, enormously experienced merchant banker".[6] Prior to being appointed to the IRC on 1st February 1968, he had worked for J. Henry Schroder Wagg. Whereas Grierson had stayed on the Warburg's Board as a non-executive director, Villiers resigned; "I feel that independence is of necessity in this job and Schroder's has a lot of industrial clients".[7] There was another important change too. Grierson had worked for nothing, possibly because he felt that he was thus preserving his independence. After his resignation a strong body of opinion apparently argued that the position should be a paid one and it was settled that his successor was to receive £20,000, a higher salary at that time than those of Ministers and nationalised industry chairmen. The fact that this was a potential embarrassment to the Government's prices and incomes policies may also explain the length of time that it took for the appointment to be announced, because Villiers appears to have been chosen in mid-December.[8] In 1970 he agreed to have his two-year term extended to 31 January 1971.[9] He was thus Managing Director for about two and a half of IRC's three most active years, before presiding over the winding up of the

Corporation.

The next changes in the Board came in early 1969. Kearton did not wish to renew his formal two-year term as Chairman when it expired in December 1968 and Sir Joseph Lockwood, a Member of the Board, was appointed his successor. Although initially he only agreed to a one-year term, he in fact consented to his contract being renewed and remained as Chairman until the IRC's formal dissolution on 31 May 1971. Stokes was appointed his deputy to take the chair when matters relating to electricals and electronics were being considered by the Board, Lockwood being automatically excluded as he was Chairman of EMI.[10] Stokes was a particularly suitable choice as he had earlier been Chairman of Electronics EDC. In December 1968, all the Members of the Board apart from J.P. Berkin agreed to further two-year terms. Three new Members were appointed to the Board as from 28 April 1969 to help spread a growing work load, and to make up the net loss of three Board Members between October 1967 when Wheeler had resigned over IRC's role in the GEC/AEI takeover battle[11], and December 1968. They were Sir Maurice Bridgeman, a Director of the National Provincial Bank; M. Clapham, Deputy Chairman of ICI; and Lord Goodman.[12] The net effect of these changes was to broaden the Board's experience: whereas all three lost Members were from industry, only one of the new ones was. However, the IRC's basic belief in the virtues of private enterprise was in no way altered: Villiers was often quoted as saying we are businessmen and free enterprises.[13] The point was further underlined by the fulfilment of Lockwood's main aim – "I don't want anyone who could remotely be described as a back-door nationaliser".[14] After these changes the composition of the Board remained the same until the IRC's dissolution. Unlike Kearton, Lockwood received a small salary. Members were paid throughout the IRC's existence, most of them earning under £2,500 a year.[15]

The Managing Director was the only full-time Member of the Board. The main part of the work on which the Board's decisions were based was done by the full-time staff who were recruited by Grierson and Villiers, probably with the assistance of the Chairman of the day. The executive team played an important part in the IRC's development largely because of a deliberate attempt to incorporate five characteristics into their collective approach.

The first three of these seem to have derived from a determination to get a certain kind of enquiring and critical attitude built into the team. First, people were recruited primarily "on the basis of their ability and personality".[16] The second aim of not letting people stay too long can be seen as an attempt to avoid any complacency or loss of edge seeping in whilst still on the job. The average term was roughly two years: some like Ziman stayed as short a time as eighteen months whereas others – Brooke, the Deputy Managing Director for example – stayed for nearly three years. Thirdly the accent was on youth. The result was a stream of people who were in their thirties. There was no one over forty in February 1969 and some appear to have joined when they were close to their thirtieth birthday. As Brooke put it – "our people must belong to the generation with an eye for the things that need changing".[17]

Previous jobs were important in that the fourth objective seems to have been to get a good mix of skills and backgrounds at any one time. People came from the private sector of industry, the commercial branch of the Foreign Office, financial journalism, the City, accountancy, the World Bank, and Transport House. There was also a lawyer for most of the time. Getting a good mix was made more difficult by the final criterion which was to keep the team small. In October 1966, there were five; in November 1967 there were eight; in June 1968 there were nine; in February 1969 there were eleven; and at the start of 1970 there were again eight. The February 1969 figure was probably as high as it was only because of the care taken when new people arrived to get some overlap between those leaving and the newcomers to work the latter into the job. One of the advantages of a small mixed group was that at all times and not just at the regular morning meetings for those in London, they were able to pick each other's brains and discuss projects that others were involved in. Apart from the Board and the executive team there were typists, back-up executives doing desk work, clerical and library staff. The library was an immensely important part of the organisation because it was where all the published material was brought together with a great deal of confidential information that was sent in, often on a regular basis, by individual firms. The library was a huge asset and probably the main reason why IRC reports were highly spoken of.[18] As a result of the increase in work a post of Secretary had to be created to handle all the routine business, leaving the line executives free for the detailed industrial work. The IRC was able to get an enormous amount of work done with a very limited staff, which never exceeded thirty.[19]

This small size, together with factors such as the way in which individuals in each of the two basic executive teams that operated in the four active years fitted together, and the drive and hard work that each of the Chairmen and Managing Directors brought to the job, combined to produce an *esprit de corps* that was probably unique in Whitehall. One can sense from Anthony Sampson's description,[20] and the enthusiasm for the Corporation's work expressed in the annual reports, that one of the reasons why it was able to achieve results was that the participants seemed to have seen their work as a race against time, almost as a kind of modern crusade.

The IRC's Own Finances

When it was established, the founders of the IRC envisaged that it could be self-supporting and be able to earn a commercial rate of return on its operations. The actual cost of running the IRC oscillated between £261,000 for the first fifteen-month period, and £303,000 in 1969/70.[21] Its operating costs were made up of the following items: amortisation and depreciation; rent and rates; office equipment and related expenses; auditor's fee; consultancy, legal and professional fees; staff salaries and associated costs; and Board Members' expenses and income. The IRC borrowed public funds but earned a surplus even after paying for its running expenses, its tax, the interest on its borrowings from the National Loans Fund and the dividend on its borrowings from Public Dividend Capital. (This is sometimes called Exchequer Dividend Capital.) This was not of course true in the first year when very little income was received from initial investments of £17 million. However in 1968-69 there was a balance left after deducting these four items from its income of £215,000. In 1969-70 it was £71,000 and in its final thirteen-month period it was £862,000.[22] It paid the Treasury a dividend of £750,000 in 1968-69 and £500,000 in 1969-70. Unlike the NRDC, which was more involved with long-term risk-taking, and the whole NEDO complex and the NBPI which yielded somewhat intangible returns, the IRC was thus able to more than cover its running expenses, which came to about a third of the annual cost of the NBPI.[23]

'Commercial' can of course be defined in many different ways, but experience proved that the Corporation could fulfil this aim in that it was far from being a loss-making body, and it managed this even though much of its work yielded no income. This question is hedged about with many complex considerations – for example the IRC had to pay annual interest to the National Loans Fund on money which it had borrowed from the Treasury, but lent to firms on conditions which allowed them to pay no interest in the early years of the loan, provided it was made up later. However the Corporation paid dividends to the Secretary of State, and in its final year earned over £7 million on total investments of £103 million, which is just about 7 per cent. By its last financial year these deferred interest payments and loan repayments were beginning to come through on a regular basis. IRC's income was £7 million in 1970-71 as opposed to £4½ million in 1969-70, and loan repayments amounted respectively to £3,800,000 and £6 million. The anticipated picture had been altered by the early repayment of half of the £15 million capital EE/EA loan following the

the GEC/EE merger.[24] By the time that it was abolished IRC was only just starting to operate at full pitch. It is not therefore possible to say with confidence whether the original theory that the IRC's £150 million would act as a revolving source of finance, and be the only money the Corporation was allowed to draw on, could have worked in practice. It might indeed have been the case, had Labour won the election in 1970, that the IRC's financial limits might have to have been raised. The Corporation was pressing for an increase in its funds in 1970,[25] thus the experiment was cut off at the point when it was getting under way. However the indications were that a body like the IRC could not only be self-supporting, but could earn something approaching a commercial rate of return on its operations.

The Role Of The Board And The Executives

Projects came from different sources at different stages in the IRC's life. At the beginning the DEA appears to have done a 'trawl' and assembled a list of problems thought suitable for the new agency. Industries almost certainly on this list include wool, footwear, cables; and parts of mechanical engineering (pumps), of electronics (scientific instruments) and of heavy electrical engineering (turbines and transformers). Once the Corporation had formally come into existence government departments continued to be a source of projects through requests to it to do specific tasks for them. Throughout the IRC's existence they remained a project source as they passed suggestions to the Corporation as to sectors it might wish to consider. Examples include vehicles, ball bearings, industrial process control and automation, and numerically controlled machine tools.

Internally the Board was handicapped initially by "ignorance about the feasibility of IRC intervention".[26] In 1967-68 executives were doing research and attempting to establish overall priorities[27] in terms of schemes that would either increase productivity, or have an impact on the balance of payments, or make better use of scarcer resources: what this meant in practical terms is discussed in the following chapter. The Board's lack of experience meant that "a systematic strategy based on rational priorities was less appropriate than sitting at the receipt of custom and welcoming all comers, pushing the boat out and using one's 'nose' to pick up a lead as to a possible fluid situation".[28]

Once the Board had gained some experience as to the sorts of situations in which it could produce practical results, then there was more scope for the IRC to take the initiative by developing its own sound sense of priorities. This came mainly as a result of the thorough investigation by the executives of the manufacturing part of the Standard Industrial Classification. Individual sectors were initially analysed by means of "such indicators as export-import balance, size distribution of firms, employment of qualified scientists and engineers and value added ratio".[29] Specific problems could then be picked out: growing over capacity in mining machinery stood out as a consequence of the progressive closure of pits by the NCB. The use of the broad criteria of productivity and the balance of payments led the Corporation to concentrate on electronics, and on electrical and mechanical engineering, and to leave on one side fragmented sectors like wool textiles and others that were already highly concentrated like chemicals and drinks.[30] Internally generated initiatives probably became the largest source of potential projects. Once the Board had some experience as to the sorts of situations in which it could be effective, criteria were developed to pick out projects that looked promising to prevent Members and executives from committing time and resources for too long before getting any return. Although the strategy of spotlighting priority sectors became more important, probably by the winter of 1967-8, the Corporation did not at any time ignore approaches from individual firms.

The way in which the IRC appears to have become steadily more accepted by a growing range of industrialists is described below in Chapter 7. It resulted in a steady flow of firms approaching the Corporation on their own initiative. Sometimes this was to discuss a narrow range of company-orientated problems; sometimes it was a request for a loan under the Section 2 (1)(b) of the Act for a specific project; sometimes the Corporation would be asked for its view on a specific merger proposal; and on other occasions industrialists would want to discuss with the Corporation the state of a whole sector and their firm's present and future position in it. The latter might then lead on to the IRC's taking the initiative and doing a full investigation of that industry, perhaps afterwards trying to arrange mergers between several of the companies. In some cases the approach came not from the firm itself but from some sort of intermediary such as the firm's financial advisors, and industrial development officer working for one of the regional industrial development associations or perhaps from one of the central government departments passing a request from a firm on to the IRC.

The IRC thus established its priorities as a result of suggestions from government departments, internally generated initiatives, and approaches from individual firms. The Corporation had to reorganise itself internally in response to the extensive increase in its overall workload if it was to remain as small an organisation as the Board wanted it to, and not be submerged. Beesley and White have analysed this organisational response:

The need was recognised for a more continuous and systematic mechanism for the development of the Corporation. In particular the stages in IRC's work on industries had to be clarified and criteria developed to facilitate the ranking of IRC's industrial priorities; also the system of progress review and work control had to be systematised.[31]

They date this as possibly taking place late in 1968. However the changes may well have been initiated during the period when Kearton was in sole charge before Villiers arrived in February 1968.

A decision to begin work on a subject area as an IRC initiative or in response to a request, seems to have been taken by the Managing Director, though in potentially controversial areas he would probably first take the matter to the Board. Once work began a specific series of steps normally followed. First, a Board Member would be given responsibility for overall control of the project or investigation. Then, working under him, an executive would greatly extend the desk work that had already been done on the industry as a whole, by himself or a back-up executive. So far as possible everything in print, whether published or classified, was absorbed so that an overall international picture emerged. The work would concentrate on

such basic information as the degree of concentration, the volume of sales, the level of technology, the growth characteristics and trends in the ratio of capacity to demand. From an international standpoint IRC needs to know an industry's direct and indirect export contribution, the rate of growth of world trade in its products; the export performance of competing companies overseas and the trends in the proportion of domestic consumption supplied by imports.[32]

The importance of IRC's library can readily be grasped. At this stage the executive would also want to pick the brains of people with a working knowledge of the industry involved: for example, meetings would often be held with the relevant EDC secretariat or with officials of the corresponding MinTech sponsorship division. In addition, oblique approaches might be made to trade associations. The use of questionnaires was eschewed because a most important part of the process was the assessment of individual managers.

With the essential background work complete the emphasis shifted to personal visits to the companies. This stage was regarded as crucial. "Desk research and statistics provide the bones of IRC's work: visits to companies and detailed discussions with management provide the flesh".[33] The visiting executive would talk to people at all stages from the board-level downwards, attempting to get the "feel" of a firm and to fill out the broad picture sketched out at the deskwork stage. Following that, individual managers were asked a range of detailed questions in order that a full picture of a firm could be built up, covering such items as the state of labour relations and training; the firm's liquidity, output per employee, P/E ratio, and results in relation to return on capital; the extent to which orders on hand, and forecast make maximum use of existing assets; the management's financial control, marketing strategies, investment and manpower plans; and grasp of issues like developing technologies, import penetration, change in market shares and plans of commercial rivals. Depending on whether a project was a merger or a capital investment scheme additional questions would be asked respectively about overall post-merger rationalisation plans and the economies of scale benefits at all levels from R&D through to distribution, or about the phasing of the scheme, its location, and the anticipated cash flow. If the inquiry being undertaken was only a general one questions might be asked about how each management team saw their firm's future in their industry and, because of the role personality factors can sometimes play in a merger situation, about their views on prominent individuals working for rival organisations. As the Corporation was concerned to get results the emphasis at this stage of an enquiry was not just on seeking information, and assessing individuals, but on looking out for practical problems.

The Board Member overseeing the investigation "exercised close oversight".[34] He would sometimes accompany the executive on visits to the most important firms, on return visits, or to conferences at IRC headquarters with groups of senior managers from different firms in the same industry. By the time a project got to an advanced stage one of the most important elements in the situation became the process of assessing managers. In some sectors the views of customers were sought: this especially was the case where the customer was a nationalised industry. The means by which control was exercised was through "virtually continuous telephone consultation" between the executives and those Board Members particularly concerned with the sector he was working on.[35] For example when he was a director Lockwood had at one point fifty long calls of this kind a month. When a project was a big or intransigent one (ball bearings, nuclear power, pumps, aluminium smelters) *ad hoc* groups of several Board Members would be involved and the Board as a whole would exercise control and direction at its regular monthly meetings. These big ongoing items took up a great deal of time. Nuclear power for example came up at eleven full Board meetings and was the subject of nine staff papers, and the bid for Brown Bayley was only launched after eight Board meetings had discussed six working papers.[36]

These detailed papers on specific projects were written as the basis for the Board's discussion and decision-taking and were thus very important. They probably contained detailed analysis using standard sets of sub-headings such as a detailed description of the project including the factors like rationalisation benefits that made it important; the position of the firm(s) in relation to the industry involved in terms of profit record, assets, market share, the import/export balance, world competition and similar factors; an assessment of the abilities of the managers involved to see the project through; the impact of the scheme on other firms and on the overall use of resources within the sector; and the importance of the project with regard to the balance of payments and the economy as a whole. McClelland has commented in this regard that "the general run of Board papers . . . was certainly of outstanding quality, thoroughly researched and clearly and incisively presented".[37]

The criticism of IRC executives as being 'brash young men' probably arose mainly as a result of the processes described above. The executive would go to a factory or firm headquarters asking questions, taking up the time of people who perhaps had not asked him there, or who were following instructions perhaps against their will from their own superiors. The executive would ask a great many detailed questions, some of which may have related to matters about which individual managers were not too proud. Because the executive himself had a heavy work load with substantial travelling, his own time was limited. It is thus fairly easy to envisage situations in which people chosen for their personality but with, in the eyes of the manager they were talking to, apparently limited practical knowledge and experience, might come to the point perhaps too quickly for the taste of men who had spent years or perhaps a lifetime in a certain industry. Executives appeared 'brash' purely because of the dynamics of the situation. Their own difficulty in this context is illustrated by Brooke, the Deputy Managing Director, who told Graham Turner that "in the early days . . . he sometimes used to take older men on visits with him in order to reassure clients".[38] It was for similar sorts of reasons that charges of superficiality were occasionally levelled at IRC's understanding of complex industrial situations: for example some SKF managers in the ball bearings industry, on which the IRC had spent considerable time between August 1968 and May 1969, were quoted as finding IRC men unable to fully follow complex discussions about its nature.[39]

The method of research described so far applies to the system that Kearton appears to have originated and which Villiers developed. Earlier, under Grierson the organisation was less centralised and the executives had more scope for taking the initiative. Much more use was then made of outsiders: for example, the telecommunications inquiry was conducted by one of the Board Members together with a senior partner from a firm of accountants.[40]

However, the Corporation still had to use outside expertise after the internal reorganisation if the executive team were to be kept small despite the increasing work load. The tactic employed was apparently to control such use by commissioning reports on closely defined subjects and by ensuring that all the 'conclusions' part was done inside the Corporation. Because the IRC was not always happy with the recommendations of these (outside) groups an overall decline in their use took place.[41] This is reflected by the item in the accounts labelled "consultancy, legal and other professional charges": £52,000 was spent in the first fifteen months, £74 in 1968-69, £35,000 in 1969-70, and £27,000 in 1970-71.[42] When it is remembered that these will have included the ongoing merchant bank and other legal and professional fees relating to the Corporation's involvement in specific projects, and that such involvement increased in 1968-69 and 1969-70, it can be seen that consultancy fees dropped as a proportion of the total. The actual decision on whether to call in outside experts was made on an *ad hoc* basis. Examples of their use occurred with the joint investigation with the Board of Trade of the textile industry which was done partly by two well-known figures in Lancashire, Mrs. Caroline Miles and Mr. Ord-Johnstone; and with the IRC's research on the effects of the taxation system on inward and outward investment, which was partly dealt with by employing "an expert in the field".[43] The Corporation also employed 'head-hunting' agencies on some occasions, to help find executives for some of the companies it was involved with restructuring.

Throughout the IRC's existence security was a permanent problem because without safeguards members would have been in a position to obtain confidential and perhaps commercially valuable information about rivals. The problem was dealt with in various ways. All executives were forbidden from buying shares. Next all schemes had code names: two that have come to light are Hedges and Butler for GEC/AEI and Mustard and Cress for Leyland/BMH.[44] This helped to prevent a Board Member from seeing papers connected with his own industry. The other precaution taken was to exclude a Member from Board discussion about projects relating to the industry in which his own company was involved. So, for example, Kearton knew nothing of the work on wool, and Lockwood was excluded from all electronics topics. At a conference Cant was thus able to assure a worried industrialist in the same line of business as the Powell Duffryn Group, Cant's own firm, that "in the IRC we have the strictest rules regarding confidence, I can assure you that if you brought your problem to the IRC I should be told nothing about it."[45] These security rules seemed to have been extremely strict and very fully observed, as indeed they had to be, because a scandal of any kind would have had immense repercussions not only for the IRC itself, but also for the Government.

At the apex of the whole system unequivocably was the Board. Although it was at first handicapped by lack of experience as to how it could use its powers, once the GEC/AEI watershed had been passed, and Grierson had resigned, the divergence of views seems to have been replaced by a remarkable degree of unanimity which Professor McClelland, with his direct personal experience, has explained as follows:

> As we got to know each other well, and as in particular the issue whether to be more hawkish or more doveish in our approaches was resolved by the success of a highly skilled deployment of the range of instruments at our disposal, a remarkable unity of opinion seems to have been displayed. This is not to say that we always started with the same point of view, but we found that discussion based on a very considerable respect for one another's judgement usually brought us to it; and I do not remember that a vote was ever taken.[46]

The Board appears to have exercised reasonably comprehensive control. It took decisions about what it was and what it was not going to support, and it gave the go-ahead on all important IRC initiatives. However, in situations in which a virtue was made out of giving executives extensive independence, and given that the Managing Director was the only full-time Board Member, decisions obviously had to be taken to which the Board was not privy. These were handled "effectively and informally through the regular meetings of executives and Managing Director".[47] For example, at some stage in every project a point was reached when a decision had to be made about whether it was worth continuing to commit resources or whether the time would be better spent on another subject. In such a situation the influence of the executive was extensive because his knowledge would be greater than that of the Managing Director or of the Board Member under whom he was working. Similarly, executives occasionally began work in an area without being directed to do so. However the greater centralisation introduced in 1968 was designed to cope with this problem. The executives had wide freedom of action but their extensive influence did not mean that they ran the organisation. Other factors were at work to control and guide their influence: the Chairman was involved almost daily; the small teams of Board Members and executives that operated meant that what were in effect sub-committees of the Board could be arranged at relatively short notice; the organisational changes that Beesley and White have identified introduced means of project control in 1968; and there was frequent telephone contact between the executive and the overseeing Board Member. In the last resort the Board would meet in between its normal monthly meetings to deal with any special problems that had arisen: such meetings were held during the GEC/AEI, Kent/Cambridge/Rank, and RHP struggles for example. The extent to which the executives were really independent was for all these reasons in the end very limited. Wilsher indeed refers to one example where "an executive was judged to have entered too deeply into a commitment, and it was made brutally clear that this must never happen again".[48] Altogether the doubts about whether or not the Board exercised effective control appear to have little foundation.

CHAPTER 6 DECIDING WHICH SCHEMES TO SUPPORT

The way in which the IRC picked specific industries as being the ones on which it was going to concentrate has been described in the previous chapter. Choosing priorities was the process of deciding where the IRC's attention was to be focused. The first half of this chapter deals with the criteria that were applied as the means of assessing the worth of different projects within the previously established priority industries. It begins with a fairly abstract description of the whole range of the criteria which the IRC aimed to use, before illustrating in more concrete terms what this meant in practice in two cases, one an agreed merger and the other a more controversial affair. The second half of the chapter describes how the Corporation used its money.

The Application of Criteria to Projects

The process of establishing criteria represented an attempt to define as closely as possible the Corporation's overall aim of strengthening the economy and restoring the international competitiveness of British industry. The factors that were used to establish which were the priority industries were applied to specific projects as criteria in their own right.[1] The first of these was the balance of payments. Every project, whether a merger, a selective investment scheme or a rescue operation, was assessed according to its estimated impact on the balance of payments through increased exports or import substitution. In some instances this factor was of critical importance. The process leading to the creation of BLMC speeded up in December 1967 and January 1968 partly because of the need to push through the merger quickly to maximise the extra export competitiveness available to the new combine as a result of the devaluation of the pound in November 1967. Because the payments crisis was not really alleviated until autumn 1969, the IRC was where possible concerned with schemes that would make an impact as quickly as possible.

The second main criterion was that of productivity and the ability of a selective investment scheme, but more especially of a merger, to put assets at the disposal of companies that would be able to make the greatest use of them: "often important activities are left to atrophy while in other more interested hands they would flourish".[2] The IRC Board argued that given competent management the post-merger rationalisation process would lead, because of the potential benefits of economies of scale, to increased productivity, and thence to greater job security and self-generating expansion of the company concerned. This meant that when two or three companies were joined together duplication could be eliminated and advantage taken of each other's strengths in different fields like research or marketing. In addition various other benefits would accrue once the firms had been integrated because the greater size of the new company would enable it to make better overall use of the total assets than the firms involved had been able to do separately. The theory was two plus two equals five and in the case of electronics it could be "six or much more".[3] Mergers meant that economies of scale could be achieved at all stages of the productive process from R&D through the purchasing of raw materials, production, to marketing and distribution systems, and a bigger company would find it easier to raise capital, install the most up-to-date equipment, and so on. The latter was particularly important when capital plant was expensive, as in super tension cables and parts of process plant. In the case of the big and the very big mergers the Board had to consider whether the reduction in competition would offset the advantages gained from economies of scale.[4] Almost always this did not apply in practice as the IRC was seeking to strengthen the UK presence within the intensely competitive international context.

Two examples illustrate the different sorts of ways in which a merger could lead to greater productivity. The amalgamation of BTR Industries and Leyland and Birmingham Rubber Company was supported because it "offered exceptional rationalisation opportunities due to the close proximity of their major manufacturing sites".[5] When they had been competing units, the firms that went into the RHP combine each had had a product range of between seven thousand and thirteen thousand types of ball and roller bearings. Following the merger this duplication was eliminated by establishing five divisions. Within two years this had resulted in a 20 per cent increase in productivity and a general cut in delivery time from up to a year for most bearings, down to between eight and sixteen weeks.[6]

In addition many other questions arose: for example would the scheme in question contribute not just to the development of high technology, but also to its application to productive processes? Would the project be likely to result in the development of more sophisticated product ranges aimed at the advanced Western European and North American markets? Would it assist the Government's regional policies? Would the proposal help solve the sector's structural problems by having ripple effects and encouraging others to merge or reorganise? There are two examples of the latter in the pump industry late in 1968. All but the last can be said to have been factors present in the three-way merger that led to the formation of Plessey Numerical Control. Selective investment schemes were judged according to the presence of such factors as "high growth, key exporters, capital goods and component suppliers".[7] This can be illustrated by the Marwin, Herbert-Ingersoll, and Kearney and Trecker schemes in machine tools. These were specialist, technically advanced companies exporting a high proportion of their products.

One further point applied with regard to the biggest mergers. There was a feeling in the late 1960s in parts of Whitehall, shared by some at the IRC, that there was a need to create huge companies in expanding industries like motor vehicles, computers, nuclear power, electronics and electrical engineering partly because international mergers were seen as inevitable, especially within the Common Market.[8] In that context it was argued that Britain needed large, and by that time fully rationalised and successful companies, that could take the lead when the time came: this was especially the case if there was to be any political horse-trading associated with the process.

The most indispensable of all the yardsticks used to assess schemes was the quality of the management concerned, and the Board's judgement of its ability to complete a project. This view was consistently maintained throughout, as is shown by quotations from respectively 1967-68, 1969-68, 1969-70 reports:[9] "the quality of management is the key to success"; "the critical element in IRC work is the capacity of industrial management to do the job – and it is above all on this that the IRC Board must be satisfied before lending its moral or material support to any form of industrial reorganisation"; and "the main criterion is a strong unified management willing and able to expand in the face of international competition". It was on the company managers that the actual outcome of a whole project depended.

In order to show what the somewhat abstract criteria were liable to mean in practice the reasons behind two mergers are now outlined. IRC supported the proposed EE/EA merger in June 1967 for two basic reasons. First the IRC argued that "in the electronics industry, which is highly research intensive, there is a strong case for concentrating more of the available resources and talent into fewer, more powerful companies, which can hold their own in world markets".[10] Claiming that "too many ideas were chasing too little money" Sir Leon Bagritt, Chairman of Elliott Automation, claimed that on their own EA had "got into whole new areas of technology but we could not exploit them."[11] IRC took the view that it would be in the national interest to strengthen a firm that had been described as "more of a brain box than a business",[12] by helping to give it greater resources and thus, it was hoped, a better chance of exploiting its technological knowledge.

The second reason was that the activities of the two firms were remarkably complementary. Lord Nelson, Chairman of English Electric, was anxious to expand by diversifying out of heavy generating equipment, a sector that faced a run-down in orders from the Central Electricity Generating Board (CEGB) over the next few years. Bagritt wanted to broaden his company's financial base. The only real clash over the two companies' products came over plans to develop competing ranges of computers. At the time of the merger the IRC was hoping, along with other parts of Whitehall, that this problem could be alleviated, as in fact it was, by putting EE's data-processing assets into the proposed ICL combine. The Corporation described the new company as "one of the largest and best equipped European groups in the field of automation and industrial control systems".[13] The announcement received almost universal press approval.

The GEC/AEI proposal was more complicated but three basic reasons can be identified. The first was that it provided the IRC with a means by which it could attempt to set off a ripple effect that would in itself lead to further restructuring in the industry as a whole. The IRC claimed that "the significance of the merger . . . was its strategic impact in opening the way to rationalisation on a number of fronts where progress has been slow . . . by facilitating the creation of stronger groupings involving other companies in the industry".[14] The Board hoped, as in fact happened in 1968 and 1969, that a GEC/AEI link up would trigger off "a whole chain of deals, bids, mergers and swops", thus reducing the duplication of effort within the industry as a whole.[15] In the autumn of 1967 an extension of this argument relating to IRC's indirect aim was that if AEI resisted GEC's bid it would be liable to try and persuade the stockholders that it was rationalising itself, and did not need to be taken over by GEC for this to happen. In this connection *The Times* commented during the takeover battle

> It is obvious that even if the bid does not succeed, it will have achieved part of the IRC's aim. AEI, forced to defend itself has gone some of the way to meet its attackers criticisms . . . even if GEC's bid fails the IRC will have succeeded.[16]

Secondly a GEC/AEI merger was attractive in itself. The Corporation's research would have highlighted the duplication in such sectors as telecommunications, switch gear, transformers, turbo-generators, microcircuits, process control and domestic appliances. In sectors like some of these where technological change moves quickly, economies of scale in R&D and production can be very great. The new firm would have the resources not just to achieve these rationalisation benefits, but to invest on a large scale to meet the challenge posed by developing technology. The merger by itself, and with the prospect of

programme of £200 million was envisaged of which the IRC's £25 million loan was an important part because it was quickly and cheaply available.[23] On some occasions the very prospect of such a loan "acted as an inducement to merge" because it increased "the attractiveness of the merger to the parties concerned."[24] Lord Stokes certainly acknowledged that IRC finance was vital to the creation of BLMC.[25]

On eleven occasions, the Board also lent money to individual companies in non-merger situations for capital investment schemes, in five cases under Section 2 (1)(b) of the IRC Act.[26] These loans were usually related to the reorganisation and expansion of existing plant. This was the case with Rootes, where a small loan was made with the offer of a greater commitment if required, and also with Herbert Ingersoll, Marwin, and the four projects that went through under the Textile Re-equipment Scheme. Two other uses to which the loans were put were the building of new integrated factories on green field sites as in the Samuel Osborn case, and the financing of strategically significant projects such as the Reed and Dixon de-inking plants which were seen as import savers. There was also a revolving £10 million loan to BLMC which was to be used "for the purpose of purchasing machine tools to modernise and expand its production facilities".[27] The aim here was not simply to assist BLMC's capital investment programme but also to stimulate investment in the machine tool industry:

> The recently announced IRC/British Leyland scheme will provide a basis on which IRC can discuss with particular companies new expansion schemes, the development of new metal-forming techniques and the manufacture of machine tool ranges not currently produced in the UK, but where the domestic market affords a sufficient base from which to promote export sales.[28]

This use of IRC funds illustrates how the Corporation did not always concentrate on promoting mergers.

A third use of IRC finance was to enable assurances to be given that funds would be available at a future date. On almost every occasion that a merger or capital investment scheme was supported the IRC appears to have said that funds would subsequently be available if the firm satisfied the IRC's usual conditions: the latter are described below. British Oxygen and Clarke Chapman/John Thompson are two examples of companies that appear to have returned to the IRC for funds several months after completing their mergers. In some cases, the Corporation (formally) undertook to make specific sums available as standby credit to be called on as the project progressed. In the RHP case for example, standby credit seems to have been negotiated not at the time of the merger but somewhat later.

A fourth way in which the IRC used its funds was to seek to take on the taxpayers behalf its share of the profits accruing from a scheme it had backed. This would be achieved by negotiating specific loans as convertible loans, not fixed interest ones. There were for example conversion rights in the loans to EE/EA, Davy Ashmore and RHP. The principle was taken further in those cases where the IRC took a minority shareholding to provide funds for new investment or for reorganisation. Although this involved a greater risk than did a fixed interest loan, the rewards were also potentially greater if the IRC's confidence in the firm turned out to be justified by an increase in profits. Being an equity holder was also attractive in that it provided the IRC, especially in a post-merger situation, with a more powerful lever to promote rationalisation of plant or management than it had in those situations where it was only one of several bankers. It is impossible on the available evidence to say which of these two factors predominated in individual cases where the Corporation acquired an equity holding: there was Rootes (15%), Nuclear Enterprises, British Nuclear Design and Construction (BNDC) (26%), The Nuclear Power Group (TNPG) (10%), Herbert Ingersoll, the Laird Group (13.6%), and Kearney and Trecker (15½%). The IRC's role in the reorganisation of the Laird Group was in fact the most decisive public example of the IRC using its position as an equity holder to effect reorganisation.

In three particular situations the IRC utilised to the full powers given to it under the Act. It took advantage of its funds in a fifth way when 'using the stock market mechanism'[29] to achieve its end in a bid situation. In the Kent/Cambridge/Rank affair it bought Cambridge shares and participated in the acceptance of the Kent offer. Its offer to the shareholders of Brown Bayley Ltd. was accepted. Finally when creating RHP it underwrote the Ransome and Marles' bid for Pollard, purchased Ransome and Marles shares in the market, and made a loan to Ransome to finance terms for its bid for Pollard. It exchanged the Brown Bayley holding in Hoffman that had been acquired when taking over Brown Bayley for a combination of loan stock, cash, and equity. It also acquired the 40% minority holding in Hoffman that it did not own to counter Pollard's argument that it could not decide which bid to accept until the third party had become involved in the takeover battle. So the Corporation put £6,504,514 of public funds into Kent, enabling it to buy Cambridge against the run of the market; it bought Brown Bayley Ltd for £5,818,300; and it used £9,461,000 to buy Pollard for Ransome and Marles.[30]

The sixth way in which the IRC used its funds was to lend money to individual companies in non-merger situations, but only on condition that the previously agreed measures were taken to reorganise the firm. This was part of the way, described in Chapter 4, in which it acted as a rescue operator. As a result of its financial involvement the IRC played an active part after the loan had been made in ensuring that its conditions were carried out. The two outstanding cases of this kind were Rolls Royce and Cammel Laird, where IRC went so far as to install or take directorships. A third case was Davy Ashmore where the serious overrun on the Immingham refinery contract, which had been awarded to Davy's Power Gas subsidiary could have threatened the firm with bankruptcy. "IRC sponsored arrangements to bridge this crisis":[31] its two £600,000 loans formed part of a combined City £5 million package. One of the Corporation's loans was for only a year and was the only piece of short rather than medium-term finance the IRC provided.

From the individual company's point of view the IRC was a useful extra source of finance at a difficult time, chiefly because of its flexibility. The Corporation was able to provide finance to suit the individual needs of companies of all sizes, by far the largest being the £25 million, to BLMC and the £15 million to EE/EA. Although there were seven sums between £5 million and £10 million, the majority of IRC's financial involvements were much smaller: eight were under £1 million and eighteen – one half of the total – were between £1 million and £3.5 million. The terms on which they were agreed varied greatly and reflected the IRC's ability to tailor its finance to suit the different circumstances of individual companies. At different times, the IRC provided subordinated loans, enabling the company to borrow elsewhere relatively easily; secured loans; convertible loans; and, most commonly, unsecured loans. Frequently interest in the early years was deferred, the IRC being ready to encourage this because it attached great importance to a firm making the maximum use of its financial resources in the post-merger rationalisation period. Earlier repayment was normally offered: usually this was at the company's option although in the Klinger/Qualitex case discretion was left to the IRC. As already mentioned the Board was prepared in some cases to share the commercial risk of the firm and undertake the subscription of equity.

The time scale of IRC finance was especially important to the individual company because one of the purposes of putting priority funds at the IRC's disposal had been to enable it to provide medium-term finance to new groupings when it was not available from the capital market, or from the normal providers of short-term finance.[32] In the event, the IRC found and filled this gap: over twenty of its thirty loans were repayable after periods of between four and seven years, putting them firmly within the medium-term bracket.

Although the IRC was a useful supplementary and highly flexible source of finance it should not be inferred that it was readily exploitable.

Viewing the situation from the inside, Professor McClelland has commented, that the IRC "never . . . had a long queue of would-be borrowers because it was known to be an exacting lender, not in the financial terms of the loan, but in the conditions with respect to commercial plans and performance".[33] This can be readily demonstrated by describing the five principles that the IRC applied to each of its financial involvements.

The Corporation's basic aim was to consider finance only when a "project would be impossible, or unduly delayed without IRC funds".[34] The Corporation made similar claims regarding its selective investment projects: it had to "be satisfied that the money is not available from other sources".[35] There were some clear-cut cases of this principle applying. When the Corporation supported the Dunford/Hadfields merger in special steels the finance came from Brandts, the merchant bankers. On the other hand there were times when the Corporation provided money only when it was not available elsewhere. Thus in the case of Samuel Osborn it acted as a lender of last resort, and on other occasions, like the Rolls Royce case, at the Government's request. In such instances as Davy Ashmore and Kearney and Trecker though, the Corporation provided money in company with other bankers, thus implying that money was available elsewhere.

However the commonest situation seems to have been that having backed a merger the IRC was anxious that its benefit should come through as quickly as possible. Often, the provision of money could accelerate this process, though the IRC had to be convinced that it really was needed. As the Corporation often had been intimately involved with pre-merger discussions, and knew the personalities and factors involved, it was in a good position to lend money because it had in fact gone through more than the basic processes of inspection adopted by conventional bankers. By lending money at that stage the IRC ensured that the new company avoided having to delay the post-merger rationalisation process, which could have been to the detriment of the economy, either because the firm had to wait for another bank to decide whether it would lend money, or because of the need to wait pending the raising of capital on the open market. So it seems to have been not so much a case of the IRC's lending money because no one else would do so, but because otherwise a project might be held up, thereby losing precious time in which advantage could be taken of the situation. This was an especially relevant consideration during the race against time to get the balance of payments situation under control, after devaluation in November 1967.

Once it was convinced that its funds were necessary the Board applied its second principle: it considered whether a project was worthy of its support. In a merger situation this had already been applied: in a development project the IRC claimed that it employed "the same overall criteria as determine its restructuring role".[36] Whatever the scheme, the IRC had to be convinced that a merger or development project was viable and that it was in the hands of managers who were capable of seeing it through. The objection may be raised that where IRC was involved in a rescue operation this principle could by definition not be made to apply. The Corporation would probably have argued that in such cases correspondingly greater importance was attached to the following precondition.

The third of the IRC's principles was that money would only be lent if the company concerned agreed to the IRC's conditions. In a merger situation this seems to have involved the IRC examining, in detail which varied from case to case apparently according to its view of the management team, the post-merger rationalisation plans. The kinds of conditions it insisted on varied enormously. On the one hand Stokes seems to have been given virtually a free hand following the loan to BLMC, whereas on the other the Laird Group had to agree to the IRC laying down strict limits as for example on the dividend it was able to pay its shareholders during the life of the IRC loan. In all cases companies had to agree to abide by IRC's follow-up procedures. The following chapter discusses the importance of the ways in which the IRC used its finance as a means of implementing its policies and as a means of exerting its influence in the affairs of the companies at a subsequent stage.

The fourth principle was that the IRC should earn a commercial return on the money it lent or invested. As regards the interest charged on individual loans the IRC summed up its position as follows: "IRC only commits funds where this is essential in pursuit of its statutory objectives; it is determined to operate on a commercial basis and it seeks the best return on its funds consistent with its objectives."[37] Where interest was deferred and payments made in addition to the normal annual rates in the later years of the life of the loan, the IRC still had to pay annual interest on the money it was borrowing from the National Loans Fund, its own borrowing rates being geared to the market rates. The practical result appears to have been that the overall rate of interest was worked out at a rate slightly higher than the anticipated cost to the IRC. The Corporation was then able to claim that it lent its money at commercial rates, meaning that it was charging enough to cover its expenses and any losses. This meant that the IRC was able to provide capital more cheaply than was available in the City, a process which was accentuated by the generally tight credit situation in the late 1960s. It was this that led to criticism of the Corporation for providing 'soft finance'.

This charge was always rejected by the IRC.[38] It would probably have argued along the lines that it did provide cheap money but that this was not 'soft' because the Corporation was attaching extensive conditions to the money it lent. Further, the IRC probably felt that it should not be judged by City standards as it was injecting the national interest into each situation, because it was concerned with the "wider benefits to the economy"[39] as well as with the long-term position of an individual firm: this is not the case with a conventional banker who is usually concerned with the period covered by his financial involvement. Finally the Board would have pointed out that it succeeded in implementing its fourth financial principle as it was making money and not losing it.

The IRC's final aim was to ensure that each of its investments was potentially self-liquidating. The Government had never intended that the IRC become a holding company like the Italian Institute for Industrial Reconstruction (IRI).[40] The aim throughout the IRC's life was to "turn its funds over as quickly as possible",[41] disposing of its holdings "as soon as the necessary reorganisation and management changes are completed",[42] so that the money could be reinvested and put to work elsewhere. The quicker the IRC turned over its funds the greater was its capacity for promoting its objectives. This aim was achieved in that the loans had a limited life, and the equity holdings appear to have had termination commitments, but it is difficult to make a final judgement because full details of all loans do not seem to have been published. While it may have remained IRC policy to dispose of such holdings as occasion offered, there might have been cases where it took a number of years before the Board considered the firm not to be in need of further IRC assistance.

Overall, it is impossible to deny that IRC financial activity distorted the capital market. It provided relatively cheap finance, thus creating a favoured group of what the IRC saw as basically well-managed but fully borrowed companies: to these it was able to give "selective exemption" from the generally tight credit conditions.[43] This was not just available to firms involved with mergers. An increase in loans to individual companies in non-merger situations took place in 1970 as a result of the Government's Textile Re-equipment Scheme, and because of the IRC's announcing that in the light of the continuing low level of capital investment it would assist by concentrating on its selective investment function. A second example of the distortion of the capital market was the way in which bankers were effectively encouraged to avoid projects about which they had marginal doubts in the knowledge that there was a lender of last resort in the shape of the IRC or central government departments. In addition the Corporation distorted normal takeover bid procedures in the Kent and RHP cases because it was known to have a bottomless purse. More generally companies thinking of making takeover bids had to take the IRC's attitude into consideration. Though to some, these results of IRC activity were undesirable because they were unconventional; it should be borne in mind that it had been intended from the beginning that the IRC should bring an element of discrimination into the capital market, and fill the medium-term finance gap.

The impact of IRC on the Stock Market resulted from the IRC being outside the City in the sense that it was not a conventional merchant bank. The Corporation was able to approach companies with its own ideas and questions, whereas an ordinary merchant bank had to wait to be asked into a developing situation: once it has been brought in it can only talk to the client, whereas IRC could approach commercial rivals. In addition whereas a merchant bank has to serve the interests of an individual client, IRC bore the wider responsibilities of interpreting the national interest in each situation by asking truly huge questions – for example should a particular industry be grouped into specialist or multi-product manufactures, what was the ideal import/export balance, and what should the role of foreign-owned firms be? Finally the Corporation's main concern was not, as is normally the case with a merchant bank, getting the maximum return on its investments or loans, but the long-term performance of a company after the withdrawal of its support. In financial terms the Corporation was not anxious to make massive profits but to more than cover its costs on the fixed interest loans, and to aim for rather more in selected cases where it took on greater responsibility as an equity holder, so as to cover its operating costs, its tax, its interest on borrowing from the National Loans Fund, and the dividend it paid to the Secretary of State on its Public Dividend Capital.

CHAPTER 7 MEANS OF IMPLEMENTING POLICIES

IRC Methods In Practice

When the Board had gone through the process of applying its criteria to a scheme and had decided that the management involved were worth backing, possibly with finance, it was then faced with having to find a means of implementing the project. Drawing on his personal experience as a Board Member, McClelland has analysed in a most useful passage what he describes as the "formidable panoply of means of influence" that the Board was able to develop and deploy. He lists these "in ascending order of what might be called the sharpness of their cutting edge".[1] They should be seen as the means used to fulfil each of the functions described in Chapter 4.

First and most common, was "sweet reason". The IRC's initial move was "normally to attempt to persuade those whose decisions would determine the matter to take appropriate action".[2] As the IRC itself put it: "the hope is that rationalisation can be by agreement".[3] This approach was effective in those cases where IRC promoted mergers by acting as a catalyst. McClelland's second and third instruments were two of the main uses to which the IRC put its funds. He describes how the provision of loan finance could be attractive, enabling the bidding company to finance its bid, or more often allowing the newly merged company to speed the post merger rationalisation process. The loan itself sometimes acted as an inducement. Thirdly "equity participation by IRC was in some cases a real . . . inducement to companies to take part in reorganisation".[4] As described in the preceding chapter, minority equity holdings were rarely used in non-rescue operation situations whereas the offer of a loan was fairly common.

McClelland defines the stimulation of third parties outside the direct relationship between the IRC and a specific company as a fourth means of producing action. This was used less often than the first three methods to influence both management and shareholders. The first example in this category is the media, especially the financial press. McClelland quotes the case of the publicity given to the IRC's meeting with AEI's institutional shareholders, where Kearton explained in detail the IRC's reasons for backing GEC's bid. Reporters gave the impression by quoting from institutional investors that the latter were impressed by IRC's rationale.[5] McClelland implies that the IRC Board saw this as a real instrument and used it on other occasions: "the fact that . . as time wore on it became known that the IRC view, if communicated to the press, might well be at the least treated with great respect, undoubtedly gave the IRC views added weight".[6] What he seems to be suggesting is that there were occasions when managers were not in agreement with the IRC, and that the Corporation then used publicity to try and persuade them to give way. As he acknowledges, this technique had to be used with care because it could so easily have rebounded, as indeed happened to a certain extent when the IRC's disagreement with a firm came into the open before the IRC made its detailed reasoning public: this was the case with Rank, SKF, and Pollard. The next type of third party employed by the IRC were the purchasers of a certain type of product. "Where mergers are likely to lead . . . to greater efficiency, the industry's customers may be expected to welcome the prospect, and indeed to collaborate in attempts to promote them".[7] To McClelland's examples can be added the co-operation which the IRC obtained from the CEGB when attempting to rationalise the heavy electrical sector into two groups with roughly equal shares of the home market.[8]

The last of the third parties mentioned by McClelland were shareholders. How far the IRC attempted to influence them in bid situations apart from the GEC/AEI case is not known, but as described later in this chapter, institutional shareholders were an important means by which IRC conducted its monitoring operations. There were occasions when the IRC used a fourth third party. This was the case when the Corporation used intermediaries in Whitehall to help it to persuade the managers involved. An example here would be the meetings which various Ministers had in 1967 with Stokes and Harriman, prior to the BLMC link-up.[9]

The fifth but scarcely used instrument outlined by McClelland was the use of IRC funds to buy equity holdings, not to take a risk-sharing minority holding as described above, but rather to ensure that further restructuring took place along the lines IRC wanted. He quotes the purchase of Cambridge and of Kent shares to support the latter's share price in the Rank battle, and also the actual takeover by IRC of Brown Bayley. Since Brown Bayley's board recommended acceptance of the IRC's offer, this instrument cannot be categorised as the IRC imposing its will on the stock market. Perhaps this class should be widened and simply termed 'using the stock market mechanism'.[10] In backing Ransome and Marles's bid for Pollard the IRC was also using public funds in a bid situation and exploiting the market mechanism to help ensure, as in the Brown Bayley and Kent cases, that restructuring took place along the path that its own analysis led it to believe would be in the national interest. In the case of Ransome and Marles's bid for

Pollard, the Corporation underwrote the Ransome's bid, purchased Ransome's shares and made a loan to Ransome to finance the terms of the bid. This was a very different type of devise from the provision of a loan to help finance acceptable terms in an agreed takeover situation. Basically the case of RHP is, like those of Kent and Brown Bayley, an example of the IRC utilising the market mechanism to achieve its ends.

In deploying its methods the IRC always began with "sweet reason". Even during the Kent/Cambridge and RHP battles, the Corporation sought to get Rank and SKF to co-operate in a mutually agreed scheme. It must be stressed that in the majority of the cases this was enough: in over half of its published projects there was no financial involvement or commitment. When this approach did not succeed, the IRC had to move on to discover whether "sweet reason" could be made to be effective in combination with another, or more than one, of the remaining instruments. At this stage a hint by the IRC of further action to come may of itself have persuaded some smaller managers to agree. McClelland may perhaps be seen as suggesting as much: "it might be a matter of pointing out to them (the board of the company involved) that the consequences of no action would be worse than those of taking the action indicated (the suggested IRC scheme)".[11] At this stage the IRC could use one of several combinations of loan finance, equity participation, and stimulation of third parties. In several cases "sweet reason" allied to finance proved sufficient. In others the use of a third party could lead to action: machine tool industrialists gave a cool reception to the IRC's ideas for their industry, but working through the BLMC loan was a convenient way around this.

In the last resort, when all possible combinations of "sweet reason", loans, equity holdings and the influence of a third party had failed, the IRC Board had to decide whether to use its powers to achieve its end, or to drop the proposal. This meant in essence judging whether the case was important enough to be worth all the controversy and possible estrangement of other industrialists, that would be likely to arise from the IRC seeking to use the market mechanism to achieve its end. In the case of Kent and RHP, the IRC did consider the issue to be one of critical importance: a Rank /Cambridge link-up would have had a strong, and in the IRC's view adverse, influence on the future development of the instrument industry; and SKF's expansion in Britain via its Skefco subsidiary led the IRC to believe that unless it took action there would be "no viable basis for a British-owned ball bearing industry".[12] On other occasions the judgement of the IRC Board seems to have been that the issues at stake were not of such supreme importance as to justify using the Corporation's full powers to promote change: this was the case with some of the industries that the IRC found to be resistant to change – wool, pumps and paper for example.[13]

The Importance of Monitoring

Once a project had gone through, and especially when the IRC had become financially involved, its job, far from being finished, had really only begun. The IRC had "more than a banker's responsibility"[14] for the security of its funds: it had "a continuous responsibility to satisfy itself that managements which had benefited from its support proceed with the plans envisaged when that support was given."[15] This reflected the IRC view that "much of the IRC's work . . . can be turned to profit and benefit through effective action by management." Hence, following initial IRC action, rationalisation or investment or changes in management and techniques are needed."[16] Consequently the IRC took the task of monitoring seriously and established a follow-up process to ensure that the exacting conditions actually attached to its financial support were implemented. Further the Corporation took advantage of this role and insisted that because its reputation was at stake, even where it was not financially involved, it must be allowed "to follow closely the implementation of the measures of rationalisation."[17] The Corporation thus took advantage of its role as banker, shareholder or backer and provided itself with a potentially powerful lever which could be used if the Board thought it necessary to directly influence the development of a company after a project had gone through. In practice, follow-up was thus the sixth and ultimately the most important means by which the Corporation sought to bring a project to fruition.

The commonest way in which IRC carried through the follow-up process was by return visits. Twice a year, at the time of interim and end year results there were "consultations with the companies concerned on their rationalisation and development plans."[18] Reports were submitted to the Board covering "all important indices of company efficiency, export performance and industrial relations."[19] If the Board was not happy with the report a return visit might be made, or action of the kind classified below be put in hand. In those cases in which the Corporation was more than usually concerned about a firm, "more frequent exchanges" were held to be "necessary."[20] It is important to note that these follow-up visits were all in the event conducted by one Board member, B.R. Cant, who no doubt gained from his experience in the sense that he would know which were the important points to look out for as the raionalisation programme proceeded. The aim of the follow-up reporting process, even before it was standardised in 1969-70, was not only to ensure that rationalisation measures were implemented, but to pick out any companies that looked like running into trouble, so that remedial action could be initiated. By March 1970 forty-eight companies were covered by these arrangements.

In eleven cases the IRC went as far as getting the company concerned to agree to having a Corporation representative on the company's board. There were IRC nominees on the boards of Rootes, Kent, BNDC, TNPG, Brown Bayley Steels, (Brown Bayley Ltd's subsidiary Hoffmann before it was sold to RHP), RHP, Plessey NC, Herbert Ingersoll, Rolls Royce, the Laird Group, and British United Trawlers. In all but the last case the IRC was financially involved. In eight of the remaining ten cases it was an equity holder, and in four of these cases it had also provided a loan. IRC nominees were thus put into companies in which the Corporation had an important stake. Apart from those companies with which the IRC had become involved as a result of a rescue operation, they were mainly ones that the IRC had played an important, often initiating, part in creating. The presence of an IRC nominee together with an above average financial commitment, indicates that they were firms which the IRC Board felt faced above-average rationalisation problems.

The presence of an IRC nominee on the Board was obviously a means of injecting a much more continuing type of follow-up process into the situation than was the case with the follow-up reports. Thus a great deal hinged on the person involved. In four cases (Rootes, TNPG, Herbert Ingersoll and the Laird Group) IRC Board Members were the nominees; in three cases (British United Trawlers, BNDC and Kent) it was an IRC executive; in two cases (Brown Bayley Steels and RHP) it was an IRC Board Member in company with IRC executives; and in two others it was an experienced outsider – Sir Stuart Mitchell, a former Chairman of the Machine Tools EDC, was the nominee on Plessey NC's Board, and Lord Beeching on that of Rolls Royce. The presence of IRC experience on a company's board meant that those who had been heavily involved with creating the new firm or solving a crisis were able to contribute the experience they had gained.

Less directly, but very importantly, the IRC sometimes worked through third parties in the follow-up process.[21] When a company, with which the IRC was involved, appeared to be moving too slowly in the rationalisation process, or reacting badly to unforeseen circumstances, the IRC Board was ready to take advantage of every means open to it to make its point felt to the board of the company concerned. The IRC worked through institutional shareholders, and probably through a firm's bankers, accountants, or economic advisers: sometimes this was in addition to its own direct approaches, and sometimes not.

The IRC used the follow-up process for two basic purposes. The first was to promote further rationalisation within the sectors in which a firm it had supported was involved or with which it was associated. In at least six cases where subsidiaries of IRC-backed companies were sold to others, not only was the post-merger rationalisation process of the original IRC-supported scheme implemented, but at the same time further restructuring of the sector concerned could be initiated: the outstanding example was the sale of the Brown Bayley Ltd. subsidiary Hoffman to Ransome and Marles, to help create RHP.[22]

More commonly, the IRC used the follow-up process to strengthen individual companies. This was especially the case where it attached exacting conditions to the provision of its finance. Thus Sir Joseph Lockwood has made it clear that "in nearly every case, we had to find a new chief executive for the organisation. In some cases we had to ask the Board to resign, or most of the Board, before we gave support."[23] The importance of the follow-up process was to ensure that the conditions attached to the finance were implemented. However it is important to stress that this was a *continuing* job. The Corporation was ready to inject sweeping management changes sometimes, as in the Kent case, in the light of developments long after the merger. On other occasions the IRC kept in close touch with the company and supplied fairly general assistance. On others again it instigated more far-reaching changes involving not only the injection of new management, but insistence on new systems of financial control, and sometimes the sale of subsidiary companies.[24] Although there is a shortage of documentary examples of individual companies which the IRC helped to strengthen, the Corporation certainly played a discreet role in other instances, working both directly and via a third party.

The Corporation attached more and more importance to its follow-up activities because it came to realise that the results of its work depended not on the number of projects it sponsored, but rather on ensuring that the later performance of companies it backed matched up to its expectations. The Corporation never underrated this task: "whilst reorganisation is difficult enough to achieve, it is still more difficult to get the benefits of reorganisation."[25] Steadily increasing importance was attached to the task; it was not mentioned directly in the 1967-68 report but by the 1968-69 it had "assumed increasing importance", and by 1969-70 the arrangements had been "standardised and given increasing prominence,"[26] affecting fifty-four out of about sixty-five of the IRC's published projects to that date. In its last report the IRC claimed that it "had intended progressively to develop its procedures". By getting a Board Member to conduct the follow-up visits the line executives were left "free for new projects,"[27] and a balance was established between initiating new projects and following up previous ones.

How effective were the IRC's instruments in terms of producing action? By 1970 ministers' earlier fears that the IRC would not have the impact they had hoped for had been proved groundless. As it gained experience, the Corporation became steadily more adept at using its techniques to produce results, in terms of action, in the most unlikely looking circumstances. It was a measure of the Board's discretion and care – these were the most important of IRC's characteristics – in using the means open to it that the IRC became steadily busier while at the same time retaining, with few exceptions, the confidence of industrialists. This was because the IRC, despite its powers, still relied chiefly on the power of reason. The provision of loans, the taking of equity and the stimulation of third parties were there to help convince, persuade, cajole, or even tempt those that did not agree with the Corporation. One Board Member has described this process very effectively: the IRC "takes the initiative only to the minimum extent necessary to maximise the initiative from industry."[28] To do all this the Corporation needed the acquiescence of at least one of the parties involved in a merger situation, or that of the Board concerned in the case of a capital investment project. This imposed a real and practical limit on its seemingly elastic statutory powers.

Only in two types of situation could the IRC *force* an individual Board to act despite its initial opposition. First, in both the Rolls and the Cammell Laird cases there was a liquidity problem which removed from the equation the company's financial independence, and which meant that they could not go on without more finance. Because there was no prospect of this being forthcoming from other sources, they were forced to agree to the IRC's conditions. The Rolls Royce case illustrates this well because its Board refused to accept the conditions the IRC attached to its offer of a loan in January 1970. It was only when Rolls could not go on without more money in May 1970, that the Rolls board gave in.[29] The second occasion on which the IRC was able, in the last resort, to insist that the board of the company act decisively, probably against its will, was in a follow-up situation when, as was the case with Kent,[30] disappointing post-merger results seemed to combine with outside factors to create a potential crisis situation.

If the IRC could produce results by persuasion or by the exploitation of circumstances without recourse to its full powers, did it in fact need those powers? Their importance was that they enabled the Corporation, if it felt the case to be sufficiently important, to force companies into stepping down. It must be stressed though, that only twice, in the Kent and RHP cases, did it have to take advantage of its full powers and use the market mechanism to achieve its ends, and even then it could *only* proceed on the basis of the full agreement of one of the parties involved. In the large majority of instances the IRC was able to complete a project without recourse to its full powers. What is often forgotten however, is that to some extent the knowledge that the IRC had such powers and had in the past used them, may have persuaded some managers to co-operate with the IRC, however reluctantly, through fear that by resisting they would lose much more. It may well be the case that the IRC had to use its powers occasionally to show it was prepared to use them, but far more significant in its growth in stature was the restraint shown in exercising those statutory powers. Such intangible factors as these should be remembered in the context of the above question.

The IRC's Relationship With Industry

The co-operation of industrialists was absolutely indispensable to the Corporation because "the whole basis of IRC's work is the relationship of trust with the private sector".[31] The preceding section has shown that with the exceptions of near bankruptcy and some follow-up situations, the Corporation could not force companies to act against their will because it could only produce action with the consent of at least one of the parties involved, and because its influence was founded not on statutory powers of compulsion but on its funds and the use of reasoned argument. As a result the IRC had to work on the basis of talking to and persuading individuals. From the outset the Board appreciated that it had "to win the confidence of businessmen, who had to be convinced that the IRC's aim was not to impose theoretical blue-prints of its own, but to work with industrial companies in a practical way to improve their efficiency and profitability."[32] For the IRC, as for all interventionist government organisations, its relationship with industry was of crucial importance.

When the White Paper was published in January 1966 the Institute of Directors and the Association of British Chambers of Commerce were amongst those industrial bodies that expressed hostility to the concept of an IRC. Davies, then Director-General of the CBI, later described the general reaction of industrialists in 1966 as follows: industry "was not deliberately against, but it was suspicious."[33] During 1966 a number of individual industrialists assured those concerned with the launching of the Corporation that in their view there was a need for such a body, and that it could count on their co-operation. The attitude of a different section of management opinion was that having failed to stop the IRC coming into existence it would be better to co-operate with it: if they refused to make the IRC experiment work then they might at a later date be faced with the much more difficult situation of an even stronger body run directly by politicians. Thus by the time the IRC Bill had become law, industry's initial attitude had been somewhat altered.

When the Corporation began talking to a wide range of firms in 1967 it was given a mixed reception. While it was given a guarded welcome by at least some parts of, for example, the electrical engineering and electronics sectors, it was met in industries like wool and pumps with a suspicion that occasionally boiled over into hostility. In 1968 and 1969 it continued to come across industries where it met with limited co-operation: bacon and paper appear typical examples. In some circumstances the situation was further exacerbated by the charges of 'superficiality' and 'brash young men' referred to in Chapter 5.

However as time went by the situation evolved from one of general suspicion to one where most were prepared to co-operate and work positively with it. There are clear indications that the IRC was able not just to establish, but to maintain a relationship of trust and mutual respect with the majority of those parts of the private sector with which it sought to be involved. Most important of all was the fact that as time went by a growing number of projects were initiated by firms and trade associations themselves approaching the Corporation. Second, even the IRC's most controversial involvements did not frighten people away: an example is the way the British Paper and Board Makers Association asked the Corporation to do a survey of its industry shortly after the controversial GEC/AEI battle.[34] Third, some of the industries that were initially suspicious – steel and pumps for example – later came to work creatively with the IRC. Next, because the IRC was seen as having only the national interest at heart, it had, unlike an intermediary who is hired by the firm concerned, no self-interest. The consequences of this have been aptly summarised by McClelland: "this quality of disinterestedness on the part of the IRC quickly came to be recognised and the IRC offices in Pall Mall accepted as neutral ground."[35] Finally, because it could only produce action with the consent of at least one of the parties involved in a merger situation or of the Board in the case of a capital investment project, the fact that it maintained a steadily increasing level of activity, irrespective of what it did for the Government, shows that in general terms, IRC established a strong relationship with industrialists in a wide range of sectors. This relationship was flexible enough to withstand the stresses and strains resulting from IRC's more controversial moves.

There were three main reasons why the IRC was able to work with some of the more suspicious industrialists. The passage of time enabled the Board not only to prove that it was there to give practical

CHAPTER 8 THE IRC's IMPACT ON THE ECONOMY

A full examination of the extent of the impact of intervention on the economy and of the benefit of that impact on industrial development is not, as the Preface explained, a central concern of this book. However, the subject needs to be touched on to help draw out some important themes that recur in the conclusions, particularly in Chapter 17.

The Corporation certainly seems to have been responsible for some things that would not have happened, or would have happened differently, if it had not existed. First, it injected £103 million (net) of funds, strategically placed, into the economy over a four-year period. Its medium-term finance helped fill a gap in the money market. Although it was not always true, this money was usually not available elsewhere. For the most part it supported viable projects that would have been unduly delayed for lack of funds, and it enabled firms to quickly reorganise themselves to achieve the chances offered by a merger.

Secondly the structure of British industry was substantially different as a result of IRC activity. In sectors like nuclear construction, motor vehicles, ball bearings, heavy electrical engineering and parts of electronics like numerical control, the IRC was associated with fairly comprehensive restructuring. In others, including pumps, trawler fleets, instruments, compressors and mining machinery, its work had some direct and indirect effect, though in some respects such sectors remained substantially unaltered for all its activity. There were other industries including for the most part wool, paper, footwear and parts of mechanical engineering like machine tools, where a great deal of work produced very little in terms of results. A great deal of empirical work would be needed before it would be possible to produce a comprehensive list of companies that would almost certainly not have come into existence but for the role of the IRC. However RHP, Kent, Plessey NC, the de-merging operation at Brown Bayley all seem obvious examples, as perhaps is GEC/EE.

However the point here is not just what would not have happened but for the IRC, but also the role of the Corporation in accelerating market forces. Chapter 3 showed that a major object of 'intervention' in the late 1960s was to hasten the process of change, and for the most part the means by which bodies like IRC sought to achieve this end was on the basis of agreement with the firm. Thus an important result of IRC activity was those mergers which it helped to bring forward in time: although they might otherwise have come about the point was that the IRC helped make them happen sooner. For example, Stokes and Weinstock with regard to the BLMC and the GEC/AEI mergers have acknowledged respectively that IRC brought the merger forward, and put the idea into their heads.[1] The way in which the IRC sought to accelerate market forces can also be illustrated by general examples of mergers it tried to push which fell through only to be ressurrected later. In September 1968 for example the IRC persuaded three boilermakers to merge, but within two months one withdrew. However in February 1974 the group originally envisaged was in fact formed.[2]

One particular survey has illustrated precisely how difficult it is to assess the extent of the IRC's indirect impact in accelerating market forces. Newbould[3] conducted an empirical survey into the reasons behind the merger boom of 1967-8. He asked executives how far when attempting to put through a merger they had been influenced by such factors as a wish to diversify, a desire to extend their company's market share, a feeling that another company's assets could be more profitably employed in different hands, a defensive desire to maintain the relative size of the company which has been reduced by other mergers, potential technological advantages or government influence. Yet the executive answering the questionnaire may not have been fully aware of the extent which an EDC circular, or talks with the IRC or with a government department had in fact influenced him in the way that Weinstock, for example, has acknowledged. It is important not to overlook this indirect result of IRC's work. In sectors like cranes, pumps, wool, boilers and other parts of mechanical engineering, discussions between the IRC and the firm were followed, sometimes fairly swiftly, as in the mining machinery case, with agreed mergers. The ripple effects of IRC activity, as in heavy electrical engineering, also occurred partly as an indirect result of the Corporation's role.

To fully appreciate the results of IRC activity, its record should be looked at, especially in the case of the more tangible ones, against a wide perspective. First is the immensely important point that the IRC's merger promoting function was based on the principle that two plus two equals five. In the 1960s a great deal was written about the advantages and disadvantages of bigger firms over smaller and medium-sized ones, and of conglomerates over firms specialising in one sector. Establishing a means of measuring the performances of companies of different sizes is a problem in itself. How for example can profitability best be measured, and what is its relevance as a yardstick of efficiency?[4] Even if common criteria are adopted to measure performance it seems impossible to draw conclusions from the literature: in different economic circumstances in different industries in different countries, small and large specialist firms and conglomerates are successful by varying standards. It has been pointed out that mergers are no substitute for organic expansion and that all too often they are a substitute for developing new products, or building new plant, or a means of reducing competition.[5] So the IRC's merger-promoting function should be seen against a backcloth of inconclusive empirical evidence that large or specialist companies gained decisively over small firms because of the benefits of economies of scale available to them.

It is important first to remember that IRC attempted to strengthen industry in many ways other than mergers, showing in microcircuits and machine tools that it could help find partial solutions that did not involve amalgamations. However it is basically true that a high proportion of IRC activity was dedicated to promoting big companies especially in industries like heavy electricals and passenger vehicles where "technological considerations meant that the minimum viable size was very large indeed, and getting rapidly larger".[6] In fact the IRC Board never saw size as having any absolute merit in itself, and frequently accepted that it had disadvantages. Despite this the IRC's basic contention was that sizeable assets enabled an enlarged firm to compete more successfully in world markets but only where it was headed by managers of real ability: "reorganisation is useless unless new management energies are released or transferred."[7] Size provided not a solution but a chance of self-sustained growth. The Board felt that these arguments were particularly relevant in expanding sectors. Racal Electronics is an example of a specialist company that grew very quickly in the 1960s, and which the IRC supported.

The fact that many mergers have led to disappointing results does not mean that all will, or that the Board's arguments are refuted. In the past many have failed because the constituent parts were not integrated and thus the potential benefits from economies of scale were not available. A classic example was BMH which, many years after the Morris/Austin merger was described as a "collection of unmerged companies." One of the reasons behind IRC's support for the creation of BLMC was to maximise the use of those assets by rationalising them.[8] Even if the IRC was only responsible for a tiny proportion of all the mergers that took place between 1967 and 1970, this does not necessarily mean its contribution was negligible. Some of these may be amongst the most important of all the mergers during those years. It emphasises the fact that IRC chose carefully which schemes to back because that, combined with the follow-up activity of varying intensity, was the only way to attempt to ensure that the key to success –

post-merger rationalisation – was fully implemented.

Apart from the question as to whether bigger is better, there is a second important factor to bear in mind, in considering the IRC record. The Labour Government quite failed to relate its work to criteria wider than the vague assertions outlined, for example, in the National Plan and the IRC White Paper; co-ordination with its own regional policies; and a belief that massive companies were desirable both in themselves and because at some future date they could provide the lead in what they saw as an inevitable tendency to move towards big international mergers. It was assumed that the right people with the right skills were at the IRC. There were no wide-ranging cross-benefit studies, and there were no economists. The Government did not attempt to link the IRC's work to a view of what would be a desirable industrial structure in manufacturing industry as a whole in ten or twenty years time. A conscious decision could have been taken to tell IRC to concentrate on particular growth sectors. Attempts could then have been made to concentrate national resources behind them, relating IRC's work to Government policies for manpower planning, R&D expenditure, and even location of industry. Instead the IRC was given a wide-ranging brief across the whole manufacturing sector, with the result that its Board judged individual cases on their merits in a vacuum.

This was because from the beginning the Government had stressed the need for action in the context of modernising British industry and solving the balance of payments crisis. That was why the IRC's work was not related to a concept of an ideal industrial structure; why it had no economists; why the Government was so impatient with it in 1967; why the IRC was somewhat chauvinistic when protecting some British sectors in order to prevent multinationals from removing control from within the UK; and why the Government did not worry about the IRC Act contravening articles 85 and 86 of the Rome Treaty, despite taking the decision to apply for membership of the EEC both before the Act was through Parliament and in 1969.[9] The purpose of IRC was to produce action to help solve the payments crisis and strengthen British industry. Provided the proposed schemes passed IRC's criteria any action seemed to be better than none.

Significantly it was along these lines that the IRC interpreted its general role. Brooke told Graham Turner

> We don't feel the need for economists . . . and we don't believe in great volumes of analysis. It is not a question of analysing a problem – there are plenty of Little Neddies and twenty-five reports on everything – what is needed is action.[10]

The Board accepted that it could not hope to revolutionise the structure of British industry with the resources at its disposal. Thus its main job became the short-term controlled intelligent '*ad hocery*' one outlined in Chapter 6.

The crucial issue arising from these aspects of IRC's job as it emerged, and the unproven case that bigger is better, is whether the Corporation backed the right firms. This depends on the ability of the managers concerned to control and direct the new companies. The IRC approach of supporting "managers of proven success"[11] did not by itself mean that maximum use would be made of the newly created firm's assets because the past records of individuals or groups of executives often within firms of a very different size, and with different problems, could be no guarantee of future success. Further, where great stress was laid on particular managers like Stokes or Weinstock, sustained future efficiency, even if it survived enlargement, may hang too much by the slender thread of one man's life.[12] If fate removed them from the scene, the IRC could have been helping to create firms that are potentially sluggish giants of the type it had helped put into new groups. The IRC reply would probably have been that successful companies attract first-class executives at all levels. In the event of such an accident there should be an adequate reservoir of talent in the company because to hold positions in such a firm would mean that the executive was highly competent. The danger here is the so-called Peter principle, that managers rise to the level of their incompetence.

The question as to whether IRC's work was worthwhile depends on the performance over a number of years in the 1970s of the companies it supported and helped to create. Where mergers are involved, and particularly in the case of huge companies, no judgement can in fairness be passed until the post-merger rationalisation process has not only been completed, but some years of stable non-cyclical trading conditions have been experienced. This is because IRC's judgement was based on the economies of scale advantages that would ultimately be available to the firm. RHP for example was created in May 1969, but it was about four and a half years before it was beginning to reap the benefits of post-merger rationalisation.[13] This underlines the fact that in many cases it will be the late 1970s before some sort of final judgement can be passed on the value of most of IRC's work. By 1974 it was evident that some companies like GEC were doing well whilst others that the Corporation had supported had met unforseen problems. Peter Dixon for example had closed its paper-making interests.

The nature of the task of assessing the IRC will in fact be fraught with problems because it will always be impossible to assess the issue as to whether companies supported by the IRC would have been better off on their own, or merged with others. In addition the abolition of the IRC meant the termination of its follow-up operation. This created a situation in which a company could produce poorer performances than the Corporation would probably have been prepared to permit had it still been in existence. The whole problem of assessment is made more difficult by the confusion about the IRC's precise aims when it began.

It should also be remembered that the IRC made an impact in a number of less tangible ways than those discussed above. These should not be forgotten because it is impossible to assess the nature of the precise impact the IRC made in these fields, and the extent to which the Corporation was responsible for contributing towards the developments that took place. One example of the IRC's less tangible uses was the way in which it developed as an advisory service for industry. The Corporation seemed to fulfil a need in this respect because as time went by the most important source of IRC projects became the approach from the firm.[14] In 1969 Davies was quoted as saying that those who had dealt with the IRC had "found its executives to be sensible and helpful".[15] In this connection the IRC fulfilled a further important and useful role. Because the Corporation was part of Whitehall, individuals working for it knew their way round very well. The IRC was thus in a good position to help a firm that wanted to find out the sort of reaction that the Government would make to some proposal by making discreet inquiries. This saved the firm time as it could avoid becoming enmeshed in bureaucratic tangles. Other areas where the IRC had an indirect intangible impact on the economy included in the way in which it influenced Whitehall and the making of some economic and industrial policies; and helped to make individual managers think more positively about the benefits of reorganisation and the opportunities offered by substantial rationalisation after a merger.

The most important intangible result of IRC activity was probably its direct attempts to persuade institutional investors to be more aware of the responsibilities that came from having large holdings in big companies; and indirectly to pressurise them by trying to change the attitudes of others like the CBI working in the same field. Spiegelberg has highlighted important developments in this sphere.[16] Fewer institutional shareholders now wield greater power than in the past. The stake of the institutional shareholders in British industry has been growing at the same time as mergers have been taking place amongst the insurance companies, investment trusts and other institutions. This appears to have gone hand in hand with a greater willingness to use that power to bring about changes either in top management as in the Vickers case, or in the way in which a company is actually run. Other factors have been present including for example the constant need for the institutions to get a better return on their investments. However the IRC's vigorous championing of this cause was seen to have made some contribution to the growing preparedness of the institutions to use their influence to increase industrial efficiency.

On a wide range of important issues that were receiving varying amounts of attention the IRC helped stimulate discussion and action in Britain, the Common Market, and elsewhere. Organisations modelled in varying degrees on the Corporation were established by governments in such countries as France, Italy and Canada.[17] The whole IRC experience proved a valuable ingredient in the process of re-examining both the need for interventionist policies in the early 1970s and the means of implementing them. The debate on the IRC that followed its abolition added greatly to the scope and depth of the Parliamentary inquiry in the 1970-1 and 1971-2 sessions published as *Public Money in The Private Sector*.[18] It also influenced the shape of the 1972 Industry Act and had a significant bearing on the Labour Party's attitude to industrial policy as it emerged in the 1970s. In the long run it may well be that the importance of the Corporation was not so much its tangible impact on the economy, but what policy-makers could learn from its experience in the sphere of means of implementing policies, particularly with regard to follow-up.

CHAPTER 9 THE IRC's RELATIONSHIP WITH WHITEHALL

The overall relationship between the IRC and its sponsoring department (the DEA) on the one hand, and the Government as a whole on the other, has to be seen against the backcloth of their relationship during the IRC's first nine months. The period is especially important because not only did it have a strong influence on the way the IRC afterwards developed, ensuring that the Corporation was to have operational independence, but it also provides valuable insight into the sorts of problems that can arise in general between a para-government body and its sponsoring government department.

The situation was extensively influenced by a certain amount of confusion as to how the IRC, for all its powers and wealth, was going to work in practice. This was indicated by the evidence given to a Parliamentary Committee by Sir Eric Roll, who was Chairman of the official committee that produced the IRC concept and White Paper, and also by the wide-ranging discussions that the IRC's Board Members had about the Corporation's future role before the Act was passed. Although Kearton had been involved from the outset with the setting up of the IRC, the man who most influenced its day-to-day operations, the Managing Director, played no part in the planning of the IRC and thus had no built-in conception of its role.

The confusion about the precise aims of the Corporation were outlined at the start of Chapter 4. The situation was complicated by the fundamentally different approaches of the Government and the IRC Board to the question of the speed at which the IRC should become active. The Government was impatient to restructure industry and get the balance of payments situation under control. This was intensified by the fact that some ministers seemed to have had exaggerated ideas about the speed with which IRC action could be expected to have an impact on the visible trade balance. However, from the start, the Board argued that controversial use of its powers would be counter-productive because it would frighten away industrialists with whom the IRC had to co-operate if it was to produce results. Thus the Board's consensus view – that research and the establishment of a relationship of trust and confidence with industry should be the priorities – was quite at variance with the Government's attitude.

IRC's relationship with its sponsor department and with the

Government was also complicated from the outset by the Rootes affair. In January 1967, the Minister of Technology, Wedgwood Benn, reacted to the prospect of Rootes going into liquidation by agreeing to the American firm of Chrysler extending its minority shareholding subject to certain conditions. One of these was that at least 15 per cent of the Rootes equity should remain in British hands. The IRC took this holding and was thus the means by which the Government achieved its end. However, Harold Lever, the newly appointed Joint Under Secretary of State at the DEA, stressed that the IRC Board could refuse the DEA's requests; and that the Board supported the proposal as being in the public interest.[1] It is true that the Board agreed that in the absence of other viable options the Minister chose the best available solution from an industrial standpoint. However it does seem to be the case that at least some Board Members felt their acquiescence somewhat taken for granted, although it would be an exaggeration to go so far as to say that the IRC had been forced into unwilling co-operation. The situation was further complicated by political factors. Not only was there the dimension of potential unemployment at the Linwood factory in a Development Area, but before the 1964 election, Wilson, Callaghan and Crossman had expressed fears that the Conservative Government's decision to allow Chrysler to take a minority shareholding in Rootes would either lead to the Rootes Group being controlled from America, or to the minority shareholding being extended. Michael Shanks later summed up widespread press and Parliamentary criticism by asserting that "the shareholding in Rootes was hard to justify in other than political terms".[2] As this was the IRC's first involvement it began to look as if it was liable to be used by the Government "to get it out of holes".[3] Whatever the absolute rights and wrongs of the situation, what mattered in practice was how the IRC appeared to those it was trying to help. In that respect, the Board probably felt that by being made to appear the tool of the Government it had been handicapped at the very time when it was trying to establish a working relationship with industrialists who were suspicious of the IRC's powers.

After this the Board acted with such caution that the Government and the DEA became increasingly exasperated, as they did with the fact that the Corporation was several times near to producing mergers in a number of industries, but failed because of its unwillingness to use its powers. The Government reacted by trying to put pressure on the IRC. It was plied with ideas, and attempts were made to change Grierson's views during his regular visits to the DEA. This Government pressure actually came into the open: Wilson described the IRC as "a fundamental instrument" on television when it had still to announce its first project.[4] He added that the IRC's job was to take small backward firms "by the scruff of the neck and bring them kicking and screaming into the twentieth century". The subsequent replacement of Stewart at the DEA by Shore, under Wilson's overlordship, meant that the IRC's sponsoring Ministers now had an even greater commitment to intervention, and a belief that devaluation could be avoided by modernising industry.[5] This probably led to further pressures on the Corporation.

The final means of Government pressure was the Industrial Expansion Bill. On 18 July 1967, Wilson confirmed that a Bill was envisaged along the lines of Stewart's speech three weeks before, which had stated that "the Government might have to take further powers to change the structure of industry".[6] The IRC Board Members first read of this development in the press. Moreover the DEA took the line that it was nothing to do with the IRC, not holding talks with the Corporation on the subject until October.[7] The Government appears to have kept the details secret while encouraging the belief that work on the measure was well advanced.[8] To some of the IRC Board Members, and certainly to Grierson, it seemed as if impatient Ministers were attempting to bypass the Corporation to achieve the results which they had earlier hoped the IRC would produce.

Three factors combined to enable the IRC to resist this pressure. First, although there were some Members who argued the case for an interventionist line in certain situations, the Board's consensus view about the need to move slowly did not change because of the existence of a faction arguing that the IRC should play a passive role. Second, this cautious approach was re-inforced by the fact that Grierson was a strong supporter of the passive school, arguing that "the IRC is purely experimental and may yield to fewer results than we expect."[9] As Managing Director, he was on a day-to-day basis implementing the policy in which he strongly believed. Finally, despite internal disagreements, the Board was united by a determination to move at its own pace and not at the Government's behest. The IRC exerted its independence in various ways: for example, it did not inform any part of the Government machine of the EE/EA merger until the money had been committed, and one Permanent Secretary received only a few hours formal notice.[10] After Wilson's television attack the Corporation took the line that it was "still in the courtship stage: the boot goes in later".[11]

The IRC's successful backing of GEC's bid for AEI was a watershed in its relationship with the DEA and the Government as a whole. After October 1967, the Government was generally prepared to leave the IRC to its own devices because it had proved it could achieve the Government's ends by its own methods. In addition Grierson's departure removed the main source of friction between Ministers and the Board, leaving the Board's consensus view much closer to the Government's and the DEA's vaguely defined concept of how the IRC should work. Grierson's resignation also necessitated new leadership – the forceful Kearton took over until the DEA found someone more suited to the task in its eyes than Grierson had turned out to be. The DEA subsequently became "a source of continuous help and advice".[12] The transformation into a more active agency was thus achieved at the IRC's own pace, and for reasons quite unconnected with government pressure.

However, there were still to be ups and downs in the relationship between the IRC and its sponsoring department. One difficult patch occurred in December 1969, when ICI announced that it was bidding for Viyella and was to have discussions with Carrington and Dewhurst concerning the terms of a merger of that company with Viyella.[13] The Ministry of Technology – now the IRC's sponsoring ministry following the dissolution of the DEA in October 1969 – decided to re-examine in the light of this development Government policy that further mergers amongst big firms in the industry were undesirable. A Committee was established to examine the industry's future prospects and the related question concerning the most suitable structure. This inquiry was headed by the Paymaster General, Harold Lever. The IRC had been intermittently involved with textiles and apparently offered to help. Within MinTech this seems to have been interpreted as an attempt to take over the inquiry in the sort of 'empire-building' fashion of which Aubrey Jones was sometimes accused at the NBPI.[14] As a result the IRC was kept at arm's length, although Lockwood was one member of the Committee: this seemed chiefly to be because he had been a member of the Committee established at the Board of Trade in February 1969 to examine the structure of the industry in the light of the Textile Council's report on its productivity and efficiency.[15]

The nearest the IRC came to being roughly treated by its sponsoring department was probably in the spring of 1970 after MinTech had asked it to investigate the cause of Cammell Laird's liquidity crisis. The IRC reported that the crisis had been caused by losses in the shipbuilding subsidiary of the whole group. The Government then appears to have tried to get the Corporation to implement the proposals in its report but the IRC was determined to act cautiously. This was because the IRC had no remit for the shipbuilding industry as a result of the existence of the SIB and it would have been aware that Cammell Laird had made an application to the SIB which had been turned down.[16] The IRC made a reality of the independence it had been promised by the Government and "insisted as a precondition of its involvement that the shipbuilding undertaking should become independent from the rest of the group."[17] As a result the shipbuilding concern, subsequently called Cammell Laird, ceased to be a subsidiary and became a trade investment of what was subsequently to be called the Laird Group. Thus the Board preserved its independence and left itself "free to promote the reorganisation and the development of the group's activities."[18]

There may well have been a significant financial twist to the Cammell Laird situation. At the start of May 1970 the IRC knew definitely that it had investments and commitments totalling £109,373,000, leaving it about £40 million of working capital out of its original £150 million allocation.[19] But not all of this £40 million was uncommitted because at the beginning of May the Board probably had a good idea of the extent of the £16.3 million that it was to be firmly committed to by its own initiative by the middle of June. This reduced its working capital to about £24 million. However at the beginning of May it probably had more than an inkling of the £10 million that the Government wanted it to put aside for the Textile Re-equipment Scheme. It also knew that MinTech wanted it to provide about £6 million to assist Cammell Laird. If it agreed to the £16 million or so involved in these two cases, the Corporation was effectively cutting its working capital to under £8 million. The IRC made a habit of careful forward financial planning, and reducing its funds to this extent would have had a severe effect on its scope for action because in merger situations finance was a crucial source of its strength, and at this stage it was increasingly concentrating on selective investment schemes. The Government does not appear to have agreed – at any rate in public, though it must be remembered that this was the pre-election period – to give the IRC more money. It is very probably the case that when MinTech made these two requests the Corporation was able to use them – and especially the Cammell Laird shipbuilding case which did not come within its sphere, as a bargaining counter when pressing for an increase in its financial ceiling to £300 million.[20] Because Labour lost the 1970 election it is impossible to be definitive about the outcome of what was an important test of the balance of power between the IRC and its sponsoring ministry.

After the GEC/AEI success the Corporation had generally a harmonious relationship with its sponsoring department. It came to be based on respect for each other's abilities, and acceptance on the Government side of IRC's operational independence. It valued its links with the Government and appears to have kept its sponsoring ministry informed of developments, there being no repetition of the EE/EA case. Contingency arrangements were no doubt drawn up for the Managing Director to have immediate access to the

Corporation's sponsoring Minister or his Permanent Secretary in controversial cases, where events moved quickly, as happened in the scientific instruments and ball bearing affairs. However the aim of such arrangements was to facilitate the smooth running of the Government machine; and the Corporation's independence was not thereby circumscribed. On its part the Government responded by providing firm support for the IRC in these controversial cases.

Finally reference must be made to the provisions written into Clause 2(1)(b) of the IRC Act. Under this the IRC could be asked by its sponsoring Minister to provide finance to individual companies even when there was no merger involved. When the IRC Bill was drafted, the powers were made very wide partly because it was not known how they would be interpreted in practice: it gave scope to the IRC and its sponsoring ministry to devise the most suitable administrative methods in any given case. In the event this Clause was little used. Chapter 6 showed how it proved to be just one of the means by which IRC finance was made available to individual firms in non-merger situations for specific capital investment projects. The actual administrative means used appears to have been that, having investigated a project, the IRC then asked the Minister to issue a formal request for it to proceed, irrespective of whether the scheme had been initiated internally or as a result of a Ministry suggestion.

The IRC's Relationships with Other Departments and Agencies

As has been shown, the IRC came into existence after July 1966 when the main emphasis of industrial policy was on strengthening British industry. In these circumstances, different departments and agencies compiled lists of problems thought likely to be suitable for the IRC. The DEA synthesised these, probably with help from the Ministry of Technology which was responsible for four important 'bridge-head' industries. It is worth noting in this connection that two IRC Board Members, Cant and Berkin, were Industrial Advisers at MinTech and the DEA respectively; Berkin was one of George Brown's closest confidants in the early days of the DEA, as was Kearton who was also a Member of the Ministry of Technology Advisory Committee.[21] Indeed at the beginning of 1967, the Corporation seems to have been plied with ideas from all quarters, and several of the problem industries examined by the DEA at the start of 1967 were passed to the IRC.[22] A typical example was the heavy electrical industry where severe overcapacity was developing as a result of a rundown in CEGB orders.

The IRC at Board and executive level possessed a blend of experience and skill that was unique in Whitehall. The result was that in various ways departments soon came to take advantage of its presence using it as a Government merchant bank. The commonest request was to ask the Corporation to hold an inquiry into a specific subject "where decisions . . . require a commercial appraisal of the facts by an independent agency."[23] Usually, this related to a situation where Government money was going to the private sector. In 1967 for example, the IRC conducted studies of the structure of the telecommunications industry and its relations with the Post Office for the Secretary of State for Economic Affairs, the Minister of Technology and the Postmaster General; of the structural problems of private steel prior to the BSC vesting day in July 1967 for the Ministry of Power; of Cunard's finances for the President of the Board of Trade before he agreed to a loan to help with the building of QE2; and of the proposals of different companies for building aluminium smelters in the UK for the Secretary of State for Economic Affairs and the Minister of Technology. But it was not just the main industrial departments that took advantage of the IRC's skills: in 1968, the Corporation examined the Army Kinema Corporation and the Royal Air Force Cinema Corporation at the request of the Minister of Defence and advised that they should be amalgamated: and in 1969, a study of the pig processing industry was completed and recommendations of "future forms and levels of financial support from public funds"[24] were submitted to the Minister of Agriculture.

In 1968, a new development took place: the IRC was asked not just to examine a specific problem and make recommendations, but to undertake itself the necessary remedial action. Thus the Minister of Technology asked the IRC to "ascertain the views of the nuclear power industry following the Parliamentary Select Committee for Science and Technology's recommendations in favour of a single organisation to design and construct nuclear power stations."[25] The IRC's investigations led it to favour two companies and in July 1968, the Minister asked it to set them up. Another typical example was Rolls Royce, where the IRC was asked to study the problem in October 1969 and to implement its proposals the following December.[26] It is extremely likely that the other assignments mentioned in the IRC reports represent only the visible tip of a large iceberg of such work, because publication was only assured when IRC funds were involved.

Even when the IRC had got to the stage where it was working independently various departments still approached it suggesting that it might be worth studying specific industries with a view to taking the initiative and trying to restructure them. The difference between this and the series of assignments described in the preceding paragraph appears to have been one of emphasis and formal procedure. Suggestions that it might be worthwhile for the Corporation to look at ball bearings or numerical control came informally from civil servants in the relevant industrial sponsorship division, and not from the politicians.[27] On the other hand in cases like Cammell Laird discussions were held at the instigation of ministers: once the Corporation had agreed to act it was then formally asked to proceed by the relevant Minister. The difference was that the Board could ignore the informal, but not the formal approach.

Departments also approached the IRC on a miscellaneous range of issues where its blend of experience and ability to move very swiftly could supplement the more limited commercial skills and slower speed of the civil service. For example, it provided advice on the commercial aspects of Government contracts with the private sector.[28] Sometimes it was able to help in finding solutions to difficult procedural problems as was the case when it was approached by the DEP over the proposed Reed/IPC merger and asked to help find a way around what would have been an infringement of restrictive practices legislation, in that Reed would have had an advantage over Bowater in the supply of newsprint to IPC. Another type of problem that the Corporation was especially well qualified to deal with arose on the occasions when the Government felt that there was a need to react strongly over the performance of senior managers from individual companies. This could occur in the presence or absence of ministers and civil servants, in slowly moving or fluid situations, with either multinational or British firms. This is an area bounded by secrecy, but two examples that have been publicised are the protracted negotiations with SKF in the winter of 1968-69 and the dismissal of ten Cammel Laird Board Members in May 1970.[29] The IRC therefore came to be approached by individual departments as a sort of universal 'trouble shooter'. However the process was not all one-sided, and it would be an oversimplification of a complex relationship to indicate that it was. In fact, there was a continuous and dynamic relationship in which both sides were ready to take the initiative.

Once established the IRC approached parts of the Government machine on its own initiative primarily because of its search for information. This was especially the case with the close relationship that the Corporation established with the Ministry of Technology's industrial sponsorship divisions. Executives made use of "surveys and reports",[30] published and classified, both when looking for areas in which to work, and when building up a picture of an individual sector at the desk stage before visiting firms. The sponsorship divisions were probably especially helpful to the IRC executives in giving them advice to help them understand current and developing technologies in industries like electronics, where research can progress rapidly.

The way in which the IRC was helped in the Rolls Royce investigation was another typical example.[31] It is also apparent that the Corporation sought the views of the relevant part of the Ministry of Technology with respect to research and development and the technical economies of scale considerations in certain specific merger cases, usually where two companies were competing with bids for a third. Overall it is probably a fair generalisation that the less complicated the technological side of the industry, the less useful the IRC executives found the MinTech (and before that the Board of Trade) sponsorship divisions. Thus the Corporation appears to have asked more questions on electronics, telecommunications, and computers than it did on machine tools or process plant; and more on the latter than on vehicles or wool.

The most regular contact of all with a department was that over monopolies with the Board of Trade (and after its dismemberment in October 1969 with the Department of Employment and Productivity). The IRC obviously did not want to be seen to be in conflict with the Board of Trade Mergers Panel, whose function it was to process all proposed mergers to help determine whether or not the President should refer them to the Monopolies Commission.[32] The result was that an extremely close working relationship was established. The Mergers Panel probably informally advised IRC executives that if certain conditions existed in a proposed link-up, or in the industry in which the new firm was involved, then the proposed merger would be unlikely to be referred to the Monopolies Commission, even if it technically came within the provisions of the 1965 Monopolies and Mergers Act. McClelland points out that in getting the IRC to concentrate on schemes that would assist the balance of payments, there was an implicit acknowledgement that large firms with their exporting capacity would be acceptable, because of their foreign exchange earnings, and because their domestic monopoly would be liable to be checked by imports of goods made or finished by foreign-owned subsidiaries, irrespective of the resulting domestic market share of the new group.[33] From this it can be inferred that the existence in the industry of a strong multinational with interests in the UK is very likely to have been one of the desirable factors so far as the Mergers Panel were concerned in the sense that it gave them a justification for not recommending that the merger be referred. This is one example from what probably amounted to a check-list of justifications.

Apart from the Monopolies Commission the IRC was also in contact with the same part of the Board of Trade and later the DEP on a case by case basis over restrictive practices. One specific example concerned the joint acquisition of the Inveresk Paper

Company's Donside Mill by Bowater and Reed, the IRC having in this case to approach the Board of Trade to obtain the necessary consent under Section 1 of the Restrictive Trade Practices Act 1968.[34]

The IRC also came into occasional contact with other departments when acting on its own initiative. There were three reasons for such approaches. The first was again the continuous search for information. Apart from contact with the Board of Trade sponsorship divisions in cases like trawling fleets and cables,[35] the IRC approached other departments for information. Typical examples include the way in which it drew extensively on reports and surveys from all over Whitehall in 1968-69,[36] and approached the Ministry of Agriculture Fisheries and Food over trawlers and pig-processing.[37]

Secondly the IRC approached Whitehall departments on those occasions when it was trying to restructure an industry in a potentially controversial and complex situation. A good example of this was the series of top level meetings held by the Corporation throughout the winter of 1968-69 to discuss the developing ball bearings situation. Finally there was a natural need to approach a department when the IRC appeared to be working in an area for which that department was responsible. Talks were also held with the DEP on the subject of redundancies following post-merger rationalisation, the object here being to establish a Code of Good Practice. This area was not an IRC responsibility but the Corporation remained "well aware of the need for companies contemplating rationalisation to ensure that any resulting redundancies are planned to take place in an orderly manner."[38] The Corporation was thus in a position to ensure if it looked as if redundancies were going to follow a merger that the DEP received notice of the likelihood of this so that the management of the firm concerned would be better able to cooperate fully with all departments concerned. This happened for example in the GEC/EE and RHP cases.[39]

IRC's sources of finance were Public Dividend Capital and the National Loans Fund, and the framework of the relationship between the IRC and the Treasury was outlined in Sections 3–7 of the IRC Act. The nature of the Corporation's brief necessitated a flexible working relationship with regard to both the availability of money and to the IRC's interest payments on its borrowings. Notice would have been needed for large sums, but by October 1969 the Treasury agreed to guarantee the IRC's ability to borrow on a temporary basis up to £1.5 million from the Bank of England in pursuance of Section 6(1) of the IRC Act.[40] There does not seem to have been a situation of the kind which otherwise so often appears to occur with regard to items of public expenditure, where a project is investigated a second time by the Treasury after it has been submitted, to see if it could be allowed in terms of its viability, discriminatory implications and so on. Had the Treasury wished to make such an attempt, then it would certainly have been stopped by ministers arguing that Parliament had agreed to the funds being made available to the IRC, and that these funds were there to be used.

The Corporation's contact with other parts of the Government machine in the search for information went beyond just reading the reports of NBPI, MC, EDCs, and the Textile Council, to confidential talks with executives from the other bodies who had done research behind the reports.[41] The material that was collected prior to the writing of some of the EDC reports was of really massive proportions. Members of the NEDO secretariat from the EDCs in fields that the IRC was working in made an especially important contribution, because they were working at the industry level from a more objective standpoint than were trades associations. The Paper and Board EDC provides what was probably a typical example. After the latter's confidential report on *Structure and Productivity* in June 1967, the Corporation was then invited by the British Paper and Board Makers Association to do a survey on the industry's structure.[42] The work and the papers produced by the EDC secretariat in the course of writing the report would have been of great use to the IRC executives at the deskwork stage of their investigation. In some cases the IRC also worked closely with NRDC, examples being micro-circuits[43] and probably the Miles Roman scheme, as this firm was partly owned by NRDC. The Regional Economic Planning Boards and Councils do not appear to have been at all involved with the IRC, though they on several occasions expressed concern about the redundancies resulting from IRC activity.

Nationalised industries were approached for two reasons. First, yet again for information, and secondly for their views on the most desirable structure for their supplier industries in specific cases; to this end the CEGB, the Post Office and British Rail Board all gave their views in the GEC/Plessey/EE struggle.[44] The nationalised industries were also of great importance to the IRC in developing situations because of their purchasing power, which was a potentially strong instrument in the restructuring process, and because of the nature of their future plans, as in the BSC case. The best example of this is probably National Coal Board (NCB) which "worked closely" with the IRC "promoting the rationalisation of the mining machinery industry."[45] The evidence suggests strongly that in the process of achieving its company mergers in this sector the IRC used a guaranteed level of NCB orders to a new group as one as the inducements to merge. Other examples are the CEGB's purchasing power with regard to heavy generating equipment[46] and the

Post Office's telecommunications sector. The Corporation's report appears to have been one factor contributing to the abandonment of the Bulk Supply Agreements covering exchange equipment and telephone apparatus.

Co-ordination

Overall co-ordination of the IRC's activities with those of other parts of Whitehall, especially where there was overlap, was the responsibility of the sponsoring department. For example, NBPI, the EDCs, the Monopolies Commission, the IRC and later the Commission on Industrial Relations (CIR) all dealt with various aspects of industrial efficiency. Being at the centre of the web from 1964, and with sponsorship responsibility for NEDC, NEDO, the EDCs, NBPI and the IRC, the DEA took on this task and approached other departments on the subject. Although a behind-the-scenes consultation system was evidently used throughout the period, it was formalised with the emergence with an inter-departmental committee to handle the formal and informal references to the different bodies, and the Government's reaction to those references. The situation was confused by the emergence of an inter-departmental dispute in 1968-69: this began over the future of the monopolies policy and the Monopolies Commission, grew to encompass the work and future of most of the agencies and indeed the whole question of monitoring the private sector, and resulted in the proposal to establish a Commission on Industry and Manpower.

MinTech also played a co-ordinating role in that it provided something of an overall framework in developing situations in those industries for which it had responsibility. For example, it kept the IRC informed on the progress of the negotiations which preceded the creation of ICL in 1967-68 because the Corporation was studying computers,[47] and it provided overall guidance for IRC and NRDC when they were both working in micro-circuits in 1967-68 prior to the announcement of a £5 million R&D support scheme. There may in addition have been MinTech guidance to ensure that IRC's work did not duplicate the somewhat different approaches of the special committees Wedgwood Benn appointed to study aspects of the process plant and machine tool industries. MinTech went beyond simply making a suggestion to the IRC, by repeatedly encouraging continued IRC activity to achieve its end, as with the attempt to get BMH and Leyland together in 1967.

A third means of co-ordination employed by the Government was to appoint to the IRC Board people who held other posts and conversely to ask IRC Board members to serve in other positions. Thus

Kearton was on NEDC, AEA, and the Ministry of Technology Advisory Committee; Schon worked at NRDC; Stokes was Chairman of the Electronics EDC; Schon and McClelland served on the Northern Economic Planning Council. It is impossible to define the extent to which this was done in a systematic fashion but there is an important indication that the Government found it useful. IRC Board Members provided three of the five members of the Advisory Committee reviewing projects applying for assistance under the Industrial Expansion Act: this was to "ensure that projects that come within IRC's province are passed to it for negotiation and implementation."[48] In addition Boxall, an IRC Board Member, was appointed to the Monopolies Commission when it was strengthened in 1969.[49]

The IRC's wide contacts within the Government machine meant the it was in a good position to integrate itself appropriately into the overall framework of the various Government policies and bodies. The Corporation's aim was to "avoid getting at cross purposes with Government departments without infringing the confidentiality of the IRC's separate dealings with companies in the private sector."[50] Typical examples of the way in which it acted as the main Whitehall co-ordinator are the trawling fleets, Rolls Royce and ball bearings cases mentioned above.[51] Informal links were also developed with the NBPI and NRDC. There was no real duplication between those EDCs working on the structure of their industries – these included Machine Tools, Paper and Board, Electrical Engineering, and Electronics – because, unlike the IRC, they lacked executive authority. Rather their work of persuading managers of the need for rationalisation was complementary in that it prepared the ground for the IRC. Catherwood, the Director General at NEDO, probably played an important role here as he had earlier been an Industrial Adviser at the DEA and was closely connected with the machinery that was set up by George Brown. By taking the initiative and approaching the nationalised industries the IRC also co-ordinated their views and purchasing power into the restructuring process.

The question of co-ordinating the Government's monopolies policies with its industrial policies was a very complex one and it has attracted a great deal of attention.[52] However, much of what has been written has tended to confuse two quite separate issues: first, could the Government logically promote restructuring, merger-producing policies while simultaneously operating strengthened monopolies legislation? And second, did the Government in fact co-ordinate the implementation of the two policies? The first is a question for economists and has been hotly disputed. What matters in an analysis of an institution is what Government policy actually was, not what it ought to have been. From 1965 the Government argued that the two approaches could logically be pursued, because every case was different and needed to be judged on its merits. When he was President of the Board of Trade, Crosland claimed that "the IRC and the Commission are working to the same objective, which is the most efficient use of resources in each case."[53] Villiers argued that "industry needs both a stimulant and a sedative."[54] Brittan explains official attitudes as follows

> the balance of payments has been the most important single reason why the Government has avoided laying down a definite ruling on monopoly and industrial policy, but preferred to rely on the judgment of politicians and officials rather than rely on a known framework of law.[55]

While Board Members could, and probably did, say what they thought of these policies – Lockwood for example was a member of the Industrial Policy Group which later attacked the apparent inconsistency between the two policies in a pamphlet[56] – in the last resort their job was to operate according to the Government's determination to judge each case on its merits. The Government's task was made easier by the vague definition of the 'public interest' in the 1965 Act.

Within the context of stated Government policy effective co-ordination was achieved in the sense that the IRC was not in open conflict with any part of Whitehall over monopolies or restrictive practices. The example regularly quoted to indicate that it sometimes was, is the IRC-backed merger of the trawling fleets of the Ross Group and Associated Fisheries (AF) in April 1969, which appeared to be in direct contradiction to the Board of Trade's decision in 1966 to support the majority Monopolies Commission decision that a full merger between Ross and Associated Fisheries would be against the public interest. However the two situations were quite different.[57] The 1969 proposal concerned only the fishing fleets and not the remaining distribution and other land-based activities of the companies. Furthermore, in the Government's view, the state of the industry by the autumn of 1968 when the IRC was asked to intervene had greatly deteriorated from its position in 1966 which had provided the backcloth against which the Monopolies Commission report was considered. 1966 and the following two years had seen increased catches but fewer fishing trips, lower prices, lower capital investment, and increasing imports. A further decline held the prospect of a deteriorating balance of payments situation, greater unemployment and social distress in the fishing ports, some of which were Labour seats. The result was a series of measures directly aimed at resuscitating the industry. There was the 1968 Sea Fisheries Act which resulted in a new subsidy scheme, increased activity on the promotional and marketing side from the White Fish Authority, and a reduction in imports of frozen fillets from the EFTA countries. In this context the IRC was asked to try to create a bigger unit to produce sustained and self-generating capital investment. The IRC activity was thus part of an overall aid package. Had Boston Deep Sea Trawlers gone into the merger as originally intended, then the 1966 and 1969 Ross/AF mergers would probably not have been compared in the same way.

Effective co-ordination over monopolies was achieved by the IRC's establishing "a more or less continuous dialogue"[58] with the Mergers Panel. The IRC tried to pick out special factors that could help the Panel to avoid recommending that a merger be referred to the Monopolies Commission (see p.99). In some instances the Board refused to give public support to a proposed merger before the Takeover Panel gave its verdict. In others the Board might effectively have been forced to drop proposals because of the ministerial support for the Takeover Panel arguments. However, where firms that were going to be big exporters were being created, the IRC support, which in the important cases always seems to have been given ministerial backing from MinTech, seems effectively to have guaranteed a proposal Monopolies Commission clearance. It is true that the Government utilised the Monopolies Commission more than preceding administrations had done, and was prepared to argue that size was no guarantee of efficiency. Nevertheless the Government usually gave merger promotion priority and was ready to approve large amalgamations on the basis of limited evidence, although the 1965 Act should have enabled the President of the Board of Trade to refer such proposals to the Monopolies Commissions. This seemed especially to be the case when the proposed firm appeared to have the potential to be a large exporter. However, it was only by the conscious taking of political decisions at high levels, sometimes in the Cabinet as in the GEC/EE case, that an outwardly consistent approach was ensured.

Therefore by means of formal committees and informal discussions behind the scenes, by taking advantage of IRC Board Members working in other parts of the Government machine, and through the IRC's attempts to work closely with various parts of Whitehall, the Government managed overall to effectively co-ordinate the work of the Corporation with that of the other ministries and agencies involved in the process of implementing its industrial policies. It would be an over-simplification to suggest that this co-ordinating process should be defined in terms of the iniative always coming from one side since the fact that both partners contributed actively to the process of working together was one of the main reasons for the effectiveness of the co-ordination. The best illustration of this co-ordination was the complex two-way process in the IRC's close and productive relationship with MinTech. This was much the most important part of

within the manufacturing sector, and with the establishment of the SIB, it was made clear that it excluded shipbuilding. However in practice, the location of these hard and fast boundaries to IRC's activity became blurred. The Monopolies Commission for example was an erratic constraint sometimes being ignored, and sometimes effectively stopping the IRC from proceeding as it might have wished. In the Thorn/Radio Rentals case for example for Corporation did not state its view until after a decision about referring the proposal had been taken, and the Monopolies Commission had given its verdict.[1] Once the Board had shown it could produce results of which ministers approved the Government consciously widened the IRC's hard and fast boundaries, thus steadily broadening the Corporation's sphere of activity, *vis-à-vis* departments and other para-government bodies. Specific one-off requests from Government departments took the IRC into areas in which it probably would not have otherwise have been active. Implementing its report on Cammell Laird is a typical example.

The IRC's internal attitude was an important third element in this overall equation. There were cases where as a result of its own initiative it moved into areas which it was not actually asked to enter. The IRC's attempt to modernise British industry when conducting rescue operations was a typical example. Other included the IRC's study of the fiscal problems involved in overseas investment, the ways in which the taxation system might have inhibited inward and outward investment, and the concept of a European IRC.[2] The IRC moved on to advocate points of view on these and other subjects within Whitehall, sometimes without being asked by the Government. Occasionally, the Government reacted formally to internal IRC pressures as when it put the clause in the 1968 Miscellaneous Finance Provisions Act allowing the IRC to make loans in foreign currencies, and when it asked the Corporation to complete and implement a full report on a subject which the IRC had either begun work, or had been pressing to be allowed to study in depth – nuclear power construction was an example of this. The Corporation was thus prepared to take the initiative and to expand its influence.

Pressures within the IRC also led in the opposite direction, to the Board's freedom of action becoming narrower rather than wider. This was the case in those instances where, for reasons discussed below, the Board imposed restraints on itself either by eliminating a potential line of action from the available options, or by refusing to involve itself at all. Because the IRC valued its relationship with MinTech and its own operational independence, it obviously did not want to offend the Government by embarrasing it, particularly if this would have threatened to precipitate any kind of backlash on itself. Thus the Corporation took "special care" in industries where government funds were already committed.[3] In those instances where the Board wanted to go ahead on commercial grounds but where the subject was potentially embarrassing to the Government, the Corporation tended to put out feelers to the Minister rather than just giving him the normal notice of a particular involvement. In some cases it may even have refrained without actually bothering to approach the Minister. For example, the two IRC involvements to which the Government had most heavily committed itself concerned Rootes and the Ross/AF merger. The Government would have been in an embarrassing position if the IRC had wanted to sell its Rootes holding, or to put together all and not just the trawling fleet parts of Ross and AF. As it was, the IRC support for the latter limited merger gave rise to considerable criticism of the IRC and the Government's mergers policies. This sort of problem was apparently one factor contributing to the failure to restructure private steel.

A second type of situation where the Board imposed restraints on itself concerned those situations which would have aroused opposition, not from Ministers but from industry. As described in Chapter 7, there were cases where the Corporation almost certainly could have achieved a link-up by similar tactics to those employed in the Kent/Cambridge, Brown Bayley and RHP situations, but where it did not. This was because on the one hand the firms concerned were not important enough to make the case one of compelling national interest in the Board's eyes, and, on the other, because to have proceeded would have jeopardised the crucially important working relationship that the IRC had with individual companies both in the sector concerned and in other industries.

The limits to the areas in which the IRC was active were steadily widened because this suited the changing needs of the Government; because of a desire in Whitehall to take advantage of the IRC's unique blend of skills; and because of internal IRC initiatives which arose partly as a result of the Board discovering towards the end of its life that its merger-promoting role was almost played out for the time being.[4] Although IRC's sponsoring ministry was at times prepared to hold the Corporation back, the overall result of the political, institutional, and internally-generated pressures on the IRC Board was to widen its sphere of activity beyond the original and more narrowly envisaged merger-promoting and selective investment roles outlined in the IRC Act.

A broadening of the limits of IRC activity, together with an intensification of activity well within those limits could imply an increase in IRC influence on Whitehall. It is impossible to determine the precise extent to which this happened, and certainly the IRC would sometimes have been disregarded. However, examples show the sorts of ways in which the Corporation appears to have been able to make an impact on Government thinking, decision-making and policy-implementation, both well within and at the edges of its sphere of activity. The most obvious is the fact that departments were presented with a wide range of reports that the IRC had been asked to prepare. These had an impact whether they were fully or partly implemented, or whether or not the department concerned asked the IRC to follow through the recommendations. It is difficult to assess their importance because they were confidential, and because Parliamentary Questions about them elicited no details.[5] However, there is evidence to suggest that the IRC reports on telecommunications, Cunard, and pig processing were amongst those which were more or less fully accepted.[6] Secondly, although it was a policy-implementing, not a policy-making agency in the minds of its creators, the IRC felt itself free to make recommendations on policy to the Government.[7] The concept of a European IRC is probably the best example of an IRC view influencing ministerial thinking, but others included the hardening attitude to overseas investment in the UK, and the lack of a known framework of law on mergers and monopolies which meant that the *ad hoc* policy of assessing individual mergers was continued. Thirdly, although even more intangibly, IRC Board Members had, as described in the preceding chapter, other jobs in various parts of the Government machine. The fact that most of the cases in the first two examples come from the later stages of IRC's active life suggests that the Corporation's influence increased. The strongest sign of its being regarded as important by those it was seeking to influence was that at some stage it was brought within the exclusive telephone network serving ministers and top officials.

In attempting to assess the IRC's claims to full operational independence, two questions arise: how far was the IRC dependent on others, and could it be forced to act against its will? As regards the first, it has been shown that the IRC drew the information on which it based its decisions from Government departments and agencies, nationalised industries and individual companies; it approached the sponsorship divisions of MinTech for technical advice; and it received suggestions for requests from parts of Whitehall to study certain problems. Although individual companies provided a lot of information, the Corporation also took extensive advantage of other parts of Whitehall, and was in varying degrees dependent on the latter. This it in fact acknowledged: "IRC's work has in many cases been made possible by the basic fact-finding that has already been carried out by others." Beesley and White suggest that IRC's dependence on MinTech lessened as time went by because of IRC's "generation of knowledge and experience."[8] However the Corporation was left by others to act entirely within its own discretion. The IRC's freedom was more seriously challenged when attempts were made to force it to act against its will. It would be wrong – because the IRC Board agreed with the Government's line – to quote Rootes as an example, but certainly the Government's impatience in the summer of 1967 was an attempt to push the IRC Board into more positive lines of action than it felt justified. Probably the nearest the IRC came to losing its operational independence was in the Cammell Laird case, but even then the Board was able to insist that the Government should accept certain preconditions before it became involved. In the Rolls Royce case the Government had accepted the IRC report but nothing could be done unless the Rolls board agreed.[9] It should be noted that in this situation one option open to the Government, which was "very worried"[10] at what was happening, was to attempt to persuade the IRC Board to alter the pre-conditions as a means of trying to get the Rolls board to agree to accept them. The fact that the IRC did not change its conditions, whether asked to or not, is a firm indication of the respect shown by the Government for its operational independence.

Therefore although its independence was circumscribed on various occasions when it was prevented from doing what it wanted to do for commercial reasons or excluded from some subject areas, the Corporation maintained its independence over what it probably saw as the crucial issue: the Government found it impossible to dragoon the IRC into lines of action against the collective will of its Board. This was borne out by Sir Joseph Lockwood: when asked to say what was wrong with the IRC he referred to its "power and independence"[11] as being the factor that caused the most disquiet amongst MPs. It is important to note that the IRC's independence applied not just to matters at the centre of its sphere of activity but also, as in the Cammell Laird case, to those at the edges. The most outspoken of the IRC's claims to independence was in the 1968-69 report: "in all cases the operational independence of the IRC has been scrupulously respected by the Government who neither insisted on nor prevented any course of action."[12] This appears to be more justified with regard to 'respect' as opposed to 'preventing'.

The IRC's ability to be independent was largely the result of the way the 1966 IRC Act was framed. In the first place, the Corporation was given executive authority, and in the second it was, unlike many other executive departments and para-government bodies, genuinely independent of the Treasury. Thirdly, the very wide powers given it by the Act enabled it to take the initiative on such questions as to how to organise itself, what sectors to examine, which firms to approach, which parts of Whitehall to ask for advise or information, and how to act in different areas. Beesley and White have also stressed in this connection the importance of the fact that the information it received from companies was confidential and not passed on to Government departments:

> It would not be unfair to suggest that the confidentiality of information, and hence its secrecy, was used by IRC . . . to maintain its freedom and independence from Government control.[13]

The Corporation's position can be compared to that of other organisations. The NBPI for example, however much it tried to get a reference, could only go into an area if the Minister agreed to give that reference; the NRDC could only act in response to a firm's or occasionally a Minister's request; and the EDCs could only discuss and recommend. By contrast the IRC had executive authority, financial independence, and an acknowledged right to take the initiative: together these enabled it to enjoy an unfettered relationship with the private sector of industry.

There were also practical developments in the relationship between the IRC and the Government that ensured its ability to continue to operate independently. The most important of these was the Board's determination from the beginning to refuse to be pushed into lines of action against its will: this was a result of the composition of the Board with its lack of Government representatives and the inclusion of some strongly-willed characters. Secondly, the passage of time seems to have produced a fairly widespread respect amongst senior civil servants, for example within MinTech, and also among Labour Ministers for the IRC's judgment, professionalism and ability to move quickly. Of course, there were exceptions, but the point seems to be borne out by the fact that IRC was given an increasing number of wide-ranging jobs to do, special attention was given to its views, and importance was attached to its ability to move swiftly in a crisis like the Cammell Laird affair, or to exploit the Stock Market and shift capital sums in a bid situation. Thirdly, by showing it could exercise self-restraint and act tactfully on occasions that could have embarrassed the Government, the IRC proved it could be trusted. A reliable body is less likely to be the subject of Government interference. Finally, underlying the whole situation, it would probably be true to say in general terms that the IRC's collective judgment and attitudes on various subjects had a lot in common with the more interventionist MinTech civil servants and Labour Ministers.

However, in the last resort, the IRC depended on political support for its ability to be influential and independent. Although there was friction at different times between the IRC and some Labour Ministers, the political constraints on the IRC's freedom of action were limited and restricted to detail because of political sympathy for the concept of an active IRC. After its GEC/AEI success the Government was happy to leave the IRC alone to get on with the job. Its executive authority, financial independence and right of initiative were thus based firmly on political support.

The 1970 election of course at once transformed this situation because the Conservative Government removed several of the elements that enabled the IRC to be independent. The Corporation's new political masters objected to some of the principles behind the IRC; they naturally lacked a respect based on close experience of IRC's work as a specialist adviser to various parts of Whitehall; and they restricted its financial independence by forbidding it to enter into any new commitments without the permission of the Minister of Technology.[14] The effective removal of its right to take the initiative was the crucial blow: the IRC's work load fell off steadily because it could not start new business. It had to withdraw from the Rolls Royce investigation when told to do so in October 1970.[15] The very fact that the IRC's scope for work was so radically diminished by the Conservative Government shows clearly that its most important source of independence was political support.

The conclusion that the IRC had fairly wide influence, full operational independence, and could not be forced to act against its will could imply that it acquired something of a momentum of its own, that it was in some way beyond the Government's control in that it was doing more than the Government had expected or wanted. This question must be considered against a wider backcloth. The fact that there was widespread criticism, based sometimes on sincere personal conviction and sometimes on political dogma, that the IRC was unorthodox, unconventional, too independent and politically undesirable does not prove that it was out of control. Since the IRC was acting within the Government's overall directives such criticism should properly be directed at the Labour Government for giving a para-government agency such extensive powers in such a broad sphere of activity. Whereas the question of political desirability is largely one of value, the question as to whether the IRC was out of control is largely one of fact.

Finally there remains the question as to how far the IRC was out of control. This has certainly been suggested by no less a figure than one of the junior ministers involved with the IRC: "The Government found that, like Frankenstein, it had little control over its monster."[16] Several incidents have come to light which, it could be argued, illustrate the point. It might be suggested for example that when the Board nominated to the Minister the successors to Grierson and Kearton,

IRC had let its independence stretch too far.[17] However, since the Board understood the nature of IRC's job and had to work with the nominated man it was only sensible to let it suggest a name. There was no question of the Minister being forced by IRC to act against his will as the Minister could have said no the first nomination and asked for a second. It could also perhaps be argued that the Corporation seemed to be trying hard to get through its £150 million before the 1970 election as a means of either getting more money out of a new Labour Government, or of ensuring that the money was inevitably injected into the economy even if the Conservatives won and either abolished the IRC or restricted its activities. This is not however, to suggest that it was not then applying its usual financial criteria. A further instance of IRC acting irrespective of Ministers' wishes might be some of the IRC projects announced after the 1970 election which appeared to be at variance with the Conservative Government's attitude at that time: the stand-by credit to RHP, the equity holding in Kearney and Trecker, and the loans to the textile firms and to Clarke Chapmen/John Thompson. Unlike the money loaned to Samuel Osborn and Marwin, these cannot be shown to have been clear hard and fast pre-election commitments. The IRC would have been able to present these to the Minister and still appear to be following his directive not to enter into any new commitments without his permission on the grounds that there had been agreement between the IRC and the firms concerned before the 1970 election. However it is quite possible that some of these cases were in fact only at a very early and tentative stage by 18 June 1970.

There seem to be two ways in which the IRC could be said to have been out of control. The first is the issue as to whether it contained within itself "the facility for self-determination",[18] and was able to carry through its own projects. The evidence from the last few chapters suggests that with regard to its own operational situation it developed into an autonomous organisation that was independent of the Government. However this has to be qualified by the point that it did depend on others as, for example, for ideas and information. There is also no evidence to suggest that it could be forced to act against its will though this again has to be qualified in that the IRC went out of its way not to embarrass the Government.

It also might be said that the Corporation was out of control in the sense that it could take the initiative and act irrespective of the wishes of Ministers. However there was no question of it being able to do anything of which the Government strongly disapproved, or of it being able to force the Government to do anything against its own will. If the limits to IRC's sphere of activity were widened by the Government as a result of IRC persuasion, then the Government had no occasion to comply if it did not want to. In the last resort it was only able to expand them when working in areas that did not jeopardise its political support: Labour Ministers were able to exercise political power and prevent the Corporation from doing more than the Government wanted it to do as they did early in 1970 over the Lever Committee investigating the textile industry.[19] Thus any action taken by the IRC was supported by the Government's tacit consent at the very least, and in the last analysis that support was essential to the IRC's work. What it boils down to is that while the IRC made a reality of its operational independence, it was doing things of which the Government approved.

The Problem of Accountability

The IRC, like any other political body, could not exist in a vacuum: it affected other bodies and was influenced by them. The controversial nature of the Corporation's work impinged on the interests and sometimes offended the CBI, the City, the TUC, all political parties and others. The IRC was answerable to the Secretary of State for Economic Affairs, and after October 1969, to the Minister of Technology. The sponsoring Minister was answerable to the House of Commons for IRC's actions. However, because the IRC was so independent, MPs were not able to make the Corporation or the Minister accountable in the classical political sense. By contrast, it seems that the only criticisms from a sectional interest that led to the IRC actually amending its policies and attitudes, rather than acknowledging and accommodating the criticism, came from the City.

It was for practical reasons worth the Corporation's while to establish good working relationships with management consultants, solicitors, accountants, merchant banks, and the City in general. Consequently it cultivated its relationship with them by wide distribution of its patronage: it commissioned reports, needed professional advice in takeover situations, had large sums in bank accounts on call at short notice, and took care to abide by the Takeover Panel's Code. It had after all to work on a day-to-day basis with the City representatives of the companies with which it was involved, and it needed to have good relationships to fall back on when it utilised the market mechanism to push through regroupings that incensed City opinion. This was especially desirable because the IRC was flouting convention by introducing the concept of the 'bottomless purse' into bid situations. There appears to have been something of an element of the Corporation's knowing it could go so far and no further. For example, after resisting pressures to publish its reasoning with regard to the industrial logic of a given case, on the grounds that it possessed confidential information, it gave way in the most controversial instances of Kent, GEC/EE, Brown Bayley and RHP.[20] This seems to have been the only occasion when the IRC fundamentally changed its attitude on a particular issue. It also effectively evaded the question when asked to arbitrate between Weir's and Studbaker-Worthington's bids for Worthington Simpson: the City did not seem to relish the prospect of the Corporation establishing such a precedent.[21] The CBI had general reservations about the way the IRC was allowed to exercise its powers, and about its lack of accountability, but it could not react in any positive fashion to the IRC because it was hamstrung by the conflicting interests and views of its members. The IRC accommodated criticism from the CBI by initiating discussions "at board level to ensure proper appreciation of the IRC's objectives, criteria and working methods."[22]

The most extensive criticism of IRC came from those whose jobs were threatened. The issue of redundancies following mergers first became really critical in February 1968. GEC then announced that it was going to close AEI's Woolwich telecommunications factory, with the resulting loss of five thousand jobs.[23] This sparked off a wide-ranging debate, that was to last well into the 1970s. It was given a further impetus in 1969 when following its merger with EE, GEC announced plans to run down several factories on Merseyside. How far should the IRC be publicly accountable for redundancies following on its mergers? How far should workers be consulted over mergers? What were the social responsibilities of firms in the private sector? Had the Government fully thought through the social implications of its policies and what was it going to do about their effects?

It is in this context that the social consequences of mergers must always be remembered. The boiler industry provides one of the most acute examples of the extent to which the ramifications of mergers can affect workers and their families for years. This particular sector was involved with many merger proposals and was also affected by the rationalisation taking place in diesels following GEC's acquisitions; some factories changed hands more than once in a year. The situation was further exacerbated not just by high unemployment in the late 1960s and early 1970s, but the fact that the rationalisation process could and did drag on for years, especially in the face of continuing low capital investment, which meant limited demand for the industry's products. The social effects on whole communities not just of a closure, but of a threatened or feared closure, could be extensive and even devastating. This was the case regardless of whether there was something of a cushion of alternative employment. The situation was even worse though, in a city like Lincoln that was heavily dependent on heavy engineering, or a small town like Annan in Dumfrieshire, where a large proportion of the workforce were employed in a factory owned at the start of the 1960s by Cochranes.

It is quite clear that from the beginning the IRC had been well aware that mergers would lead to redundancies if benefits deriving from economies of scale were to be realised.[24] So even before the issues were publicly raised the Corporation had made special attempts to take into consideration the views of the unions. The telecommunications inquiry was probably not the only one completed for the Government in which the union's views were sought and considered: in that case the Post Office Engineering Union naturally held strong views.[25]

The main effect of the Woolwich and other cases was to make the IRC all the more sensitive on this issue, so that while it was not mentioned in the 1967-68 annual report, by 1968-69 the Corporation was acknowledging that it was "acutely conscious" of the "far-reaching implications for trade union members".[26] Observers were sent to the 1968 Trades Union Congress, where Cannon from the platform rejected as he was bound to do, claims that IRC should be responsible for the results of its actions. The Corporation probably took advantage as well of the personal connections with union leaders of both Cannon and, for the time that he was with the IRC, of Robinson (who had been a research worker at Transport House) to put across arguments such as the greater job security for those not made redundant that could result from the IRC's work.[27]

There was in fact little the IRC could do because the extent to which it could take the initiative in this field was very limited. It could not give union leaders advance notice of a merger on account of the need for secrecy as dictated by Stock Market considerations. It is impossible to say without a great deal of empirical work how far it was successful in insisting on firms entering into consultation not negotiation, with unions as soon as possible after the announcement. When such talks took place they would not have been binding on the company. Where there was an open bid situation, as in the GEC/AEI case, the Corporation did insist on early talks.[28] Detailed post-merger plant closures and rationalisation schemes do not seem to have been worked out in detail before a merger was supported. The IRC claimed it took account of regional considerations when examining a post-merger review.[29] Judgment on the reality of this claim must remain suspended until tingible evidence is revealed. In the meantime the claim seems dubious. It seems that, with a few exceptions, the decision to close factories was made on commercial grounds without social considerations being taken into account. Individual firms did not go into a merger bound by conditions over redundancies imposed by the IRC. That is why the Corporation's response to this problem amounted to attempting to accommodate the criticism, not amending its policies.

Where the Corporation was itself directly involved as a result of taking over Brown Bayley it attached great importance in having a model relationship with "full consultation on all matters that significantly affect the work force."[30] The approach was implemented both before and after the sale of the Hoffman subsidiary, and the Brown Bayley Steels unions in Sheffield, apparently much impressed by the IRC's attitude, established a negotiating committee through which to put its views to the IRC. This was a process of consultation not negotiation.

The second effect of the publicity which the redundancies issue attracted was the talks which the IRC initiated with the TUC Economic Committee in 1968 and 1969 with a view to drawing up a code of good practice in merger situations:[31] its practical value appears to have been limited because it could not be made mandatory. Apart from this the TUC was not itself involved with the IRC Consultations about redundancies which took place directly between unions and management at local level: there were such talks at Chelmsford with RHP, and at Woolwich and on Merseyside with GEC.

The concern of the unions was focused on the House of Commons: there were marches of soon to be redundant workers, petitions, and sit-ins; lengthy editorial comments in the specialist financial press and in the general press; radio and television coverage; and an expansion of the middle management union – the Association of Scientific, Technical and Managerial Staffs.[32] In the House itself there were questions and debates on the Rootes and Kent affairs, but these were not concerned with redundancies as such.[33] The fact that IRC's representatives answered questions on its role in the reorganisation of the nuclear power sector put by the Select Committee on Science and Technology, had no practical effect on the Corporation.

Overall the criticism made no real impact in the sense of influencing IRC activity. The Corporation itself took steps to accommodate it, but apart from publishing its industrial logic in a few cases, made no concessions. This was understandable in the sense that it was only one arm of the Government's industrial policies and its task was to get on with its restructuring role. It could be left to other parts of Whitehall to cope with the results of IRC's actions. Theoretically the Minister from the sponsoring department was responsible to Parliament for the IRC's activities. The Corporation published an annual report and as a result the Minister had very little extra answering to Parliament to do.

In practice, appreciating the extent to which the IRC relied on its independence, he became a buffer between the IRC and the public pressures on it. He was the only person who had the power, under Section 2(5) of the IRC Act, to give the Corporation general directives.

When he did so decisions were taken within Government and not as a result of any external or Parliamentary pressure. The IRC experience showed how such a body could be independent. It also showed clearly that while it was to some degree accountable to its sponsoring Minister, Parliament exercised little detailed control over it. The situation contrasted sharply with the institutional arrangements introduced under the 1972 Industry Act. As a result of the latter all decision-making was located within the Industrial Development Executive *within* the Department of Trade and Industry. In that situation the Minister could be, and indeed was, questioned much more closely on the floor of the House about his work, than the IRC's sponsoring Minister had been about the IRC's actions a few years earlier.

PART III

THE 'DISENGAGEMENT' EXPERIMENT 1970-72

CHAPTER 11 THE DEVELOPMENT OF THE CONCEPT OF 'DISENGAGEMENT' 1960-70

Chapter 1 showed that when the Conservative Party left office in October 1964, it was as a Party committed to government intervention and economic planning. Yet, by 1970, when the Conservatives fought the June election campaign, their attitude had become:

> LESS GOVERNMENT
>
> There has been these last years an explosion of Government activities; The bureaucracy – central and local – has soared; boards and committees have multiplied; new laws and regulations cascade – and impose huge burdens of comprehension and compliance on all. Each individual purpose may be defensible on its own, though some are not – but in aggregate the spread of government intervention is an evil which must be reversed before it stifles enterprise.
>
> Government should limit itself to getting the general pressures right, withdrawn from inessential activities, and keep its legislation to what is really necessary.[1]

What was the origin of this 'disengagement' philosophy? How did this develop during the 1960s?

Conservatism and 'economic planning' were in one sense never wholly compatible bedfellows. Though the leaders of the Party were converted to planning in the early 1960s, or became convinced, particularly through the French example, of the important role the Government should play in industrial policy, yet there remained some Party sceptics. Enoch Powell, for instance, remained outside the planning ethos.

> If ever the history of economic hallucinations comes to be written, the idea that governments possess the knowledge and power positively to determine the rate of economic growth through the technique of central economic planning will be revealed as one of the most widespread tenacious and harmful of errors.[2]

Nor was Powell alone. Even at the height of Conservative acceptance of 'Interventionsm' therefore, when the Party leaders were almost without exception committed to a closer relationship between the state and private industry, there existed a corpus of opposition to them.

For the majority of the party, however, the chief criticism of the Labour Government at this early stage after the election, 1964-6, was not that they were doing too much, but that they were not doing it effectively. Sir Edward Boyle, for instance, was careful to distinguish between economic planning and Labour's National Plan.

> The fact that there is a wide gap between the National Plan and reality – and many businessmen realise this clearly – does not mean that industry rejects the whole planning concept. I believe that public opinion in Britain wants to see a greater sense of national purpose in the conduct of our economic policy.[3]

The majority of both parties, and certainly each of their leaderships, were close to a common 'planning' approach at this time. The change-over from 'intervention' to 'disengagement' was a *volte face* which took place between 1964 and 1970.

One of the many pressures for change was seen in October 1964, when the Conservative Political Centre (CPC) became an official part of the party organisation, to exercise a dynamic role analysing policy-making within the party and through local committees, to act as co-ordinator of the two-way traffic of ideas between centre and constituency. Mr David Howell was appointed Director of CPC in December 1964. Under him it was to be "the spearhead, as you might say, of our philosophic advance".[4] From the beginning of 1965 one can begin to identify the emergence of a 'new ideology': a gradual rejection of the 'planning' commitment of the Conservative leadership; a call for the abolition across the board of economic planning controls; the progressive development of the 'new style of government', which was ultimately to be adopted at the Selsdon Park Conference as official policy before the June 1970 election campaign. Initially this search for new ground involved an attack on established positions, an attempt to return to a pre-planning era of liberal *laissez-faire.* It was epitomised by the pamplet *A Bonfire of Restrictions,* an attack not just on Labour planning, but on the whole planning approach. It called for greater competition, using the Monopolies Commission and the Restrictive Trade Practices Court more vigorously; abolishing the Iron and Steel Board and minimum price supports in agriculture, and reviewing transport legislation. It advocated the abolition of monopolies in the nationalised sector; of the licensing laws; of restrictive shop hours; and of limited bank opening hours. It was a castigation across the board of the 'restrictionist' mentality. In the 'new style of government' therefore, there runs one strand of the old liberal Conservative tradition: the wish to restore a competitive free market economy and individual enterprise.

Grafted on to this old stock however were new developments: the introduction into government of business methods and modern management techniques, principally cost effectiveness and management-by-objectives. After the 1964 election defeat Ernest Marples went to Washington for the Conservative Central Office to make a detailed study of cost saving methods developed in the

United States. This report helped to produce a new Conservative attitude to public expenditure and the nationalised industries. Also, in July 1965 Edward Heath replaced Sir Alec Douglas Home as leader of the Party, and during the 1966 election campaign pledged a "War on waste in government". It was a two-pronged attack: to make sure the public sector was efficiently run and to review it as a whole to see if it could be reduced. The essentials of 'Disengagement' were clearly formulated by the new Party leader in 1966.

A five-point plan for the public sector was put forward in January 1967. It was squarely couched in management terms:

> (a) A Central Cost Effectiveness Department, responsible to the Prime Minister, to keep a constant watch to see that money was spent to the best advantage.
> (b) A Cost Reduction Target for each minister to be established. Ministers would be responsible for achieving specified financial savings. The results would be independently checked and published.
> (c) Further consultation with outside experts before huge sums of money were spent. This would involve sweeping away much Whitehall secrecy.
> (d) The use of the Total Systems Analysis approach. This complex sounding procedure has three main steps. First a clear definition of the objective. Second, a listing of the alternative methods of achieving the objective. Third, choice of the most practicable and economical method is necessary with the aid of a computer.
> (e) New methods of government contracting. The government is a huge purchaser of goods and services, and must ensure that it gets the best value for taxpayers and save money. This would be done by introducing new forms of contract . . . Advance techniques of control like Critical Path Analysis would be applied to all large projects.[6]

To fulfil the second criterion, to reduce the area in which public money was spent, two remedies were put forward. The Conservatives wished to reverse the innovations introduced by Labour, like steel nationalisation, and 'creeping nationalisation', whereby bodies like the Transport Holding Company were taking over private road hauliers. In addition they wanted to reintroduce private enterprise wherever possible, as for example by giving private airlines opportunities to compete with state airlines. Thus there steadily developed in the Conservative Party from 1964 an emphasis on management techniques, efficiency, and cost-effectiveness, which was fairly well-developed by the beginning of 1967.

The second component of the 'new style' was added during 1968. Management-by-objectives was inter-related with cost-effectiveness, but the Conservatives only seemed fully to appreciate this with the publication of the Fulton Report on the civil service. Prior to the publication of the Fulton Report, a Party document concerned with civil service reform adopted a predictable attitude:

> . . . a Conservative Government will reverse the socialist tendency to extend the government sector of the economy. This means a bonfire of controls and putting nationalisation into reverse.[7]

By December 1968 the key tenets of the Fulton philosophy, management-by-objectives, accountability, and hiving-off, had been successfully incorporated into CPC thinking. The Fulton Committee had been set up to suggest reforms in the structure of the Civil Service, but very early in their Report they stressed the inter-locking of state and private interests as a characteristic feature of the modern mixed economy.

> The increase in the positive activities of government has not been solely an extension of the powers and functions of the state in an era of technological change. There has also been a complex inter-mingling of the public and private sectors. This has led to a proliferation of para-state organisations; public corporations, nationalised industries, negotiating bodies with various degrees of public and private enterprises, and voluntary bodies financed from public funds. Between the operations of the public and private sectors there is often no clear-cut boundary.[8]

The origins of 'hiving-off' are clearly seen in suggestions for reform of the Civil Service:

> . . . to conclude that large-scale executive operations cannot be run effectively by government departments, and that they should be 'hived-off' whenever possible to independent boards.[9]

The Fulton Committee considered that there was not necessarily a distinction to be made between those activities for which a minister was responsible and those for which he was not.

> There is indeed a wide variety of activities to which it might be possible to apply the principal of 'hiving-off'. They range from the work of the Royal Mint and air traffic control, to parts of the Social Services . . . we think however, the possibility of a considerable extension of 'hiving-off' should be examined and we therefore recommend an early and thorough review of the whole system.[10]

Following this publication Conservative Party ideas about denationalisation and increased efficiency in public spending crystalised further, making the connection between 'hiving-off' parts of the public sector to para-state boards, and following logically to the 'privatisation' of some of the nationalised industries.

The main influences on the Conservative Party in the formulation of 'disengagement' have, therefore, been mentioned. It remains to see how committed the party was to this policy before the June 1970 election, and what specifically the policy meant.

In the public sector the policy became much more than a desire to denationalise, or 'privatise' the major nationalised industries. The objective became a basic reappraisal of the whole range of government functions and services, of the vast supportive structure which had grown up, not only under the Labour Government since 1964, but since the mid-nineteenth century. An essential document[11] analysed a future government's role. It stressed the crucial role the Civil Service would play in the thorough analysis of government activity which would be undertaken. Further Civil Service reform would be needed. A new 'capability unit' would be established at the highest level to supervise the internal changes. Administrative change would lead to tighter control, and financial control would develop con-commitantly. Services and functions would be subject to cost-benefit analysis, using new accounting methods. Reorganisation would produce clearly defined blocks of executive responsibility. The new capability unit would be based in part on the Treasury Management Accounting Unit. To accompany departmental reorganisation, ministerial reorganisation would take place, with fewer ministers presiding over wider areas of responsibility, such as 'Industry', 'Protection' and 'Conservation', but smaller in terms of personnel, since many existing departmental responsibilities would have been 'hived-off' into executive agencies.

> The vague desire to interfere with and subsidise industries on an *ad hoc* basis would be replaced by the creation of specific task forces to deal with specific industrial situations.[12]

Conservative policy towards the nationalised industry sector of public policy had three objectives: first to end nationalisation; secondly, to ensure that remaining industries would be run more efficiently; and thirdly to return certain parts to private ownership. So that, under the first heading, dock nationalisation would not go ahead; under the third heading, recenly nationalised sectors such as steel and the road haulage industry under the 1968 Transport Act, would be returned to private enterprise. The second part of the policy, increased efficiency, was very much part of the ideas of the 'sixties, as has been shown. Recommendations to effect this were, however, less clear except that the government should provide a general framework within which the industries worked, and within which management should be allowed to manage, subject neither to political pressures, nor to detailed interference by government departments. This was nothing new, and left undiscussed the difficult problem of the accountability of such 'Arm's length' government.

The new component of the policy lay in the commitment to 'privatisation', to return certain industries to private ownership.[13] The difficulties inherent in this were recognised and various alternative solutions offered. A 'Volkswagen' solution, where no private investor was allowed to buy more than ten shares, was suggested, or a 'BP' solution in reverse, when instead of the government buying 49 per cent of the shares in a private company, the government would allow that proportion of the nationalised industries to be sold, and private shareholders to elect Directors to the Boards. Other alternatives were that ancillary or subsidiary activities should be sold separately from the parent company or that regional divisions should compete with each other. Lastly, rather than sell a state concern, private firms could be encouraged to enter into competition with a monopoly industry. Although these various alternatives had been mooted within the Party, the 1970 Manifesto itself made mention only in vague terms:

> We will progressively reduce the involvement of the state in the nationalised industries, for example in the steel industry, so as to improve their competitiveness.[14]

The attitude towards the private sector emphasised the government role of 'creating the climate' in which private industry operated. Labour Government intervention was specifically condemmed on two counts, that it was ineffectual, and that it was doing a job inappropriate to government. The emphasis on individual initiative masked the very real repercussions which the public sector cuts would effect on private firms:

> A policy of intervention distracts ministers from their essential task of getting the general pressures right. A Conservative government will create a climate that encourages spontaneous industrial progress and adaptation. The emphasis and the instinct will no longer favour intervention. The emphasis and the instinct will be to get the general pressures working coherently to stimulate enterprise and wealth creation at all levels of income and to encourage spontaneous industrial progress and adaptation.[15]

However, it was not suggested that government should abandon the regulatory activities it undertook with regard to industry. On the contrary, these might actually increase:

> A policy which promotes competition is not the same thing as *laissez-faire* (or doing nothing). In some respects it does mean an absence of government intervention: for example allowing people to spend their own money as they think fit. But it also implies positive government action to foster competition.[16]

More vigorous use of the Monopolies Commission and the Restrictive Trade Practices Act, the reform of company law, the encouragement of labour mobility, additional training schemes, and fiscal changes favouring income tax, and abolishing SET, would all act as incentives at both personal and company levels. A Small Business Development Bureau would be established to give training in modern management methods, and to put small firms in touch with sources of finance. So that although many intervening Boards or Departments would be curbed or scrapped, it was believed that government would support competitive private industry. The full implications of the promise[17] to cut dispensable government activities and subsidies, and to review regional investment incentives could not be foreseen. The Conservatives also accepted that certain private industries which were not competitive would inevitably need some government assistance.

> . . . some industries such as aircraft, shipbuilding and parts of electronics, need special treatment. The US tax payer pays for almost all American high technology research and development out of defence and space funds. While we stay on our own and in the high technology fields we are more or less forced to do the same – and with a smaller choice of firms. We recognise that as client or through NRDC governments should back carefully selected new developments beyond the timescale of private enterprise.[18]

Industry was promised that there would be "determined, tireless government action".[19] The irritants (bureaucratic departments, forms to fill in, and SET) would go, but the support would stay, and specifically guaranteed in the case of certain high-risk high-technology enterprises. That these policies might have a real impact on the private sector was little appreciated. The full implications of the public sector policy could have been deduced,[20] but Sir Keith Joseph, Opposition Spokesman on MinTech matters, did not spell these out.

While in opposition, then, the Conservatives put forward a blueprint for future action. In the nature of party politics, little significance was attached to it. There was an active policy of 'disengagement' which made up the 'new style of government', but which came to seem important only retrospectively when the Conservatives won the General Election and began their attempts to implement it. It is important not to overemphasise the ideological commitment to 'disengagement'. It was a party political programme: the prime objective of a party is to win the next election. The philosophy was adopted not only for ideological reasons, but because it strengthened the platform for the election. Within Britain's broad, centrist parties many divergent strands of thinking can be accommodated. 'Disengagement' was a development of one particular strand, a response to a disillusionment with economic planning when it was understood that this would not provide the panacea for all economic ills; a response to a search for a real alternative to the Labour Government's increasingly interventionist policies in the late 1960s;

and a natural desire to capitalise on the inevitable dissatisfaction of the electorate with the party in power. The election was won by the Conservatives in June 1970, but it is by no means clear what part 'disengagement' played in their victory, nor even how far the electorate understood the Conservative programme. 'Disengagement' did add up to a coherent programme for a Parliament, but this was little understood in June 1970. Nevertheless the Government believed it had a mandate to introduce its policies.

new departments, therefore, had a major role to play in 'disengagement'.

It has already been said that aerospace R&D, procurement, and sponsorship was taken out of the DTI in October 1970. On a temporary basis a Ministry of Aviation Supply was set up, while Mr. Heath's advisors rationalised overlapping departmental responsibilities. However on presentation of the report in April 1971,[5] responsibility was again divided, between DTI and the Ministry of Defence. The most significant development, however, was the establishment of the first of the 'hived-off' agencies: the Defence Procurement Executive. This body, as its name suggests, was made responsible for procuring defence equipment, and for implementing policy, but was not itself involved in policy-making. This was made the responsibility of a new inter-Ministerial Aerospace Board, a non-statutory body on which sat the Defence Secretary, the heads of DTI, the Department of Education and Science and the Minister for Posts and Telecommunications. Individual ministers, however, remained responsible for matters effecting their departments. In October 1970 the aviation industry had broadly welcomed the setting up of the Ministry of Aviation Supply as a single body to deal with its special problems. In Spring 1971 the outcome of the review had redivided responsibility between two or more ministries. Functional unity had been overridden when an additional inter-departmental committee had been set up which four senior ministers were entitled to attend. One of the purposes of giant departments, to reduce inter-departmental conflict, had been obviated by establishing an agency responsible to several of them. If a 'hived-off' agency cannot make policy decisions its creation can increase ministerial work-loads. On the other hand if it can make policy decisions the problem of accountability to Parliament becomes acute, as Chapter 10 showed in the case of the IRC. Some of the difficulties inherent in executive agencies were pointed up by this first example. In trying to solve old problems, it is difficult not to create as many, and as intractable, new ones.

To the Conservative Government, and particularly to the Prime Minister, these changes were of vital importance. Structurally they were intended to initiate a chain reaction of reform progressively through the lifetime of a Parliament. Every minister was to review his department's existing responsibilities, decide whether they were a necessary part of the government function, and if so, rightly established in the organisational framework. He was to define responsibility and accountability at senior levels. In the aim for 'less government and better government', according to one commentator

> The likely outcome may or may not be better government, but it almost certainly will not be very much less government,

and, except in a marginal way, it is unlikely to be carried out by fewer people.[6]

The second report of the Civil Service Department[7] suggested that the number of civil servants, admittedly a difficult figure to determine accurately because of the problem of consistency in classification, had risen again following initial cuts after October 1970. As this report pointed out however, surely the important criterion was how well civil servants carried out the essential jobs allocated to them, rather than a crude numerical calculation, taking no account of competence.

Concern for efficiency did, of course, also play a major part in Conservative thinking. Many of the most substantial changes, however, can be said to derive not from Conservative re-thinking but from a consensual agreement encompassing both major parties and the Civil Service itself. They can be related to an evolution of ideas about management methods and government structure which dates back at least to the Plowden Report on the Control of Public Expenditure in 1961. The pursuit of efficiency in government, as a theme, can be traced through Plowden and the Labour Government as for example through its acceptance of the Fulton Report, and equally importantly through Sir William Armstrong, head of the Civil Service, and Sir Burke Trend, Secretary to the Cabinet, both of whose terms of office have encompassed governments of different political persuasions. Many of the ideas owe more to the continuity of the civil servants than to their political masters:

> Foreign and Commonwealth Office; Ministry of Defence; DTI; DoE; and the Department of Health and Social Security.
> Note that the first two of these have been developing, stage by stage, for many years; that the last was created by the previous administration; and the 'giant' DTI replaced the 'giant' MinTech, and that the post-election statements by the previous administration favour DoE; so the approach to 'giant' departments has certainly been an all-party one.[8]

To acknowledge the continuity in the evolution of government structure is not to underestimate the change in attitude introduced by the Conservative Government. The structural changes could equally well have been introduced by the Opposition, but in intention they remain sharply differentiated. The Conservatives aim was to reduce the overall amount of government and to lessen the role of the state. Success in such a leading enterprise would virtually have reversed the long-term and lengthy bi-partisan trends of the previous twenty years. The assessment must be, however, that of the two aims of 'disengagement': one, governmental reforms for efficiency, was beginning to be implemented; the other, to lessen the role of the state, eluded the Conservative Government.

In the public sector also, ministers indicated from the outset that they intended to exert their control to promote a system of free competitive enterprise. This was taken to mean a reversal of the state role which had developed not only under the previous Labour Administration but since at least the Second World War. The Conservative Government wanted to ensure

> that the powerful influence of government is exerted to create a climate in which free competitive enterprise can flourish, not to draw more and more power into the hands of the state itself.

It intended to do this by

> the cutting of public expenditure; the reining back of state intervention and control in industries; reduction and reform in taxation.[9]

In providing 'less government', the possibility of actually winding up some existing boards and agencies obviously had great attractions. In the event some important agencies were closed, and continuing departmental reviews may have been expected periodically to add to this list, but the relatively small number gives some indication that, in this sense at least, 'disengagement' did not measure up to Conservative expectations.

Soon after taking office the Land Commission was abolished. It was followed by the NBPI. The pre-election manifesto had not mentioned this possibility, though the party antagonism towards it had been well-known. There was some suggestion at the time of the closure that its demise had been precipitated by Conservative antipathy to Mr. Aubrey Jones, Chairman of the Board, and an ex-Conservative Minister who had taken office under a Labour administration. Certainly it seemed difficult to justify the closure on grounds of expense alone; costs over its five year existence had been £3,800,000, and no attempt at cost-benefit analysis appeared to have been undertaken before it was abolished. On the other hand its closure, like that of the Consumer Council, which followed it, can easily enough be explained in terms of philosophical antipathy, and the exposition soon after of the Conservative Government's hostility to a voluntary or statutory prices and incomes policy.[10] In the terms of 'disengagement' it was no proper part of a government's activities to make decisions which would be better made in the market place, and theoretically neither in the private nor in the nationalised industries should there be the need for a body such as NBPI. Events after its abolition, however, proved that some way of determining wage increases was essential. Having abolished the statutory body, the Government began to establish independent commissions on an *ad hoc* basis, particularly to settle disputes with public sector employees.

Between 1970 and 1972 postmen, miners and electricity workers, for example, all took their wage claims to independent tribunals set up by the Government, each time after considerable disruption not only to the consumers but to the economy at large. The establishment of these independent commissions made the point that by abolishing an agency one does not necessarily abolish the work it did.

In fact the Office of Manpower Economics, a non-statutory body linked with the Department of Employment was widely thought to have risen like a phoenix from the ashes of the NBPI, taking over many of the board's staff and performing at least some of the same administrative functions. Initially set up as the review body for the pay of doctors, MPs, and civil servants, its wide-ranging terms of reference included provisions for it to look broadly at problems of pay, productivity and conditions. During the difficult political period after the 1970 election it developed on a limited basis. Gradually the Government was forced by the growing seriousness of inflation to initiate a regulatory body into the wages situation. Independent commissions backed by secretarial help from an unpublished government agency temporarily filled the gap until a more formalised structure was introduced, with the Pay Board and Prices Commission. Meanwhile the 'disengagement' policy having been put into effect dramatically with the closure of NBPI, the retreat from the policy was equally dramatic. One part of the NBPI remit had been pay; the other part had been price increases and here too the Government tempered their ideological commitment because of the unprecedented rate of inflation. With the establishment from November 1972 onwards of Phase One, Phase Two, Phase Three, Pay Board (especially with its enquiry into the relativities aspect of the miner's pay claim in February 1974), and the Prices Commission, it seems fair to say that the 'disengagement' philosophy had not only been abandoned but a more actively interventionist approach than even the Labour Government had attempted had been introduced. The Conservative Manifesto for the election in February 1974 warned that it might be necessary to stiffen the statutory wages and prices policy further.

Although the abolition of NBPI was intended to presage a thorough review of public sector activities, the extent to which change was achieved was limited. For instance, in the Central Office of Information (COI) a review was carried out by the editor of the *Financial Times*. COI, was already in effect an independent 'hived-off' activity, and in the event the unpublished report to the Government was understood to have recommended its retention, but the transference of some of its work back to within the DTI.

A similar review of the EDCs led to only six of the twenty-two being abolished, and in 1973 a new one for shipbuilding was subsequently established. Industrialists and civil servants apparently found these bodies to be useful. On the other hand, the British National Export Council was abolished, but in its stead the British Overseas Trade Board was formed. The former had been an executive agency, comprised of professional and voluntary efforts; the latter was placed again within DTI and at several times the previous cost. Another closure was that of the Public Trustee Office. The Hutton Committee, a three-man enquiry set up by the government, recommended its closure,[11] as there were adequate alternative facilities available, so that the government's service was unnecessary. As the Trustee Office competed directly with the private sector the closure has diminished rather than enhanced competition. It is also noteworthy that it was not a burden on the taxpayer, since it paid its own way by making economic charges. In its review of different organisations the Government often encountered intense opposition. In 1973 for example an alliance of, amongst others, architects, surveyors, ramblers and film-makers forced the Secretary of State for the Environment to back down from his attempt to make the Ordnance Survey financially less dependent on the Treasury.

Apart from the closures of boards and agencies, another way to effect cuts was by a reduction in staffs and services. The Ministry of Agriculture, Fisheries and Food, for example, published a White Paper in January 1971[12] which placed its emphasis on cost-effectiveness; but outside Whitehall it was seen as something of a political as well as a managerial revolution. A reallocation of existing work was announced, in an attempt to achieve greater efficiency, and some services previously provided free were to be provided on commercially economic rates. Some cuts too were made, such as the Pennine Rural Development Board, and the three hundred committees of the County Agricultural Executive. A number of grants ceased, such as those for agricultural machinery and for vermin clearance. Total savings were expected to amount to £15 million within three years. The Institute of Professional Civil Servants reacted by calling the plan scandalous, doctrinaire, and based on pseudo-statistics.[13]

In the DTI reviews, possibly the Conservatives expected more positive recommendations for cuts than in fact emerged. Though recommendations for greater accountability to government by research associations, for instance, were made, this confirmed previous thinking and was not in any sense 'disengagement'.[14] The Labour Government's proposal for a British Research Development Corporation, for example, was based on the concept of hiving-off outlined by Fulton.[15] Those reviews to which access is possible, as for instance in evidence before a Common Select Committee, confirm that the process was a continual one.[16] 'Disengagement' played little or no part in policy-making. During 1971, the continual threats of future cuts diminished and then stopped. Most of the advisory services developed by Labour and referred to in Chapter 2 emerged unscathed. By 1972 the Government was introducing new ones, as for example with the Small Firms Advisory Bureaux. Some incentives, like the Pre-production Orders Scheme were expanded.

In the more explicitly interventionist areas of industrial policy, the DTI was involved with what was initially one of the more successful attempts to implement 'disengagement'. The 1971 Industry Act marked a symbolic rejection of Labour's interventionist strategy of the late 1960s. The IRC and Industrial Expansion Acts were repealed. The SIB was also abolished. A fundamental part of the philosophy of 'disengagement' was the belief that Labour's interpretation of the role of the state was too broad. It was argued that governments did not need to be, and should not be, involved in such a way, because the competitive pressures of the market would release forces to which companies would have to respond.[17] In addition, the sight of public funds being used to support one side in a takeover bid, as in the Kent case, was anathema to the Conservatives. There were also sound practical reasons for abolishing the IRC. The Conservatives had seen and were probably advised as to the difficulties that have been explained in Chapter 9 of co-ordinating the implementation of restructuring policies, and policies designed to promote competition. Finally in the Autumn of 1970 there was a political need to cut public expenditure. The Corporation argued that to operate it had to have money. As attempts to raise it from both the Treasury and City failed, there was no option but to cancel it, even though pre-election statements only referred to curbing its powers.

However this success was short-lived. In the Winter of 1971-2, as unemployment climbed and capital investment remained stagnant, a political decision was taken at the highest level to reverse previous policy in a bid to promote expansion.[18] A White Paper entitled 'Industrial and Regional Development' was published in March 1972, and followed by a bill in May.[19] Although this was concerned with regional policy, it was also designed to enable the government to provide selective financial assistance anywhere in the country, and to make money available to the shipbuilding industry. A measure of the extent to which it echoed Labour's approach of the late 1960s was the opposition that the bill aroused in the CBI.[20] Comparisons with the IRC were inevitably made when the Secretary of State announced that an Industrial Development Unit (IDU) was to be established within the DTI, and that an Industrial Development

Advisory Board (IDAB) would be set up. The industrial sponsorship and regional policy divisions of the DTI were reorganised into an Industrial Development Executive (IDE). Even though the Secretary of State argued that he still did not intend to support uneconomic ventures, it cannot be denied that the 1972 Industry Act represented a complete rejection of one of 'disengagement's' main strands.

In regional economic policy Mr. Anthony Barber, the Chancellor, changed the direction of existing Labour policies; investment grants were abolished to be replaced by allowances; Corporation Tax was cut in two steps by 5%; REP was to be abolished with effect from 1974; SET was reduced in 1971, prior to its full removal. However, here too, 'disengagement' was quickly put into reverse. Late in the Winter of 1970-1 when unemployment reached unacceptable proportions new Special Development Areas, mainly mining areas with higher than average unemployment, were singled out for selective treatment. Public sector purchasing was increased as with naval orders to provide employment. The combination of high unemployment, inadequate industrial investment, with the depressed areas of the country exaggerating every downward trend, led to repeated attempts to reflate to encourage industrial investment and consumer spending, and to give an added boost on each occasion to the more deprived regions. This naturally eroded the Conservative fiscal and economic policy developed in opposition. Finally, in the Spring 1972 budget, and with the publication of the White Paper mentioned above, the Conservative Government produced policies that discriminated more in favour of deprived regions than Labour's. Since March 1972 firms in the assisted areas have had a wide range of sources of assistance. A strong regional differential was introduced through free depreciation, and other tax allowances were made available; in addition grants were available for modernisation schemes, not just for an incoming firm, as before, but for an existing one wishing to expand. Mr. Christopher Chataway, the new Minister, described the new resources as "the biggest package of help regions have ever had." The 1972 Industry Act made over £1,400 million available between 1972 and 1977, no less than £1,013 million of which was for Regional Development Grants.[21]

Underlying the Conservative Government's approach towards the public sector as a whole was an attempt to reduce public expenditure. The Labour Government had left plans, in their last White Paper,[22] for public expenditure to increase at an average annual rate of 3 per cent until 1971-2, and provisionally at 3½ per cent from 1973-4. In January 1971, the Conservative Government announced proposed cuts to 2.6 per cent. By the White Paper of November 1971,[23] however, increases in public expenditure of £482 million in 1971-2 and £718 million for 1972-3 were announced. The Budget proposals for Spring 1972, and the massive regional development programme were further moves away from reducing public expenditure. The selective cuts in public spending in early 1971 had seemed to confirm the Government's determination to carry 'disengagement' through this field. However, the turnabout and the Conservative back-bench pressure in 1973 for greater control in this sphere went far to show that they had rejected any such straightforward approach.

The effect of 'disengagement' on the general framework within which private industry had to operate has been briefly examined. Previously it was seen that this Government came to power with a clear philosophical outlook and overall policy. It wanted to withdraw as far as possible from policies of government 'intervention'; 'hive-off' government activities, and act only in the setting of a broad framework within which market conditions would determine the size, structure and profitability of individual industrial concerns. An attempt was made to implement this when the government took office: reviews of public sector boards and agencies began, some bodies were closed down, and some funds were reduced. The next chapter describes the Government's reactions to the Rolls Royce and Upper Clyde Shipbuilders (UCS) crises that erupted together in February 1971. From then onwards the retreat from 'disengagement' was under way: in some cases new agencies arose to perform functions of those which had been closed; in regional and industrial policy the first policy changes had been reversed, and what were essentially 'interventionist' policies were reintroduced. In legislation 'disengagement' was overshadowed by two massive and controversial Bills – that to amend Industrial Relations, and that dealing with British entry into the EEC. This initially left little parliamentary time for other reforms. However, the Fair Trading Act did reach the statute book in 1973. On the other hand the Companies Bill was lost as a result of the election that was called in February 1974. Although the hard-line doctrinaire commitment to 'disengagement' was rejected for the most part with, for example the 1972 Industry Act, there were some isolated cases, as with competition policy of the original remaining. Overall the role of the state was in fact expanded.

The Impact of Disengagement on the Nationalised Industries

Conservative policy towards the nationalised industries had three broad components: to stop further nationalisation; to 'steadily reduce the involvement of the state . . . so as to improve their competitiveness'; and to privatise certain parts which could be developed more effectively in partnership with private enterprise. Having ensured, with the dropping of Labour's plan to nationalise the ports, that no further nationalisation would take place, three further aims for the nationalised industries were put forward: first the shedding of peripheral activities; secondly, the introduction of private capital into shareholdings; and thirdly, improving management efficiency.[24] The two basic tenets of 'disengagement' – reducing the role of the state, and improving efficiency – can again be seen. Each of the three objectives will be looked at in turn.

'Hiving-off' had two meanings with regard to the nationalised industries; first the sale of the whole of a government enterprise back to the private sector; secondly selling back part of a large undertaking, where that part could be regarded as peripheral to the whole. Sir John Eden, Minister for Industry, aimed to start selling off parts of the nationalised industries in 1971 and a review was put in hand. Certain 'hiving-off' measures were accomplished in due course. The Government confirmed the sale of the Carlisle and Scottish state-owned public houses, not of great importance to state assets, but it nevertheless raised some important questions of principle in the 'privatisation' policy. If undertakings were to be returned to private enterprise with the aim of increasing competition, that was by no means guaranteed. If the state public houses were sold off to the major brewers, which seemed likely, competition would in fact decrease, and consumer choice would be restricted rather than widened. Another minor but again instructive example of 'privatisation' occurred with Thomas Cooks & Son, and Lunn-Poly, both state-owned travel agents. One of the reasons given for the sale was the hope of greater profitability in private hands, though in the travel business slump of 1971, Cooks' profits compared favourably with those of other major tour operators. The Government sold the firm to a consortium, made up of the Midland Bank, the Forte Hotel Group, and the Automobile Association, which had put in a bid of £22½ million. Several of the major travel firms had been involved in earlier stages of the negotiations, but had either withdrawn or been eliminated. The problem of to whom to sell Cooks posed a dilemma. To sell the firm to an existing travel agent might have given an unfair advantage and decreased consumer choice; on the other hand a non-travel group might not have been able to honour Cooks' obligations. To sell off a profitable concern with large and undervalued assets proved easy. Lunn-Poly was unprofitable however. Having made losses of £1,600,000 since 1969, it was sold to Cunard for £100,000 in July 1971. In these three examples the reasons for 'hiving-off' were apparent: they were identifiable and coherent packages, not intertwined in a large nationalised industry, and consequently easy to sell as a business to private industry. In none of these cases, however, was there any question of a state monopoly. In fact, selling to the private sector may have decreased competition. They are interesting examples of 'privatisation', but hardly in the mainstream of the nationalised industries.

'Hiving-off' ancillary activities was canvassed in such cases as British Rail's hotel and shipping interests, the NCB's brickmaking works, and its computer-ticket agency. The paradox in the Government's position was that only profitable concerns would readily find a buyer at a realistic price, and yet they were the areas where much ingenuity and initiative had been employed to try to ensure that the nationalised industries were not only a rump of the unprofitable or declining industries. They were a useful part of the industries as far as attracting management talent was concerned. They were not in any sense monopolistic. Rather they were in direct competition with the private sector, though of course the latter could not always be expected to approve of competition from a public body.[25]

The problem of defining an 'ancillary activity' became relevant in the case of BSC, which had certain peripheral activities in non-steel-making, such as constructional engineering and chemicals. However there were also steel-making activities as with the special steels division, which the government was thought to class as 'ancillary'. However, by the time the BSC development plan was put forward, the retreat from 'disengagement' had occurred, and the Minister announced that the plan was not 'hiving-off', but rationalisation to which both BSC and the private firms involved had agreed.[26] The attitude to 'hiving-off' in June 1971 was contrasted with that of June 1970:

> in those days the Government dismembered first and consulted afterwards. This time Mr. Davies had accomplished a 'hiving-off' by consent. This is a different and more sensible operation, and much more likely to produce good results.[27]

Eleven of the BSC brick-making works were sold in two lots, and at the same time the wholly-owned subsidiaries in the construction engineering division were formed into separate companies so that private capital could be injected should that be deemed desirable. The rationalisation with Firth Brown could not be described as 'hiving-off', since BSC gained as much as it lost. In total the agreement left the balance of ownership between the public and private sectors fundamentally unchanged. What had promised initially to be hard line 'disengagement' became reduced to rationalisation, agreed with the private sector. Two positive explanations suggest themselves for this particular shift in policy. First, the steel industry was suffering extensive closures as a result of reorganisation, and was therefore presumably anxious to make any sacrifices which might alleviate its problems. Selling off or rationalising its peripherals was not the greatest of its worries and it reluctantly worked with the government to find an acceptable basis for agreement. At the same time, the Government did not push its 'disengagement' policy uncompromisingly. With time, DTI's policy changed, in this as in other areas. In fact, in many of the undertakings where a simple 'hiving-off' was widely canvassed, for instance the retail showrooms of the Gas and Electricity Boards, in fact no proposals emerged, after many 'leaks' to the contrary.

In fact, as the example of the National Freight Corporation showed, talk of disposal of assets had all but ceased by mid-1972, and there was by then some evidence that the trend was in the reverse direction. A new Chairman had been appointed to the National Bus Company, and he appeared interested in expanding the Company's activities, by entering the private car rental market. So 'hiving-off' as a way of decreasing the role of the state had only a brief honeymoon after 1970. Much was discussed but little materialised.

A second way to reduce state concerns was to provide competition where previously none had existed. In this area the development of the 'second-force' airline, British Caledonian, in competition with British European Airways/British Overseas Airways Corporation (BEA/BOAC) is instructive. To establish British Caledonian as a successful second force meant giving them routes previously run by the state airlines, thus reducing an established monopoly. The formal policy statement setting out the Government's intentions[28] stated that preference should be given to the second force airline when licensing an additional carrier. It was almost inevitable that the promotion of British Caledonian would have some adverse effect on BEA/BOAC, which was already in a vulnerable position, but the Government justified the move by the enhanced competition which it believed would result. Other private airlines viewed the development of British Caledonian with as little enthusiasm as BEA/BOAC. Two of them, Skyways Coach Air and Lloyd Aviation both called in the Receiver in 1971-2, blaming British Caledonian's promotion for their decline. It would be inaccurate to classify the Government's airline policy as 'disengagement'. To promote one airline in the private sector it is necessarily to single it out at the expense of others, and the policy can best be said to have been directly interventionist.

The reasons the Government advanced for wishing to sell off ancillary activities were that they tended to denude the major concerns of scarce management talent, and also that competition should be increased. Opposition to 'hiving-off' was mounted on many grounds. It has been suggested, for example, that lengthy arguments between the Government and nationalised industries in 1970-1 absorbed a disproportionate amount of time:

> Lord Melchett and his colleagues on the Steel Board have for months past been too busy fighting political battles to be able to give any thought to improving the efficiency of their undertakings; the Coal Board is now being forced to turn its attention from mining, which employs nearly 300,000, to such minor activities as brick works, which employ 1,500. It is ironic that those in charge of the nationalised industries are being forced by the Government to devote a quite disproportionate amount of time to the peripheral activities which Ministers say they ought to give up because they divert their attention from more important matters.[29]

As the examples of 'hiving-off' have shown they were by no means only those where the state had a monopoly: and their scale did not necessarily involve an increase in competition. In many cases the ancillary activities were profitable, and a decline in morale had properly to be faced if they were sold, leaving a rump of declining, or less profitable, activity. Furthermore if the penalty for profitability was to be returned to the private sector, then an incentive to improve management and profitability had been removed. Similarly many of the ancillaries were in newly developing industries, with good prospects of fast growth, whereas their parent company was often in a declining industry with little or no growth potential. If the objective was to increase competition, this was not guaranteed. If the objective was efficiency, this too was elusive. 'Hiving-off' as initially promulgated can therefore be said to have had a doctrinaire basis in a desire to reduce the state's role. That the Government quickly recognised its impracticality can be seen from the rapid retreat from the policy. Little reference was made to it after the middle of 1971.

A second part of the Government's policy towards the nationalised industries was to introduce a 'BP solution'. This was to bring equity capital into them, in order to instil the best qualities of management practice, and to force the public corporations to go to the stock market for additional finance, in other words to be subject to the same restraints as a private firm. The advantage over 'hiving-off' would be that the size of the corporations would be retained allowing economies of scale and the benefits of continuity. This effectively was the solution proposed for most of BSC, and in the Iron and Steel Bill of December 1971 provision was made for private shareholding in some specified areas. Far from being a major determinant of the future of steel, however, it was introduced as one small element in a complex situation. The other major industry in which this solution was learned to have been mooted was in gas, presumably as a direct result of pressures from private capital, since the discovery of North Sea Gas and the monopoly in distribution had made the Gas Board much more attractive. Yet the Conservative Government, in the Gas Bill of January 1972, retained the *status quo*, and disappointed private industry, despite its commitments to reducing the role of the state. The shareholding solution, like 'hiving-off', seemed by late 1972 to have substantially faded as an instrument of Government policy.

Even had all the ancillary activities of the nationalised industries been shed, and those which could attract private capital actually done so, there would nevertheless have remained a very large nationalised sector. For this the Government's objective, consistent with its 'disengagement' philosophy, was to improve efficiency and the quality of management. To this end 'accountable management units' were established, for example in the AEA. The Fuel Division and the Small Isotope Laboratory were formed into separate companies, totally owned by AEA, but the possibility of future sale is there to be seen. Similar companies were established in the chemicals and constructional engineering divisions of BSC. Management independence for sectors of the industries was, in the light of Fulton, as much a Labour as a Conservative policy. Under the new Conservative Government the process was hastened and the aim appeared to have changed: the possibility of 'privatisation' always appeared on the horizon. Similarly with the new British Airways Board, a new umbrella Board was established, exercising strategic control over both BOAC and BEA. The aim was to make the airline more independent of Whitehall by having the Board act as a buffer between airline management and civil servants. It has been argued that in this context the government is chasing a chimera:[30] there has never been anything but tenuous control over nationalised industries by ministers.

However much the Conservative Government tried to alter the structure, management or market of the nationalised industries, they could never really be comfortable with this sort of compromise. The Government were trying to minimise the scope of the nationalised industries, yet they were forced to use them as part of their broader macro-economic policies, and this led to increasing intervention in their affairs. A typical example occurred in March 1971 when the Steel Board announced price increases of 14 per cent, the Government reacted by halving the increases. Subsequently all the nationalised industry chiefs were called on to limit price rises to 5 per cent in pursuit of the CBI price restraint policy. Here, government control of the commercial freedom of the nationalised sector was unequivocally demonstrated. From 1961 governments have nominally expected nationalised industries to behave in a commercial way, to borrow at current rates of interest, and make a return on capital equal to the private sector. Yet here the government interfered with the market mechanism by reducing price increases. Concern for price inflation over-rode the determination to make the nationalised corporation self-sufficient. The dilemma was an old one and repeated itself through many of the nationalised industries during 1970-72. One commentator wrote:

> There has never been a government as determined to regard the nationalised industries as the 'commanding heights of the economy' as the Heath Government has been – the present government . . . is using nationalised industries' pricing policies as a major instrument of national economic policy to moderate inflation.[31]

The dilemma of pricing can be matched by the dilemma of social costs: purely economic costing must be balanced, so it is generally said, by social costing, as in the carrying of essential services like gas and electricity to isolated rural areas. It has been said of the 1964-70 Labour Government, even though it was approaching this in the opposite direction:

> The practical problems of making the public sector efficient undermined many of its preconceptions about the importance of 'ownership' as such.[32]

The 1970 Conservative Government was deeply concerned with ownership. It opposed the nationalised industries more or less on principle, preferring that any activity be performed in the private sector. Moreover shortly after winning the 1970 election the Party's attitude to the industries seemed to have hardened. Hiving-off and shareholding assumed a much greater importance for a shorter time than had been anticipated. The halting and partial reversal of the policy from mid-1971 shows up in greater contrast because of this. Of the three parts of the policy – hiving-off, shareholding, and management efficiency – marginal changes were effected in the first two. It was marginal in the sense of affecting small proportions of the total capital in the nationalised sector, and marginal also in the extent to which schemes were implemented. The third component was tackled with every sign of determination through internal reviews. Actual day-to-day control may have been in the hands of the managers, but overall policy-making had never been closer to the Government. Nicholas Ridley, the Under-Secretary of State at the DTI, has described "how 'monitoring' of the nationalised industries has virtually reduced the Chairman and Boards of these concerns to front men for Whitehall." He particularly mentions the case of the 'Steering Group' established late in 1970 to moniter BSC investment.

> All it succeeded in doing was to infuriate the Board of BSC and delay decision-taking for at least one and a half years. One result is our chronic shortage of steel capacity and another the relative inefficiency of the plants we have.[33]

Thus the aims of 'less government' and 'more efficient government' were not found compatible. Indeed they were contradictory because, while 'less government' implied leaving the nationalised corporations to run themselves, promoting the aim of greater efficiency led ministers to interfere extensively with their management. In the last resort the aim of efficiency overcame the political attachment to 'disengagement.'

In all its policies towards the public sector, therefore, it can be said that the Government experienced reverses and discovered, sometimes painfully, that the commercial and political realities were often such as to defeat even the most determined attempt to implement the political component of 'disengagement'. The role of the state was not reduced.

CHAPTER 13 'DISENGAGEMENT' AND THE PRIVATE SECTOR

It was at the Conservative Party Conference in Blackpool in October 1970 that Mr. John Davies, then Secretary of State for Trade and Industry, gave the first major indication of what the Government industrial policy changes were to mean in practice. He spoke of applying much greater stringency than had the Labour Government, before granting state support: he would not "bolster up or bail out companies where I can see no end to the process of propping them up".[1] But he, too, excluded certain industries; aircraft production, and to a lesser extent, shipbuilding, though a warning note on these was sounded for the first time. The Minister believed that they needed "a supporting hand" but he would not be commited to "an open-ended liability". This approach subsequently became known as the 'lame ducks' policy.

The changes in industrial policy introduced by the new Government were outlined in the preceding chapter. They impinged directly on many small and medium-sized firms. The health of such firms naturally depends also, often crucially, on the general economic climate, and therefore on the health of the giant concerns, for whom many of the smaller firms manufacture components, provide tools, and sub-contract for services. The ramifications of even the potential collapse of one giant firm are correspondingly enormous. In the wake of the collapse of Rolls and UCS there followed a catalogue of redundancies, debts, empty order books, short-time and great uncertainty. Despite the intended boost for private industry in the cutting of Corporation Tax and repeated in the Government's attempts to encourage investment, the basic uncertainty reflected by such collapses as those of Rolls Royce and UCS in large measure overwhelmed the encouragement. The new Government's attitude had been much tougher than industry had expected, and industry in general did not react favourably. Economic indicators did not in the event really begin to recover until after drastic revision of the Government's industrial policies and the announcement of the 1972 Industry Bill. The cases of Rolls Royce, Upper Clyde Shipbuilders (UCS) and Harland and Wolff can be said to have acted as catalysts in altering the Government's attitude. In addition these case studies raise important issues that are discussed in the following chapters. One minister at the time later acknowledged that the UCS case in particular "killed" the 'lame ducks' policy.[2]

Rolls Royce

When on 4 February 1971 the Government announced the appointment of a Receiver, and an intention to nationalise 90 per cent of all the Rolls Royce (R-R) Divisions, it was the RB211 contract which was blamed for "the most spectacular crash in living memory"[3] The contract had been signed with Lockheed (United States) in March 1968. For Rolls this had been the culmination of a long and expensive sales campaign, which had begun in September 1966 and cost over £400,000. Rolls had regarded the contract as vital if it was to have a future in the manufacture of the larger aero-engines.[4] The airbus was believed to be the aircraft of the future, and forms of it were being developed both in Europe, with twin engines, and in America, with three. Rolls had not yet become involved with either market, and had therefore to aim at an international contract. Rolls won the RB211 contract against the competition of two rival engines by paring down its price to £350,000 per engine, and by its advanced technical design.[5] This design consequently included many developments still unproved, and although some provision was made in the contract price for the unknown amount of research and development involved, there was no accurate way of costing this.

The value of the RB211 contract was put at £98 million initially, but with additional aeroplanes beyond the first batch, and taking into account spares, it was expected that this figure might rise to £350 million. Launching costs were estimated in 1968 at £65 million and under the launching aid scheme of the Ministry of Technology, the Minister agreed when the contract was signed, to provide 70 per cent (£47 million) of these costs. It seems clear that the Ministry of Technology was at the least very helpful in the securing of the contract. There is certainly no doubt that Rolls wanted the contract very badly, and little doubt either that the company knew it was taking a risk, though in the words of Sir Denning Pearson, at that time Chairman:

> When we signed the contract and got our board's final approval to the contract we were entirely confident that we had a good contract, that we had the capacity to carry it out, that it would be profitable, and, in particular, that we had recourse to adequate financial resources to meet our maximum cash requirements.[6]

Lockheed must presumably have thought that Rolls had the capability to carry out the contract, though the American company's judgement may well have been affected by the fact that they knew the backing Rolls Royce was getting from the British Government. But there was some ambiguity in the position of the British Government:

> I think that Rolls Royce were, rightly or wrongly, convinced they had got enormous resources behind them when they did start because they thought the Government was fully

committed to being a participant in the project.[7]
It may be noted here that one of the major lessons to be learnt from the Rolls Royce crisis is the difficulty, and the necessity, of defining both how far a private company is responsible for its decisions when large sums of government money are involved, and how far the government has a responsibility to discover, and to make public, the various problems as they arise.

In retrospect it is possible to see that two related problems had emerged even at this stage. The contract between the Government and the company limited the Government's share of the costs to a maximum sum. This meant that any overrun was the company's responsibility. Sir David Huddie later admitted this was at the root of the problem.[8] One commentator subsequently wrote: "It was the terms of the contract with the Government, not the deal with Lockheed that finally broke the company."[9] Yet the Government had concentrated on negotiating the contract, and not on examining the strengths and weaknesses of the firm, and its ability to see the project through. It has been suggested that the vital lesson of the RB211 affair is the need for Government to inform itself thoroughly about the contracting firm before agreeing to give launching aid."[10]

The first unequivocal indication that R-R was in difficulties came in October 1969 when MinTech asked the IRC to look into the Company's affairs. The IRC nevertheless offered a loan of £10 million with a promise of a further £10 million so long as its conditions were fulfilled.[11] The management changes included placing Mr. Ian Morrow an accountant, and respected 'company doctor', and Dr. Beeching, on the Board, and Mr. Morrow was to complete a report on the company's financial position before the further sum was released. The DTI inspectors subsequently put a lot of the blame on poor internal financial control.[12] In due course Mr. Morrow found that a serious cash flow shortage would be inevitable by 1973. For this he blamed inadequate procedures, though he also felt in this regard that the situation was much the same as in many other companies he had served.[13] The December 1969 balance sheet actually showed a profit of £2½ million, but bank overdrafts of £37 million from R-R's two bankers, Lloyds and the Midland, acceptance credits of £17 millions (loans from merchant banks) and debts of £62 million, owed to over one hundred companies, together comprised a very pessimistic underlying picture. Before Mr. Morrow could make a final report, another critical cash shortage overtook the company, and in November 1970 it turned again to the Government for aid. Projected launching costs of the RB211 had by now risen from the original £65 million to £135 million. Although a much less sympathetic hearing for R-R might have been anticipated from the changed

Government, a further £42 million aid was in fact offered, to make the launching aid up to the original level of 70 per cent. This replaced the IRC's second £10 million loan which was never paid. Since the Corporation had been excluded from the project, Cooper Brothers were now introduced to investigate.

However the Secretary of State was anxious to distinguish the case of Rolls from the Government's industrial policy in general:

> We have made clear that we dissociate ourselves and wish to disengage from an excessive degree of intervention in private industry. Equally, we wish to bring about a reduction in public expenditure . . . There is no doubt that the aircraft industry presents important problems which are different from those of any other industry. I have never made a secret of that . . . To try and pretend that Rolls Royce is just like any other company is laughable to the point of the ridiculous.[14]

Mr. Davies thus argued that the Government's policy in the case of Rolls was consistent with its overall industrial policy. *The Times* and *Financial Times* agreed that the Rolls case was unique, and that at this stage it did not mean the 'disengagement' policy had been abandoned.[15]

The new financial assistance again had certain conditions attached to it, including the appointment of Lord Cole, formerly of Unilever, as Chairman of the Board. The aid was also again dependent on a satisfactory accountant's report, re-examination of the contracts, and limitation for a period of any distribution of the Rolls' share capital. All sales of the RB211 were to bear a levy to be paid to the Ministry of Aviation Supply. But those conditions were to be overtaken by events and this particular sum of £42 million was not in fact paid.[16] To further ameliorate Rolls' cash shortage, the Government also persuaded the City to provide further finance. It was announced that the City would make available £18 million but this proved to be somewhat misleading, in that the sum was made up of £8 million from the Bank of England, and £5 million each from the Company's existing bankers, Lloyds and the Midland. To compensate for the additional £5 million loans, the agreement was that similar amounts would be withdrawn from R-R's day-to-day overdraft facilities with their bankers. Perhaps this was what finally brought the company to collapse. R-R had arrangements with both banks for overdrafts on current account of up to £25 million each and although the additional £5 million loans announced in November 1970 were not paid over, in mid-January it seems that both banks reduced their overdraft facilities to R-R by the agreed £5 million. This interpretation, however, can only be conjectured.[17] Ian Morrow, on the other hand, has argued that there was no immediate cash shortage in the autumn of 1970.[18] It appears that it was on 22 January 1971 that Lord Cole visited the Ministry of Aviation Supply and agreed that R-R would not continue trading. The Cabinet, after numerous preliminary meetings, finally decided at a three-hour meeting on 3 February 1971 to nationalise most of Rolls' assets. By then, launching costs for the RB211 had risen to £170 million.

In deciding to nationalise R-R, what were the main considerations which must have weighed with the Governmnet? The Chancellor argued that:

> This Government are responsible to the taxpayer and we are not prepared to provide the massive sums required to keep the company as such in business, with or without the RB211; nor were we prepared . . . to acquire the shares of the company because this would have involved assuming in full the company's huge liabilities, again at the expense of the taxpayer.[19]

The Government were also unwilling to accept any risk to Rolls not least because of its size and economic significance. With a work-force of over 80,000, Rolls was the fourteenth largest employer in the country. To have allowed the Company to go into liquidation would have meant widespread and massive unemployment. Some 80 per cent of R-R turnover came from its aero-engine divisions and many of these divisions were in areas already sensitive to unemployment, or with few alternative job opportunities, such as Central Scotland and Barnoldswick, in the North East Lancashire Intermediate Area. Another important consideration was the extent of the defence and international commitments of Rolls. In addition to the RB211 contract, other divisions of R-R were responsible among other things for the Olympus engine for the Anglo-French Concorde, the Adour engine for Anglo-French Jaguar, the RB199 for the Anglo-West German-Italian multi-role-combat aircraft, the M45 for the West German 614 air liner, and the VTOL engine for the Harrier jump-jet. The defence capability of the UK and of very many foreign air forces depended in part at least on R-R. The need to maintain Britain's own defence capability, and the political desirability of fulfilling obligations to foreign air forces, would probably by themselves have dictated that R-R should be kept in being. Furthermore, in addition to its own six operating divisions, five in aero-engines, R-R owned the Bristol Aeroplane Company, Bristol Aircraft Holdings, Bristol Siddeley engines, H.J. Mullin and Park Ward. The company also held a 20 per cent holding in BAC, and Bristol Aeroplane had a 15¼ per cent holding in Short Bros. and Harland of Belfast. There were thus the very best economic, political and social reasons for not letting R-R go into real liquidation.

On the other hand if the Government had not wanted the company to be wound up they still in principle had another alternative to nationalisation, namely to continue funding R-R as a private company.

The Government, however, rejected this alternative because the technical problems with the RB211 engine meant that there would inevitably be a delay in delivery of the engine to Lockheed, and the original contract had severe penalty clauses for default. At the time of nationalisation it was thought in fact that the engine would be between six and twelve months late, and the damages even for a six-month delay were of the order of £50 million.[20] But by setting up Rolls Royce (1971) Ltd., all existing contracts were voided, and an opportunity was opened up to renegotiate that for the RB211. The Government appear to have concluded that there was no time to renegotiate the contract.[21] An approach to Lockheed the day before the Receiver was put in led nowhere. If the contract could not be renegotiated then it stood, and ministers were anxious about the position of the company and the Government under Section 332 of the Companies Act, which deals with trading while knowingly in deficit:

> Section 332 absolutely penalises this responsibility. Whereas a public company is a limited liability company, under Section 332 the directors are personally and generally responsible to the limit of whatever resources they have, and can be at risk on a criminal charge . . . The Government would have been at risk under Section 332 to the extent that they would have become liable for the whole of the liabilities of Rolls Royce . . . This was the advice we had.[22]

Could the immediate paradox of a government following a policy of 'disengagement' while simultaneously nationalising one of the country's largest industrial concerns be reconciled? In one obvious way the Government's action over R-R was entirely contrary to policy and some concluded that "certainly no Government in Britain today will any longer be able to pursue a policy of industrial disengagement." On this view, the Government's decision represents "the triumph of pragmatism over ideology". The affair could thus be seen as having initiated the Government into a new maturity:

> the industrial realities today have made the party political debate about state ownership redundant. The issues are so great and have such repercussions that a pragmatic approach is the only one. Governments must protect national interests – among them a defence capability, the industrial lifelines which generate modern technology, and the future base of advanced industry. It is as futile for Conservatives to insist on non-intervention as for Labour to hark back to Clause 4. Both must operate a mixed economy efficiently.[23]

The Cabinet's initial decision had been to stop funding the RB211, thereby accepting a default on the contract, while salvaging the rest of

R-R. Negotiations with Lockheed to find a more acceptable basis for the RB211 were formally initiated only after the collapse. The ramifications of the original decision, on R-R itself, on its sub-contractors, and on Lockheed had by then begun fully to emerge and the Government responded by continuing the RB211 contract despite the problems resulting from the original decision.

The Government appointed a Committee to investigate the situation. On 11 February 1971 Sir William Cook, ex-Chief Scientific Adviser to the Ministry of Defence, Sir St. John Elstub, a director of ICI, and Professor Douglas Holder of Oxford University were asked to advise on the prospects for the RB211. The Government were sufficiently impressed with their report that two of the three were asked to serve on the new R-R (1971) Ltd. Board, and to go to Washington to help conduct the negotiations with Lockheed. The succession of internal reviews from the IRC onwards suggests that Whitehall lacked the resources to carry out meaningful follow-up checks to ensure that the Rolls management were in control, and that the project was proceeding broadly as intended.

The Receiver was instructed to nationalise about 90 per cent of Rolls' assets, and to sell off the car and oil divisions. A manpower reduction plan had been introduced in January 1970, in consultation with the unions, and this had resulted within the first year in a cutback of 5,000 workers. On 8 March 1971 the Receiver announced a further 4,300 redundancies, 2,900 among white-collar workers. This represented a further 5 per cent cutback, not connected with the RB211. Had the RB211 been abandoned, and there was a real possibility of this at the time, a further 12,000–18,000 jobs would have been lost. One immediate consequence of the nationalisation, therefore, was a great uncertainty about future work and in a time of rising unemployment, this added further instability to the situation. With the Government still undecided whether or not to continue the RB211 programme the full complexities proceeded to reveal themselves. The danger of losing skilled workers, a more serious risk in the case of R-R than in that of UCS, was equalled only by the difficulties involved in getting suppliers to continue sending materials. The reluctance of sub-contractors to continue sending vital parts was also understandable. Only later did the Receiver persuade the Government to pay enough for the Company to enable the creditors to be covered in full, or to be promised such payment. At the outset the problem was that unless parts and supplies continued to be delivered to R-R the capacity to build the engine would inevitably be steadily eroded, skilled workers leaving for more secure jobs.

In addition Lockheed, too, was put at risk. To Lockheed, the Tri-star L10-11 for which the RB211 was intended, was as vital as the

RB211 was to R-R. In the sixties, Lockheed had come to rely exclusively on contracts for defence aircraft, but this had led them close to financial ruin, and it was in this context that they had determined to re-enter the civil aircraft field. They had in fact been involved in four contractual disputes with the Pentagon, and their losses of $480 million had been met by a settlement of only $290 leaving them in a dangerous financial state. Lockheed's downfall had been the 'fixed-price', hard-fought contract, a contract of the same kind that the company themselves had forced on R-R. Despite the antipathy in the US to government intervention, the American Government agreed in effect to bail Lockheed out, and by one vote on 2 August 1971, the Senate approved this, making $250 million in aid available to Lockheed. As Mr. David Packard US Deputy Secretary of Defence put it:

> It was necessary to determine whether bankruptcy or corporate reorganisation under the Bankruptcy Act was, or was not, in the interest of national defence. We found that the Company's operations were so entwined with many other companies that also contribute to our national defence effort that it was necessary to consider the chain reaction upon other companies as well.[24]

The parallel between R-R and the UK Government and Lockheed and the US Government could hardly have been more exact. Orders for the Tri-star had not reached the break-even point. For Lockheed to survive the L10-11 had to succeed and this meant that the RB211 had to be completed. Mr. Daniel Haughton, Lockheed's Chairman, did refer to the possibility of using alternative engines, and approaches were apparently made to both Pratt & Whitney and General Electric. But Mr. Haughton's optimism on this point was almost certainly more a manoeuvre in the negotiations than anything else because the costs of redesigning and rebuilding the L10-11 to accommodate either of the alternative engines made the proposal unrealistic. In any case neither of the aero-engine firms had much spare capacity in the short term. Lockheed had therefore virtually no alternative but to renegotiate the RB211 contract, under pressure naturally from its scheduled customers, always hoping to keep the price increases and the delay to a minimum. The contract was eventually renegotiated, adding $548,776 to the cost of each aeroplane.[25]

Negotiations between R-R and the British Government resulted in the Receiver's having £30 million between February and August 1971, to continue work on the RB211. On the formation of R-R (1971) Ltd. another £130 million was put into its development. Estimated costs for the engine continued to rise reaching £190–195 million by January 1972, excluding the sums expended before nationalisation.[26] Formal transfer of R-R assets to R-R (1971) Ltd. took place on 17 February 1972, but negotiations between the Company and the Government about the purchase price of assets having broken down, an independent assessor was called in on 6 April 1972. On the 17 April, Mr. Heseltine, the New Minister for Aerospace, announced that the Government had paid £1 for the RB211 engine.

To the extent that the Tri-Star, with its RB211 engines, is now flying,[27] commercially the salvage of R-R can already be considered a success, but the whole episode was a deeply disturbing one. The Government was undoubtedly faced in early 1971 with a number of uncongenial options and in response made what seemed a most remarkable decision, to nationalise. It has been suggested that the Government did this to gain effective control of the way public funds were being spent, but Mr. Ian Morrow and Lord Beeching were put on to the R-R Board by the IRC, and Lord Cole was made Chairman as part of the agreement with the Government when the £42 million was promised in November 1970. The one clear-cut consequence of nationalisation which could be construed as an advantage to the Government was that Lockheed both lost the compensation due to them and was forced to renegotiate in a situation so extreme that failure to agree would have almost automatically ensured that company's own demise. On the other hand, experience has shown that the act of nationalisation has solved nothing by itself. The major problem of monitoring the use of state funds has been as real a problem after nationalisation as it was before.[28]

Upper Clyde Shipbuilders

UCS was formed in February 1968 by the amalgamation of five Upper Clyde shipyards, in accordance with the criteria laid down in the Geddes Report,[29] and as a result of an SIB working party report. It certainly seems that some, if not all, of the companies were financially very unsound when they formed UCS.[30] UCS was initiated with a burden of debt, every one of the consituent companies having a deficiency of net current assets as at August 1967.[31] Contracts had been undertaken as was usual in the industry, on a fixed-price basis, and inflation in both materials and wages had meant that they would all be completed at a loss. A sizeable loss-making order book would consequently have to be worked through before any new orders, on a profitable basis, could be undertaken. Mr. Hepper, the new Chairman of UCS, who had been invited to take on the job after completing the SIB working party Report, of which he had also been Chairman has since said that he made it quite plain:

. . . to the Government and the SIB at the time that in my view, the

> formation of the Upper Clyde Group could not possibly be considered as a financial venture . . . The question you have to ask is whether . . . you want to have a shipbuilding industry on the Upper Clyde or do you not? If you do, they you have to go through at least four or possibly five traumatic years to make all the changes that are necessary.[32]

There were many other problems to be solved, in addition to those deriving from the order book: the SIB saw the need to rationalise berths; to reduce the labour force; to improve management; and to improve financial and accounting procedures. These tasks were put in hand. Within a year of UCS's inception, the original twenty-one berths, making everything from the QE2 to oil rigs, had been reduced to ten, and the labour force, with the co-operation of the Unions, was reduced by 2,500 to 8,500, saving about £5 million per annum on wages.[33]

Initially the Government paid £3½ million for a 48.4 per cent equity holding and promised £2 million for modernisation. In March 1969 a further £3 million was provided for working capital, but in May 1969 UCS again approached the SIB for further grants and loans. This time £5 million was provided, conditional on certain changes in senior management and on the Board.[34] As a result, Mr. Kenneth Douglas, Managing Director of Austin and Pickersgill on the Tyne, where he had effected rationalisations which had changed a loss to a profit-making situation, was brought in to UCS in the same capacity. However, late in 1969 yet another approach was made to the SIB. After consideration the SIB refused any further sums, and the request was then passed to the Ministry of Technology. Mr. Wedgwood Benn finally made a direct loan of £7 million in February 1970. In return he insisted on monthly management accounts, weekly production statistics, and periodically, on a cash flow forecast, profit-projection and production bar charts.[35] So by the time that the Conservative Government came to power UCS had received some £20 million in loans and grants. Much of this had been passed to previous shareholders to buy equity capital, and what remained had largely been used as working capital. The amount of actual modernisation and investment in equipping the yards had been abysmally small. In the meantime, MinTech and then the DTI did not get very deeply involved with the monitoring processes.[36]

There was also still a considerable way to go before profitability could be expected. The last of the old orders was scheduled for launching in January 1971, and it was hoped that the £90 million worth of orders negotiated subsequently would show profits in 1972. Unfortunately the 34 new orders had also been accepted at fixed prices because this was standard practice, and it was exceedingly difficult for one company to break the prevailing pattern. There was one improvement in that the new ships were largely of two classes: twenty-one bulk carriers, and nine Clyde-series, a yard-designed, off-the-peg cargo vessel. Nevertheless, future benefits did not improve the chronic liquidity problem, and in late 1970 the Company again approached DTI, to inform them of their financial difficulties.[37] Further aid was granted on 11 February 1971.[38] The chronological proximity of this crisis to the Rolls Royce crash, and the fact that UCS was rescued yet again may not be coincidental. Apparently in November 1970 DTI had refused to guarantee further credits to shipowners, thus cutting off much of UCS's income.[39] One of the principal determinants of the continued existence of UCS in February 1971 was the restoration of these credits, and this crucial factor lay wholly within the power of DTI. In addition one of the component companies of UCS, Yarrow Shipbuilders, was allowed to leave the Group, and return to its former owners, Yarrow Shipbuilders and Engineers, who were primarily concerned with defence contracts.[40] On 11 February Mr. Davies announced that a grant of £4 million over three years would go to Yarrow to enable them to undertake defence contracts, but no further capital was forthcoming for the main body of UCS. In fact, on 8 March 1971 Mr. Davies indicated that he had no intention of advancing further sums to UCS. Indeed, in the *Guardian's* view:

> The shipbuilding industry is the original 'lame duck'. When Mr. John Davies, Minister for Trade and Indsutry first used the phrase to attack his predecessor's policy, he was undoubtedly thinking of companies like Upper Clyde Shipbuilders and Cammell Laird which together have absorbed nearly £30 million of public funds.[41]

To try to ease the financial problems the Board of UCS had turned unsuccessfully to the shipowners in an effort to renegotiate the prices of the ships still to be built.

The Company had, at the insistence of the Government Director, Mr. MacKenzie, called for a financial statement on 7 May. This was produced on 7 June and showed that the Company was then, and had been for some time, trading in deficit. This situation was made known to the Government, and also UCS's feeling that additional working capital of £5-6 million would see them over the difficulty.[42] The Cabinet rejected the plea. UCS asked for a Liquidator to be put in and the Government then announced that the Company would be 'reconstructed' after its bankruptcy. Mr. Davies told the Commons that Mr. Hepper had seen him on 9 June to inform him that the Company could no longer pay its wages bill, and would be in deficit to the extent of £4-5 million by the end of August. The Government had therefore guaranteed the payment of one week's wages to enable further discussion to take place, but it had not been possible to reach any further agreement. A provisional liquidator had then been appointed and Mr. Davies also set up a three-man Committee to investigate the situation as he had in the case of Rolls. These three, Mr. Alexander MacDonald, Chairman of Distillers, Sir Alexander Glen, Chairman of H. Clarkson, Shipbrokers, and David MacDonald of Hill, Samuel, merchant bankers, were later joined by Lord Robens.[43] The liquidators' estimate of liabilities was £32.2 million and approximately £500,000 per week was needed to keep work in progress, Mr. Davies and the liquidator having decided that the yards would be kept in existence for at least seven weeks. The liquidator met considerable difficulties in trying to ensure the continued delivery of supplies. Approximately a thousand creditors of the previous Company were reluctant to incur further debt, and the liquidators found that only by paying in advance could some supplies be obtained. An initial £4 million was made available by the Government and work proceeded.

The Government's original apparent intention to close UCS, and put it into liquidation, before selling off those sections attractive to private firms, was said to be closely in accord with the so-called Ridley Report, which the *Guardian* reported in its issue of 15 June 1971 had been drawn up by Mr. Nicholas Ridley, Under Secretary of State at the DTI, while in Opposition.[44] The Report of the four-man committee on the other hand issued on 29 July 1971 recommended that while two of the four yards should be closed, (Clydebank and Scotstoun), the other two yards should be retained and modernised.[45] These were Fairfields, where so much finance and effort had already been expended on modernisation and improving industrial relations, and Linthouse, the steel fabrication yard. This report, whose proposals were estimated to cost £10 million, was initially accepted by Government though strongly criticised by the management and shop stewards of UCS, and by the Opposition. The shop stewards' unique response to the threat of 400 immediate redundancies, and ultimately a workforce of only 2,500 instead of 8,500, was a work-in at all the former UCS yards, but especially at Clydebank which was only finally terminated after fourteen months when the retention of all four yards was assured. During this time, the leading shop stewards Mr. James Reid and Mr. James Airlie, maintained a continuous attack; Mr Dan McGarvey Chairman of the Shipbuilding section of the Confederation of Shipbuilding and Engineering Unions (CSEU), actively sought for an alternative solution acceptable to both sides; the Scottish TUC set up its own Committee of Enquiry as a symbol of dissatisfaction with the Robens Report, and leading members of the UCS management appeared before it and openly criticised the Government.[46]

Some attempt was made at this time to find an alternative buyer for the yards. Mr. Archibald Kelly, a Scottish businessman and owner of the Liffey Dockyards in Dublin had meetings with Mr. Nicholas Ridley, but by the end of September 1971 he had dropped his offer for Clydebank.[47] DTI proceeded with their plan based on the Robens Report for the re-construction of UCS into Govan Shipbuilders by appointing three of the leading management team: Mr. Hugh Stenhouse, Chairman; Mr. Archibald Gilchrist, Managing Director; and Mr. Kenneth Douglas, Deputy Chairman. Mr. Stenhouse, Treasurer of the Scottish Conservative Party, in the short time before his tragic death in a car accident, worked very hard on Govan's behalf. He overcame the deep initial distrust of the shop stewards, and indeed, gained their co-operation. Mr. Davies also pledged at this time that he would give guarantees to shipowners to enable the outstanding contracts placed with UCS to be completed. On 27 October 1971 Irish Shipping accepted for its four ships the new terms offered by the Government. Early in November the CSEU took the unprecedented step of guaranteeing to the owners that these four ships would be delivered on time.

The Belgium-based Breaksea Tankships of Houston, Texas announced they were interested in the Clydebank Yard. When the negotiations with the DTI began to seem sluggish, Mr. Jack Service, the Secretary of the CSEU made a direct approach to Mr. K.G. Arkwright of Breaksea Tankships, and early in 1972 he and Mr. Dan McGarvey went to Texas in person. While there they also made contact with the Marathon Manufacturing Company who expressed an interest in making oil rigs at Clydebank, and when Breaksea Tankships more or less dropped out of the negotiations, Marathon took its place. Mr. Wayne Harbin of Marathon visited DTI and Clydebank on successive days in late January 1972, and in February the Government agreed to meet all of Marathon's requests for finance through the Local Employment Act Finance Advisory Committee (LEAFAC). Lord Strathalmond, who had been appointed as Chairman of Govan to replace Mr. Stenhouse, met with the shop stewards and Union officials, now satisfied that all four yards would be retained, and also on 16 February 1972 with his new Board.

The feasibility study which Mr. Davies had agreed to initiate at Mr. Stenhouse's instigation had been undertaken by Hill Samuel, Merchant Bankers, and was in his hands by mid-February 1972.[48] An announcement was made in the House of Commons on 28 February 1972, that £35 million was to be injected into Govan Shipbuilders, and it was also stated that the firm would include the old Scotstoun yard. Of the £35 million £17 million was assigned for losses on existing orders, and £18 million for reconstruction. Mr. Harbin of Marathon made an overall agreement with the UCS liquidator to buy Clydebank which was finalised on 28 April 1972. The sum was not disclosed, but Mr. Harbin had made known that in view of the Govan settlement, he felt that on a *pro rata* basis he was entitled to approximately £12 million in aid at Clydebank, and he formally asked for aid through LEAFAC on 20 March 1972. In the budget statement at the end of that month, the Government announced that £50 million in 'tapering grants' would be available to the shipbuilding industry over two years under the Industry Act. In June Booz-Allen and Hamilton were appointed to carry out the study of the shipbuilding industry's long-term prospects that had been announced in April. The Government having made another £1 million available to the liquidator in April and a further £300 000 in June, Govan became operational on 1 July 1972. Mr. Davies, in a written reply, now promised support for 'five years or until the Company was on its feet – whichever was less', and an interim injection of working capital was made to enable the new Company to obtain supplies for new ships expected to be ordered, but no specific sum was mentioned.

Therefore, by mid-1972, all four of the original UCS yards had been saved, with 6,300 of the 8,400 jobs intact. With this eventual outcome was the whole bankruptcy/liquidation process really necessary? And is the new organisation likely to fare any better in the long term than did the old? It is worth noting in this context that the Annual Report of the SIB whose financial year had ended just ten weeks before UCS collapsed, gave no indication of any unsurmountable problems on the Clyde. It saw signs of improvement and like the management it too believed that the corner had been turned.[49] Nevertheless, it appears that the DTI recommendation to the Secretary of State for Trade and Industry was that UCS should not be allowed to continue trading; in this connection the following extract is perhaps enlightening:

> I think Sir Antony (Part) did say, among other things, that there was a certain change of emphasis as between the present Government and the previous Government as to disposition to make money available to the private sector. Of course, both the Department (DTI) and the Treasury equally take account of the general philosophy or doctrine of the Government of the day. It is part of our function to advise and to put positive propositions to the Government but it is also part of our job to take note of the Government's own general thinking.[50]

The original request by UCS in June 1971 for working capital was said to be £5 million or £6 million but the Government did not believe that this sum would make the company viable.[51] However, within the next year, the government gave £7,800,000 to the liquidator, announced £35 million in aid to Govan, and granted an undisclosed sum for Marathon, which may have amounted to £12 million or more. Financially, although one payment of £6 million might not have brought to an end UCS's demands on the government there must have been a real chance at the outset of keeping the final commitment considerably below the figures eventually reached. Furthermore, the reconstruction of the yards was also at great cost in other than purely monetary terms. When UCS was declared bankrupt and trading stopped, the debts were £32.2 million, owed to over one thousand firms. Many of these were small and medium-sized firms who could ill afford their losses. The multiplier effect on Scottish industry was inevitably considerable. In an area where one in ten adult males were already out of work the problem was a very serious one for the Government. Certainly, it appeared that the unemployment problem, coupled with the long, determined and vociferous opposition from the unions, was a principal determinant of the Government's *volte face* over UCS: Mr. Davies indeed later said as much.[52]

There also remains a question mark over the future of Govan. Included in the Hill Samual Report was a study by Maynards, specialists in shipyard management, which postulated a basic minimum of £20 million for reconstruction and modernisation: in the event Govan was given only £18 million. Mr Heath's justification of Govan –

> Now that we have good management, now that we have a proper scheme for modernisation, the prospect should at least be brighter provided, always provided, that unions as well as management learn from the past.[53]

– could find unhappy echoes in the setting up of Fairfields, and later in that of UCS itself. The Secretary of State told the House of Commons on 28 February 1972 that "in contrast with arrangements made by the previous Government, I will see that this vast investment of public money is properly monitored and accounted for."[54] Less than three weeks later he "was unable to give any details of how this would be done."[55] The UCS case, like the Rolls one, illustrates clearly the importance of monitoring the use of funds to detect when plans are beginning to go astray, so remedial action can be initiated before the situation gets out of control.

Harland and Wolff

In 1966 Harland and Wolff (H & W) were saved from liquidation by a loan of £3.5 million from the Northern Ireland Government. Subsequently the Company decided to concentrate production on giant tankers and large bulk carriers, and to this end decided to build a new dock. The SIB then made a further loan of £8 million for this purpose and some £16.5 million was spent not on paying off losses but on the new dock and its attendant steel plant. The large capital programme, plus a loss-making situation on current contracts similar to that already noted in relation to UCS, meant that the Company again faced bankruptcy in late 1970. They thereupon approached the Government for £8.5 million for the period to the end of 1973 and the SIB granted them £3.5 million on the understanding that the Government would provide the rest.[56]

Following the resignation of the Chairman of the Board in December 1970, the Government initially took control of the yard in line with the policy of 'disengagement' and invited applications for it. The successful tender in fact came from the existing owners who anticipated the need for a further £3 million of government aid. This proposal, retaining ownership of Northern Ireland's largest single employer in local hands, was strongly supported by the shipyard Unions. On 3 March 1971, the Government accepted the H & W offer, and on 6 July, Mr. Robin Baillie, Ulster's Minister of Commerce, announced to the N.I. House of Commons that the Government would buy at par four million £1 shares for a 47.6 per cent holding in the company. He also promised a further £2-3 million aid later in the year. That this help was not governed by straightforward commercial criteria is demonstrated by the fact that, at stock maket prices obtained on the day, the Government could have purchased all the equity for £1¼ million. Mr. Baillie emphasised that there was no question of any further aid being made available if the company got into still more difficulties and he added that it was the Government's intention at the approprate time to dispose of its shareholding.[57]

However, in May 1972, while £35 million was being made available to UCS and £3 million with promises of further sums to Cammell Laird, it was stated that the Government would make a substantial, though unspecified, contribution to H & W's £35 million modernisation programme. A separate amount, said to be £14 million, was promised at the same time to pay off losses on existing contracts. H & W's managing director said at the time that it was expected that the modernisation programme would generate 4,000 new jobs directly, and many more indirectly, and in the desperate unemployment situation of Northern Ireland, this must have weighed heavily with the Government.

By October 1971, the *Guardian* judged that the Northern Ireland Government had already turned the 'lame duck' policy smartly on its head,[58] and by May 1972 Peter Hill was concluding that:

> Although the Government justifies the lavish assistance to the Belfast Group in the context of the Prime Minister's promise to revive the flagging economy of the Province, it seems to underline still further the burying of the 'lame duck' philosophy in regard to shipbuilding.[59]

Unlike the R-R and UCS cases, the salvage operation took place before H & W was declared bankrupt, thus avoiding any massive disruption of confidence or major social upheaval.

* * * * * * *

An examination of the Government's attempts to cut back on the provision of assistance to private industry shows that, as with the case studies, it met with little overall success. That is not to say, however, that the policy had no impact during 1970 and 1971. The Government for example refrained from rejoining the European Airbus project.[60] In the summer of 1971 it refused to provide assistance to build a nuclear merchant vessel, and began to phase out its support for the British film industry.[61] It also refused to provide aid for the Herbert Ingersoll project, and in the Autumn of 1970 the DTI declined to support the Mersey Docks and Harbours Board (MDHB).[62] A year later it was left to the banks to pull Birmingham Small Arms (BSA) through a cash crisis.[63] Yet in March 1973 the Government provided £3,500,000 to MDHB, and £4,800,000 to BSA.[64] In the meantime a £50 million scheme to encourage mineral exploration in Britain had been announced. Although there were some cuts many of the advisory services of the type described in Chapter 2. continued to operate as before. The NC scheme run by the Royal Aircraft Establishment at Farnborough was stopped for example, but the Production Engineering Research Association, The Royal Radar Establishment, and the Engineering Industry Training Board continued to provide varying kinds of assistance to the machine tool industry. Other advisory services like the Computer Aided Design Centre based at Cambridge were actually expanded.[65] The retreat from 'disengagement' began in February 1971 with the crisis of UCS and Rolls. By the end of that year various pressures had led the Government to adjust its hard-line approach to the extent that work had begun on the Industry Bill that was to follow the budget in the Spring of 1972. The policy reversal is underlined by the public expenditure figures. In January 1971 the Conservatives planned to spend £820 million (at 1970 survey figures) on assistance to private industry during 1972-3. In 1972 this estimate was revised to £1,478 million (at 1972 survey figures), largely as a result of expenditure planned under the Industry Act.[66]

PART IV

CONCLUSIONS

CHAPTER 14 CHANGES IN INDUSTRY AND WHITEHALL

The Evolving Mixed Economy

During the period that has been discussed many alterations took place that collectively amounted to a qualitative change in the nature of the mixed economy in Britain, and to government's view as to the relative importance of the public and private sectors. The first major change has been the increasing attention paid to the private sector by government. It has been shown how it has been subjected to a variety of detailed controls and regulations over such matters as prices, wages, and competition. Governments have substantially altered the economic and legal framework in which firms operate, and the net effect seems to have been that a company's freedom of action was more tightly curtailed by 1974 as compared with the early 1960s. It has also been shown how advisory services were provided on an increasingly detailed scale. Successive governments have made public funds available in a widening variety of ways, including Pre-production Order Schemes, the use of public purchasing power to further restructuring in private industry, loans, grants, credits, the purchase of equity holdings[1], the supply of fuel at cheap rates, and R&D contracts, some of which have been handled jointly by the government institutions involved, like the AEA, and the firms concerned.

This variety, and the extent of the increasing attention paid by government to the private sector are both underlined by the public expenditure figures. It is impossible to tell precisely from the early public expenditure White Papers exactly how much was spent on trade, industry and employment in the private sector. However in 1963-4 it was estimated that less than £170 million would be spent (at 1963 survey prices)[2]. By 1964-5 less than £271 million was spent on private industry (at 1965 survey prices)[3]. In 1969-70 the Labour Government spent approximately £1,498 million (at 1974 survey prices).[4] In 1971-2 the figure dropped to £1,286 million (at 1974 survey prices).[5] However the Conservative administration spent about £1,482 million in 1972-3 (at 1974 survey prices). The increasing importance of public expenditure on private industry is underlined by the rise in expenditure on trade, industry and employment in the private sector as a percentage of total public expenditure: it increased from approximately 1.5 per cent in 1963-4 to 4.6 per cent in 1969-70, before falling back to about 3.8 per cent in 1973-4.[6]

The second important feature of the evolving mixed economy at this time was the limited nature of one particular change. There was little expansion of the nationalised industries into manufacturing industry. The main exceptions were BSC and Rolls Royce. Despite the limited de-nationalisation described in Chapter 12, the main attempted expansion came in the service sector and public utilities, where the National Bus Company and the National Freight Corporation[7] were established, and an attempt was made to nationalise the docks. What is important with regard to the nationalised industries is that successive governments refused to nationalise certain industries, which were facing a variety of problems, and which there was pressure to nationalise. The Labour Government of 1964-70 for example refused to nationalise telecommunications, Rootes, aerospace, process plant, and pharmaceuticals. For its part, the Heath administration refused to nationalise the shipbuilding industry. Successive governments were thus basing their industrial policies on working through the private sector rather than by extending nationalisation into manufacturing industry.

However, during the period that has been analysed, it became increasingly hard to define where the public sector stopped and the private sector began. Public sector purchasing was important in that strict design specifications affected industry supplying various parts of the public sector with such items as telecommunications equipment, power stations, computers, and defence equipment. There were also joint ventures between nationalised industries and private sector firms. The British Gas Corporation became involved with exploration for oil in the North Sea, and the National Bus Company were actively involved with BLMC's bus-building plant in Cumberland. Nationalised industries and private sector firms were also in direct competition with each other: the NCB was involved with manufacturing bricks, and British Caledonian was in direct competition with BOAC/BEA, as for example on the North Atlantic routes.

There were many other changes in the nature of the mixed economy in Britain in the 1960s and early 1970s. Amongst the most important was the impact on the structure of industry of merger activity, particularly in the late 1960s. The 100 largest manufacturing firms increased their share of Britain's net output from 38 per cent in 1963 to about 50 per cent by 1970. This compared with 15 per cent in 1909, and it has been estimated that if the same trends continue the 100 largest companies would account for about two-thirds of net output by 1980.[8] This concentration of power was significant in itself, but it was of even greater importance when it went hand in hand with the growing influence and independence of the multinational corporations. This subject arose at various points in the IRC case-study. The decision-making of such companies can be taken anywhere in the world, but it can profoundly affect an economy like Britain's. The growing importance of institutional shareholders has already been discussed towards the end of Chapter 8, and that subject will be returned to in the very last chapter.

Between the late 1950s and the election in February 1974, successive governments had a common approach to industrial policy in that their basic underlying attitudes were the same. They attempted to adapt capitalism to the context of the mixed economy through a system of what might be termed 'state-supported capitalism'. Although there were some exceptions, further nationalisation was for the most part rejected, and governments worked on the basis of competitive market forces, of the profit motive, and for the most part, of firms that obtained most if not all of their funds from internal or conventional market sources rather than from the government itself. Different governments took action designed to overrule or accelerate market forces in order to correct emerging imbalances.[9] In the case of the nationalised industries there were attempts to model them on the concept of private enterprise. Governments attempted for example to get them to adopt a more commercial approach as outlined in the 1961 and 1967 White Papers,[10] and there were spasmodic attempts to leave the management of their day-to-day affairs, as opposed to their strategic decisions, to the corporations themselves.

In a modern mixed economy all firms work in varying degrees in the context of some uncertainty. This arises from a variety of factors including for example government's success in handling macro-economic policies, the plans of business competitors, changing markets and technologies, and the availability of materials. In the 1960s and early 1970s *the increase in government measures and in the state's involvement with the affairs of industry has greatly complicated the climate of uncertainty in which industry operates,* because they have added to the number of unknown factors with which a firm has had to cope. The main element in this situation has been the way that different governments have changed their policies on such issues as controlling wages and dividends, the level and form of company taxation and investment incentives, all of which are vitally important to industry. An important part of this has been the way in which governments have revised the levels at which for example, Corporation Tax and investment grants have been set after they have been introduced whilst businessmen have tried to work out their corporate plans on the basis that these would not be altered. Chataway's constant assurances that the incentives offered by the 1972 Industry Act would be available until 1977 marked government recognition of the importance of stability for the business community.

The discriminatory approach to industrial policy during this period has introduced further uncertainties. The arbitrary way in which governments refer proposed mergers to the Monopolies Commission, take sides in contested takeover battles, and distribute selective financial assistance, are unsettling for industry. This is because government operates according to unknown or only vaguely defined criteria. In such circumstances it can be extremely difficult for the firm to predict how Whitehall will react. Some firms have been driven to call off their plans once Whitehall has intervened. Whessoe is an example of a firm that dropped a takeover bid (for Capper Neill) once it had been referred to the Monopolies Commission. Other firms have feared the unpredictable use that the state is liable to make of the influence gained within a firm in which it has an equity holding or to which it has lent money. The fact that there is delay while government considers a firm's application for financial assistance or an Industrial Development Certificate does not stop that delay being frustrating and introducing uncertainty into the situation. Those sectors like special steels that compete with a nationalised industry have known uncertainty in the shape of what they have seen as unfair price competition from that nationalised corporation.[11] Other sectors like heavy engineering and shipbuilding have experienced an erratic and unreliable supply record from the BSC, that, it has been argued, would have resulted in a private firm becoming bankrupt. Finally the expansion of industrial policy has led to several reorganisations of government departments and a proliferation of other agencies. One of the central recommendations of the Way Committee on machine tools was that the scattered parts of the government machinery dealing with the industry should be brought together to make it easier for the industry to communicate with government.[12]

Individual interventions may make sense by themselves, but collectively they create a new climate of uncertainty, adding to that in which industry already has to work. This has been an important side-effect of industrial policy as it has developed since the beginning of the 1960s. It has influenced, and at times embittered, the relationship between government and industry, as when the relationship between the Government and the CBI broke down in 1967.[13] It has also done much to undermine business confidence which is crucial to the sustained capital investment and industrial expansion which successive governments have aimed at.

Whitehall's Response

From the early 1960s onwards an increasing number of detailed, often interventionist policies began to be implemented. The response of successive governments to the growing complexities of running a mixed economy has been to alter the institutional framework and to introduce new methods. With regard to the former, the basic departmental framework has been constantly altered. Sometimes previously established departments like the Treasury and the Board of Trade have been adapted to new tasks, and sometimes new departments like the DEA or MinTech have been established. Yet no settled position has emerged as the functions have been repeatedly reallocated. The gradual expansion of MinTech into the mammoth DTI only led to its progressive unscrambling. Before the election in February 1974, the Conservatives established a Department of Energy, and after it, separate Departments of Trade, Industry, and Prices and Consumer Affairs were established.

An important and more consistent feature of administrative change in the economic and industrial field has been the steady growth of para-government organisations. Although some, like the NRDC and Monopolies Commission, had been established earlier, the 1960s and the early 1970s witnessed the creation of many new organisations. These were set up to cope with specific problems like wages and prices, or industrial efficiency, and were given varying degrees of independence from their sponsoring departments. Examples include the British Productivity Council, the Council of Industrial Design, the Commission on Industrial Relations, the English, Welsh, and Scottish Tourist Boards, the Pay Board, and the Price Commission. Distinctions need to be drawn between those like the Restrictive Trade Practices Court that regulate, those like the Economic Planning Councils and the EDCs that have advisory functions, those like the government research establishments and the NCC that offer advisory services, and those like the IRC, SIB, the Highlands and Islands Development Board, and the Northern Ireland Finance Corporation which have executive functions and their own financial resources.

The problems posed by the increasingly detailed nature of industrial policy have been one of the contributory factors to the way in which Whitehall has adopted new methods. There has been increasing emphasis on the formulation of objectives, reviews of how to carry them out, and the corresponding allocation of resources. The Public Expenditure Survey Committee was established to help allocate resources between departments. However the problem of examining what each department was proposing to do within the confines of its own boundaries remained.[14] The Programme Analysis Review system was introduced so that statements of objectives and priorities could be submitted for central consideration before the process of allocation of resources started. In the industrial context the development within MinTech of the Programmes Analysis Unit was later seen as significant by Wedgwood Benn after he had left office.[15] This is an important example of the way in which new methods were devised to cope with the emerging problems not just of resource allocation or project appraisal, but of monitoring.

The third basic change within Whitehall that has come largely because of the increasing complexity of industrial policy has been the attempt to bring into the decision-making process people with skills and experience that the general administrator of the 1950s had lacked. In the first place there have been changes within the Civil Service itself. The Centre for Administrative Studies was established in 1963 largely to provide crash courses in economics for the Administrative Class. There was some breaking down of the barriers between administrators and specialists. Within MinTech, for example, there was some success at getting administrators and scientists and engineers to work together in the same hierarchy and not side by side in different ones.[16] About a third of the Direct Entry Principals in 1961-6 had experience of private industry, and in 1968 a scheme for two-way exchange with industry and commerce was started.[17] There were nineteen economists in the Civil Service in 1963: this had risen to 106 in 1967 and to 196 by 1970.[18] Nearly a third were in the Treasury and a further third in the Board of Trade, MinTech, and the DEP. Finally non-civil servants came into Whitehall on secondment. Examples included ministers' own advisers, Industrial Advisers, academic economists in the Government Economic Service, and the 'irregulars' who worked in the DEA.

Outside the main government departments a variety of non-civil servants worked in connection with the variery of para-government bodies that were established during the 1960s and early 1970s. Some worked full-time as executives within NEDO or the IRC for example. A larger number of people were involved in a part-time capacity while holding down full-time jobs. Members of NEDC, the EDCs and various committees of enquiry were involved mainly in an advisory or exhortatory role, while members of the SIB, IRC, NRDC, and ITBs were more directly involved with spending money and implementing policies. The majority of these people, especially the part-time ones, were businessmen, although there were others including academics from the social sciences and business education, accountants, management consultants, and trade unionists. The IRC, UCS, and Rolls Royce case-studies provided many examples of the ways in which Whitehall relies on outside expertise when formulating and implementing policy because it lacks the skills to do the jobs that have to be done.

The impact of outsiders has varied enormously. The whole policy of restructuring British industry into bigger units appears to have been largely based on the advice of scientists and engineers. They argued that only big firms could support sufficiently large R&D units within industry.[19] Executives from the chemical industry appear to have had a particular influence as for example when they were asked to give first-hand advice to the official delegation representing Britain at one of the Kennedy Round negotiations.[20] At the other extreme some members and chairmen of EDCs resigned because their fellow-members or the government department with which they were dealing were giving them little chance to make any impact. The major problem that outsiders face is that:

> A precise but complicated machine like Whitehall is programmed to extrude or absorb anything which interferes with its smooth working. New men, new ideas, new forces are bound to be treated by such a creature as irritants to be dealt with in the time-honoured fashion [which is] neutralisation by absorption.[21]

The importance of the use of outsiders in the period that has been studied was not their limited number or their erratic impact. Nor was it the fact that they had not been used before. They had for example been employed in such organisations as the Board of Trade Advisory Committee and the NRDC. Economists had been in Whitehall before, particularly during wartime. *The significance of their increased use was that it showed that Whitehall had in practice to rely on them.* In the 1950s and early 1960s their usefulness was questioned, but the growing complexity of industrial policy was to show that institutional adaptation and greater specialisation within the Civil Service were not enough, because there were jobs that had to be done which civil servants had not the skills to deal with. This is especially true of project appraisal and monitoring, and of actually managing companies with which government has become closely involved. Chataway, the Minister for Industrial Development, point this out:

> It would be wrong . . . for government to think it had a monopoly of wisdom and wrong for us to keep teams of management consultants. In the main it will be outside experts who will be called upon where it is quite clear that failure is due wholly or partly to management deficiencies, and where a precondition of putting the firm right is to get decent management.[22]

Governments needed outside expertise to help implement their increasingly more detailed policies. As part of the institutional arrangements announced with the 1972 Industry Act an Industrial Development Unit was established within the DTI. This was manned by people from the City, accountancy, industry and so on. Because the IDU was at the heart of the DTI's new interventionist strategy, its very existence marked a recognition on Whitehall's part of the impossibility of implementing detailed industrial policies without having outside expertise at hand to rely on.

CHAPTER 15 THE REASONS FOR INTERVENTION

During the period since the Second World War in Britain a close link has developed between a governing party's chances of re-election and its ability to convince the electorate that it has been managing the economy successfully. Accordingly successive governments have laid great stress on trying to solve the recurrent balance of payments deficit, to stabilise the capital investment cycle and the oscillating unemployment rate, to reduce regional imbalance and the rate of inflation, and to increase industrial productivity and economic growth to match those of Britain's competitors.[1] They have argued that success in these spheres and a stable payments surplus would raise living standards and provide the means to pay for wide-ranging social programmes. This chapter analyses the reasons behind the responses of successive governments since the early 1960s to the continued existence of these problems. It does not attempt to unravel any fallacies in their arguments.

(i) During the 1950s governments attempted to solve these problems by concentrating not on intervention but on using conventional Keynesian methods of managing demand and the balance of payments to provide an environment in which business could thrive. However, growth in production and incomes were accompanied by rises in the imports of food, manufactured and semi-manufactured goods, and raw materials. This led to a fast-growing balance of payments deficit because imports rose faster than exports. Although such a deficit could be temporarily financed through borrowing, the point was reached sooner or later where a stop had to be imposed by the Treasury to reduce the rise in imports. Public expenditure cuts and other deflationary policies, including higher interest rates and a credit squeeze, were introduced, as in 1955, 1957 and 1961, to cut back demand, production, and the growth of imports. Such policies had generalised effects which hit all parts of the economy and could not be made to discriminate between, for example, different regions, and industries doing large amounts of export business. They were maintained until the balance of payments was roughly in equilibrium again when the economy was reflated in an attempt to solve the basic economic problems outlined in the preceding paragraph.

The main reason for the growth of detailed, often interventionist, policies in the 1960s was *the disappointing impact of previous policies on the basic economic problems.* Whitehall's response to their continued existence under the governments of Macmillan, Douglas-Home, and especially Wilson, was to supplement macro-economic policies by developing more detailed industrial policies to improve the performance of industry. The aim was to get behind the economic indicators – the index of industrial production, the declining share of world trade, and the statistical international comparisons that put Britain's economic performance in such poor light, – and to provide policies designed to improve what were seen as the *physical* causes of industry's disappointing performance and lack of international competitiveness. To begin with governments intervened in response to *ad hoc* problems, as was the case with the developing over-capacity in textiles and aviation in the late 1950s.

This move towards developing detailed policies both for individual industries and for specific problems like industrial training received a powerful stimulus between 1962 and 1966 from the attempts to solve the basic economic problems through indicative planning. The process of communicating with industry, and drawing up the planning documents, revealed a number of difficulties inherent in the strategy of fast economic expansion. The implementation of the plans and thus the solution of the basic problems largely depended on Whitehall taking the initiative and attempting to devise policies to help solve the emerging difficulties. The main features have been outlined in Chapters 1 and 2. The advent of a Labour Government gave added strength to the belief that a direct physical attack was needed on the structure of industry. The formal abandonment of indicative planning in July 1966 severed the link between intervention and planning.

Between 1966 and the election in February 1974 increasingly detailed policy-making graduated from being the means of implementing the plans to become by itself the central plank in the attempts of successive governments to solve the basic continuing economic problems. The Wilson and Heath administrations concentrated on the more *ad hoc* approach of examining the difficulties facing specific industries, and problems like training, competition and prices and incomes. Such policies were implemented with vaguely defined aims and were no longer linked to a set of planning targets. Chapter 2 showed how this was the case in the late 1960s and it was certainly true of the period after the 1972 Industry Bill had been introduced. Within a year the DTI had conducted or initiated detailed examinations into the shipbuilding, machine tool, ship repair, motor cycle, carpet, and other industries. However it is important to stress that for all the rhetoric the disengagement period was no exception as policy-makers did not stop concentrating on devising detailed policies. John Davies acknowledged that the Government had no choice but to continue providing financial support for such industries as computers and aerospace. *Thus two different governments with totally opposed views as to the utility of intervention came round to the view that in order to solve the basic economic problems they had no option but to develop increasingly detailed policies.* This goes to underline the fact that all governments intervene. The difference between them is the fact that they attach differing degrees of importance to intervening to alter the framework in which all firms operate as in the 'disengagement' period, and intervening more directly in an attempt to alter the performance of industry through wide-ranging restructuring, as in the late 1960s.

(ii) What then has been the justification for the promotion of detailed policies for specific industries from the standpoint of increased efficiency? The purpose of aiming to strengthen and modernise industry has been to contribute to the solution of the basic economic problems through improved productivity, increased exports, and so on. The nub of the problem has been that governments have concluded that they must try to alter a situation in which many firms are content to run well below full capacity when orders are available; to remain overmanned; to carry on with out-dated equipment; to fail to apply available technologies and new productive processes, and so on. Successive governments have tried to increase industrial efficiency by devising policies to persuade firms to pursue new lines of action. They have sought to cajole and even bully firms on such matters as investing in the most up-to-date equipment and the most relevant technologies, lengthening their production runs, and concentrating more on marketing, especially through increased exports. Governments have been ready to provide funds for apparently viable projects rejected by conventional financiers. Above all governments have tried to persuade firms to rationalise their assets to lower their unit costs, and where appropriate to emulate their overseas competitors on R&D, productivity, marketing, exports and profits.

Policies designed to increase industrial efficiency in these sorts of ways have involved restructuring at two levels. First, governments have sought to alter the firm structure of specific industries to maximise the use of assets, as for example in the sectors the IRC concentrated on. Secondly governments have sought to restructure individual firms. Usually this involves trying to persuade managers to alter their attitudes on such issues as those outlined in the preceeding paragraphs. This is done directly through exhortation or indirectly through providing incentives to re-equip or export more. Where governments are involved as shareholders or financiers they occasionally interpret restructuring at the firm level in terms of working, often with other interested parties, to change the top management. The IRC was responsible for some of this, as were the Conservatives in 1971-2 when helping to appoint new senior executives to such firms as ICL and Harland Wolff. In attempting to modernise industry through these two main types of restructuring, governments have concentrated on various industries. Expanding sectors like electronics have attracted much attention, especially where they are large exporters as with wool textiles. Another group are industries that closely affect others. The fortunes of the consortia constructing power stations, the chemical industry and the groups exploiting North Sea oil and gas are closely linked to the performance of the process plant sector. Governments are also ready to support industries that are going through exceptionally difficult trading periods, as was the case with machine tools in 1972.

In the period between 1962 and the first election in 1974 each government has adopted very similar basic attitudes. The politicians in charge of industrial policy have all argued along the same lines – Heath as President of the Board of Trade in 1963-4; George Brown through the National Plan and the IRC White Paper that emanated from the DEA; Wilson as Prime Minister; and Shore and Wedgwood Benn from the DEA and MinTech in the late 1960s; Davies and Walker as the first two Secretaries of State for Trade and Industry in the early 1970s, and Christopher Chataway who was appointed as Minister for Industrial Development in April 1972. Their approaches have all been based on the argument that *the performance of British industry must be improved to face up to the intensification of international competition.* The difference between successive governments in this context is the extent to which they are ready to take the initiative and, in the face of inaction, whether they are prepared to force through what they want. Different governments have also adopted similar approaches to their financial involvement with regard to the industries discussed so far. Where they have provided financial support the aim has been that the assistance should be temporary, often with the money being repaid to the government, and that in future firms should obtain their funds from internal or market sources rather than from the state.

(iii) On the other hand there are *other industries which governments subsidise in whole or in part on a continuous basis.* This arises when a government provides finance but accepts that there will either be a very limited economic return and quite possibly a loss on the investment, or that the return will only come in the long term. This is the case for example with the high technology industries of aerospace, computers, and nuclear power. Government finance is made available both for specific projects like a particular aircraft, and for ongoing research programmes which examine developing technologies that may have future industrial potential. The reasons why governments continue to provide extensive support are varied. There are the strictly practical reasons that the sums involved are both beyond the capacity of private capital and usually involve a longer time lag between the R&D process and the selling of the end product, than conventional financiers are prepared to countenance.[2] Financial support is occasionally mobilised within the City, as was the case in October 1970 with Rolls Royce. However these practical reasons, together with the high-risk element inherent in these advanced technology industries make such occurrences the exception rather than the rule. Why then do governments consider it necessary to develop these industries? It is argued that computers, nuclear power stations and successful planes can make a substantial contribution to the balance of payments through big export earnings. Governments have considered that there are strong defence arguments in favour of maintaining an independent presence in aerospace and computers. These appear to be the two most important reasons for a national presence in these advanced industries, though others including for example the technological spin-off effects, and the more intangible prestige benefits do exist.

The other main reason why industries are subsidised is the social one of providing work in contracting industries located in some of the more deprived regions. In the late 1960s and early 1970s ministers stressed that shipbuilding firms had to be independent and could not rely on continued financial aid. However, when faced with a choice of massive unemployment or further subsidies, both Labour and Conservative governments chose the latter course. Governments have delayed the closure of coal pits and steel works for similar reasons in the public sector, and have adapted this approach to the special circumstances of Ulster. In 1972 when ICL wanted to close a particular factory, the Government chose to purchase it from the firm and subsidise its operation rather than condone the loss of 1800 jobs.[3]

(iv) The often unspoken assumption underlying the reasons for intervention that have so far been cited is that governments cannot permit market forces to go unchecked in a modern mixed economy. From the standpoint of industrial efficiency market forces cannot be relied on to solve the basic economic problems by ensuring through a process of spontaneous adaptation that maximum use is made of resources in both declining and expanding sectors. Governments resort to intervention as a means of prodding strategic parts of the economy. They try to iron out deficiencies such as under-utilisation of assets and the laying off of skilled men at one stage of the economic cycle, and labour and materials shortages when factories are approaching full capacity at the other end of the cycle. Sometimes market forces are supplemented, as for example when the state acts as a lender of last resort, or in providing huge sums beyond the capacity of the market. On other occasions market forces are accelerated. This was the case with many of the mergers where the IRC acted as a catalyst, accelerator or steersman. Occasionally market forces are overridden, as for example with the subsidisation of uneconomic industries for social reasons as outlined in the preceding paragraph. Governments also act to seek to control some of the undesirable effects of market forces that run counter to government policies. Through competition and regional policies, for example, governments seek to control the abuse of monopoly power and push investment into deprived regions. Intervention is thus based on a belief that *the impact of market forces on economic development in a modern mixed economy will be erratic,* and that a government needs to be ready to act to correct what it sees as emerging imbalances.

(v) Governments have also developed their industrial policies, often in an interventionist way, because of *international factors.* Since the mid-1960s the fundamental reason for supporting a British computer industry has been that without government support it could not face the consequences in international competition of the dominating position of such multinationals as IBM. In addition the fact that overseas governments provide aid in various ways for their domestic industries has led British industrialists to argue that if their competitors in fierce international markets are being helped then it is only fair that the British government should act to assist British companies which are facing what amounts to unfair competition. British shipbuilders have repeatedly pointed to the aid that governments in Japan, America, Italy, and other countries provide for their domestic industries. In the early 1970s the British ball bearings manufacturers objected to the ways in which the Japanese Government appeared to be overtly encouraging its own companies to export their products to Britain at cheap rates. They successfully pressed the British Government to insist to the Japanese Government that these exports to Britain should be limited. Another line of argument has been that the British government should introduce similar measures to those being implemented abroad. The British machine tool industry has suffered for many years from a situation in which orders fluctuate between a peak which it is beyond the capacity of the industry to meet, to such a low level that it is making very limited use of its assets, and is often forced to lay off skilled men. For most of the 1960s and at the beginning of the 1970s the machine tool manufacturers pressed the government to introduce a system somewhat akin to that which Sweden had introduced to cope with a similar situation.[4] The fact that governments have to attempt to stimulate investment in the more deprived regions means that they cannot avoid competing with other governments to attract mobile foreign investment. H. Stephenson quotes from a speech before the 1970 election by Nicholas Ridley, who subsequently became a junior minister at the DTI:

> Of course some types of international industry go to those countries which offer them the biggest bribes, and it will be

necessary for the next Conservative Government to match those inducements.[5]

Finally the scale of the costs and risks involved in such high-technology fields as nuclear energy and in the civil and defence areas of aerospace has led successive British governments to become involved, or think seriously of becoming involved, in a variety of collaborative projects with other governments involving British and foreign companies.

(vi) Ministers have always been ready to acknowledge the reasons behind the growth of the more detailed, often interventionist policies that have been discussed so far – the lack of impact of previous policies on basic economic problems, the industrial reasons, the need to support high technology and to subsidise other industries, the inadequacy of market forces, and the international factors. However there is one other factor in the overall equation that they are often less ready to acknowledge. Towards the end of Chapter 3 it was argued that the process of implementing detailed industrial policies was likely to be *self-generating.* This is because once a government becomes involved in an industry like shipbuilding or a sphere like prices and incomes, pressures combine to force it into further action. Thus an advisory service of the type outlined in Chapter 2 needs to be reviewed to fit customers' developing needs. A typical example was the way in which in the early 1970s the Computer Aided Design Centre, previously established at Cambridge, extended its facilities by establishing a national network. Sometimes policies for specific problems have been introduced on such a wide range that Whitehall has established committees of enquiry to review the situation. For example in 1969 the Bolton Committee was established to examine the problems facing small firms, and the Way Committee was set up mainly to examine "the interaction between the Government and the (machine tool) industry".[6] Both enquiries showed clearly how providing assistance and developing more detailed policies has created further, often unforeseen problems which needed remedial attention. The enquiries clearly influenced subsequent government policies. Thus, a series of Small Firms Advisory Bureaux were established,[7] and some of the suggestions of the machine tool industry were later to be incorporated in the 1972 Finance Act[8]

The commonest way in which industrial policies become self-generating concerns finance. Whitehall's estimates of the cost of a project are often overtaken by events. ICL for example received three instalments of money for R&D between 1968 and 1973, with a further amount to come in 1974.[9] Successive governments have also supported the Hovertrain. It is not just with the more advanced technology industries that financial estimates prove to be inaccurate. The Pre-production Orders Scheme for machine tools and the Hotel Improvement

Scheme both proved more expensive than anticipated. UCS was the extreme example where near-bankruptcy repeatedly sent the firm back to Whitehall. International collaborative projects like Concorde and the RB211 tend to create a momentum of their own, requiring support substantially beyond the original estimates. In aerospace the principle that the government will accept a large part of the responsibility for new projects has become established. Electronics is a typical example of the way in which previous government support seems to be used as a precedent helping firms when they approach a government for further help. MinTech provided £5 million between 1968 and 1972 for R&D in microcircuits. Late in 1970 a group of these industrialists approached the DTI for further assistance. In December 1972 the Government announced it was providing a further £7 million over the next six years to encourage the development of integrated circuits.[10] Once firms know that a government is prepared to provide finance in some way, the result is a flood of applications. In 1973 the Government received many applications for drilling rig schemes following its announcement that it was ready to assist with North Sea projects. Finally, once some industries receive help, other industries are liable to press for similar kinds of assistance. The machine tool, shipbuilding, electrical engineering, aerospace and process plant industries all pressed for public sector orders in 1971-2, once it became apparent that the Government was ready to bring forward such orders. It is probable that there were industrial pressures to extend the Pre-production Orders Scheme to the sectors apart from machine tools mentioned on page 27.

The argument here must not be exaggerated however. Individual projects that have received financial support from the government have of course subsequently sometimes been refused further assistance. In 1969 the Labour Government effectively withdrew from the European Launcher Development Organisation.[11] The Herbert-Ingersoll machine tool project at Daventry, supported by the IRC, was subsequently closed partly because the Conservatives would not provide adequate further assistance. Instances like these do not disprove the point. Rather they show that naturally there are limits to the self-generating nature of industrial policy. However the substantial point about detailed industrial policies being prone to create a momentum of their own, demanding further responses from government, stands. The failure to implement the 'disengagement' approach over a period of several years illustrates this clearly. Although there were cuts and the nature of industrial policy changed in the short term, in the long term the Conservatives fell back on finding new ways to implement that to extend the policies initiated by both parties in the 1960s.

The self-generating nature of detailed industrial policies appears to be underlined by two administrative factors. Once in existence, some specific parts of government departments, and some para-government agencies tend to seek a *raison-d'etre* for a continuing role for their organisation even if it is a different role. Beesley and White have argued this in the case of the IRC for example.[12] The second factor is the influence of civil servants. This is because when ministers first take up office in an industrial department they lack, whatever their backgrounds, the detailed knowledge and experience of the civil servant. During the time a new minister takes to get on top of his job, he relies to a greater extent than he will subsequently on civil servants, especially if they have been working solely on a specific subject like monopolies or the chemical industry for many, many, months. Even when he has mastered his department there will be parts of it about which he knows nothing. Crosland, for example, was President of the Board of Trade for about two years, and never came into contact with the part of his department dealing with patents.[13] Once an individual has been there for some substantial time he begins to reinforce the process, because for political reasons, he is usually unwilling to admit to a mistake and is thus bent on developing a policy he has initiated. The process is further reinforced because busy ministers, trying to make an impact and so stand to gain political promotion, have unavoidablly found they have had to concentrate on a smallish number of subjects. There are, of course, occasions when ministers override their advisers. It has been suggested that this was the case in 1970-71 with the switch from investment grants to allowances, and with some of the cuts in the finance available to the AEA.[14] However these factors together with the move to huge departments have meant that for the most part much of the work of a department has been left to manage itself. Thus civil servants have been left to develop policies that have been initiated. The role of ministers appears to have been restricted to taking the initiative on a few subjects, prodding civil servants into extending policies, and only becoming deeply involved if a crisis develops or looks like developing.

Thus a combination of factors lies behind a growth of detailed, often interventionist, policies in the 1960s and early 1970s. The basic underlying reason has been the continuing existence of the basic economic problems of the lack of growth, the balance of payments deficit and the other economic problems outlined at the start of this chapter. Politically, the most highly sensitive of these problems has been unemployment. In the period after the winter of 1962-63 and during the winter of 1971-72, different Conservative governments responded to steep rises in the unemployment rate with a succession of detailed policies and increased financial aid to industry. The way in which this can also be a delicate problem in a localised context, where redundancies result from state intervention or from a refusal to intervene, is discussed in the next chapter.

It has not just been unemployment that has triggered off government reaction to the failure of macro-economic policies to solve the other problems of lack of growth, continuing regional imbalance and so on. The lack of an alternative economic strategy that would not involve high unemployment, has led successive governments to conclude that they apparently have no option but to concentrate less on manipulating the framework in which firms operate, and more on developing more detailed, often interventionist non-regulatory policies. This was the fundamental reason that underlay the abandonment of the 'disengagement' experiment. It is not to say that macro-economic policies and other regulatory measures of the type described in Chapter 2 count for nothing. Governments have continued to rely heavily on them, and they have sought to improve them and make them more detailed and relevant, as for example by introducing more vigorous competition policies and adopting theories relating to the importance of the money supply. However they have found that in order to try to solve the continuing basic economic problems, thus enhancing their prospects of re-election, *they have increasingly and apparently unavoidably had to supplement macro-economic policies and other regulatory measures with more detailed industrial policies.* This happens at different levels. To begin with governments concentrate on exhortation and developing advisory services of the type described in Chapter 2. However when a government is faced with a continued existence of the basic economic problems, it responds with measures designed more directly to change the ways in which firms are behaving so that the benefit to the economy of their research, production, and exports will increase. In this connection it is important to note that while the 1964-70 Labour Government had a basic instinct to intervene, its successor had exactly the opposite instinct. Yet in both 1966-67 and 1971-72, from completely opposed standpoints these different governments adopted the same approach. Exasperated ministers faced pressing economic problems, an apparent lack of impact of their policies, and an unwillingness or inability by industry to respond to their policies by investing and expanding production, by developing and applying its research, and by exporting more of its output. In each of these two cases the response was a preparedness to bypass the 'bottleneck' of the type described in Chapter 3. Labour and Conservative governments were ready, through for example the IRC and the 1972 Industry Act, to forge a more direct link with individual firms. The extent to which each needed to act varied according to the extent to which the capital investment cycle began to pick up. If firms begin to respond independently there is then less need for government to seek to generate movement and new practices at the firm level. Even if economic growth had not been seen to be so important, the situation probably would have been little different because problems like the balance of payments would still have remained and would still have needed to be solved.

CHAPTER 16 PROBLEMS FACING POLICY-MAKERS

Once a government has decided that it cannot avoid implementing detailed, often interventionist industrial policies, it has to come to terms with the problems that arise as a consequence. The decision to intervene, like the decision to nationalise, solves nothing by itself. Rather it opens a Pandora's Box of further problems. During the often lengthy process of formulating and implementing detailed policies, a government has to work in the context of various constraints on its ability to implement those solutions that, from a purely industrial standpoint, make the best sense. This chapter outlines these constraints and ends by discussing some of the issues which arise.

The Range Of Constraints

(i) The first main constraint facing a government arises from a straightforward lack of knowledge about the way in which the economy works at the firm level. The first aspect of this is the way in which a government is handicapped in its attempts to formulate detailed industrial policies by the fact that the quality of the information at its disposal is extremely variable. The mid- and late 1960s saw a wave of mergers that transformed the structure of many industries. Yet Whitehall had to continue to rely on the 1963 Census of Industrial Production for basic information on the structure and evolution of an industry. The Business Monitor Series provides basic data on a monthly or quarterly basis on such items as stocks, exports, output, consumption of raw materials, and so on. However, this does not provide policy-makers with the basic information that they need. The 1968 Census was actually undertaken before the 1963 one had been fully processed.[1] The Bolton Committee Report on Small Firms was published in 1971. Even though it commissioned a number of research projects to try and improve the position, its findings for a changing sector, which had many complaints against the way Whitehall operated, were based on the 1963 Census. The extent to which the situation can be improved is limited by the conflicting demands from industry:

> There is on the one hand a demand for more detail, at more frequent intervals, of closely defined products, in respect of narrower market areas; on the other there is a resistance by many firms to supplying even the more limited data which is needed

for even the current statistical programme, and any relaxation of the confidentiality rules, which themselves limit the amount of detail that can be provided.[2]

The need to enable British firms to compete in fierce international competition has been a constant aim of British industrial policy during the 1960s and early 1970s. This has imposed a need for international information. In preparing policies for industries like motor vehicles, electrical engineering, computers, and shipbuilding where competition for markets is intense, policy-makers cannot proceed effectively without data about the foreign and multinational firms against which they are trying to get British firms to compete. The IRC for example, commissioned research overseas, particularly in America.

The result of a lack of up-to-date information is that government and its agents have to establish enquiries or commission them from outside the government machine to assemble as much up-to-date data as possible, before embarking on policy initiatives. This is in itself a tremendous problem in an industry like machine tools with a large number of small firms. But even in an industry with a fairly small number of large firms like shipbuilding, information is quickly outdated. In 1972 for example the Booz Allen Report was started on the shipbuilding industry only six years after the Geddes Committee had been established.[3] Even before the Booz Allen Report was published in the Spring of 1973, its work had in some respects been outdated by the rapid rise in shipbuilding orders. Thus, not only does the time it takes to do the research delay the time when decisions are taken, but even the most up-to-date information, assembled from direct approaches to NEDO, individual firms and trade associations, can turn out to be an unreliable basis for decision-making. Clearly the impact of a set of measures will be limited if it is based on inaccurate information and forecasting.

An additional aspect of the way in which a government is handicapped by its lack of knowledge about the way the economy works at the firm level, is the fact that economics is an inexact science. In practice a tenuous link exists in many fields between economic theory and what decision-makers at the firm level actually do. The IRC case-study, for example, discussed the belief that 'bigger is better' in the mergers field. Chapter 8 took this further, referring to the fact that whatever the theory, firms often merged for the wrong reasons and failed to take advantage of the opportunities through post-merger rationalisation. In other fields, there is sometimes little theory on which to base policies. It has been pointed out for example, that in the mid-1960s MinTech was handicapped in its attempts to encourage the more intensive application of science and technology to productive processes in industry because there was "no established foundation of knowledge" on which to base policy. "It was reasonable enough to believe that a relationship existed between R&D, innovation and industrial performance; but this did not tell the Ministry where to push."[4]

There is one further important example of government's straightforward lack of knowledge about the way in which the economy works at the firm level. This is its inability to forecast acurately the response of industry to specific measures. The way in which governments have sought to influence the extent to which the capital investment cycle fluctuates is a tremendously important recurring example. The response of industry during the 1960s to the range of regional incentives, and to the cuts in taxation and other incentives in the Conservative budgets of 1970, 1971, and 1972 were erratic. Capital investment was slow to pick up, especially in the early 1970s, and fell far short of ministers' hopes and expectations. The same principle has applied to more detailed schemes. Interest in the IRC Textile Re-equipment Scheme was lower than anticipated whereas the Pre-production Order Schemes have been oversubscribed. Any government is thus crucially handicapped by its straightforward lack of knowledge about the way in which the economy works at the firm level. It lacks up-to-date data on which to base policies; it lacks knowledge about the link between economic theory and industrial practice; and it is unable to predict how individual firms will react to various measures.

(ii) The second basic constraint is the practical one of the real world of industry and commerce that faces a government when it reaches the point of implementing detailed industrial policies. No government can implement policy in a vacuum. Every government has to coexist with the real world and implement policy in the context of the way in which private industry and the City operates. A wide variety of practical constraints on a government's freedom of action arise from this situation.

First is the way that managers at the firm level look at the problems inherent in what government is wanting them to do. Sometimes these problems of the real world in which industry and commerce operate on a day-to-day basis can be commercial. The ICL merger is an example of this. From its earliest days, MinTech was trying to engineer the ICL merger, but this did not finally transpire until March 1968. This was partly because International Computers and Tabulators' computer system was incompatible with those of Plessey and EE. This question of incompatability could not be solved according to the industrialists concerned before the next round of computers. Thus from the firm's point of view there was a technological reason why they could not immediately fall in with the government's wishes.

The second type of practical difficulty that arises from the real world in which industry operates is the sheer length of time it takes to implement a policy. This means that a government is handicapped in its ability to implement policies which will have an immediate and tangible impact on specific economic problems like increasing exports or improving industrial productivity. Creating new companies like ICL, BLMC and GEC for example, does not solve a problem overnight, if at all. Such companies have to undergo a period of reorganisation lasting perhaps several years, before the theoretical advantages of a merger can be reaped. The same principle applies to finance for capital investment, where there is a considerable time lag between government approval and the plants coming into operation. Three years elapsed between the Government's formal financial commitment to the companies involved, and the opening of the first aluminium smelter in 1971. In the case of extended industrial training measures, changes in quality standards, and other measures of this type described in Chapter 2, the impact of a policy will only build up over time, and even then it will be hard to measure it. The time lag that occurs in cases like these is often overlooked. The situation can be made even worse when the administrative machinery has to be established or reorganised. It has been suggested for example that the time it took to carry through the reorganisation of the administrative structure into which the government research establishments fitted limited their impact.[5]

A third type of practical constraint that occasionally arises is when events move swiftly and government is forced to react to new circumstances. One example is a takeover bid from a domestic or multinational company for what Whitehall sees as an important firm in a vital industry. Thus in the cases of Skefco's bid for Ransome and Marles and Plessey's bid for EE, the IRC had a view as to the ideal solution. In order to keep its options open it was forced to react before it was fully prepared to implement the policy it had chosen for these particular industries. In these two situations the takeover bids in fact sparked off a chain of events that enabled the Corporation to implement its own solutions. However a government's freedom of action is not always widened in such circumstances. In the case of Chrysler's bid to extend its holding in Rootes in 1967, the Government was forced to react to new circumstances. However, it found on investigation that its preferred solution of a link between Rootes and a British company was not possible. While it might have been possible to push such an amalgamation through over a period of time, it had no option in the circumstances but to allow Chrysler's partial bid to go through.

A potential bankruptcy is a further practical constraint. When a company like Cammell Laird or UCS or Rolls is in the midst of a liquidity crisis, a government or its agent has no option but to respond swiftly. The pressures to find a solution, especially when large numbers of jobs are at stake, are such that the danger is finding an instant solution which may not necessarily be viable in the long term. Although he does not give examples, Sir Richard Clarke, the former MinTech Permanent Secretary, has suggested that some companies have waited until their liquidity problems are so bad that there is very little time left before lay-offs will result, before going to the government so that the necessity for speed can be used as a lever on Whitehall.

The question as to whether organisations or institutions within the City can make a government act, perhaps against its will, is sometimes raised. Leaving aside the debate about this on the wider front of economic policy generally, the situation with regard to industrial policy is that the day-to-day way in which the City works is part of the framework within which government has to operate, when formulating and implementing policies. The most important way in which the mechanisms of the City can act as a practical constraint on government is an extension of the point in the preceding paragraph. Events can sometimes move so quickly in the City that Whitehall has to react to them before it is necessarily ready. During the winter of 1972-73, the IDE studied the problems of BSA. It had not completed its work when, on 14 March 1973, a Stock Exchange leak sent the BSA share price plummeting from 18p to close where it was suspended at 5p.[6] The Minister for Industrial Development then had to reveal his plans for a merger between BSA and Manganese Bronze, before they had been finalised. The collapse of the share price undermined the confidence of BSA's suppliers and customers, thus greatly complicating the discussions between the IDE and the two companies. The situation had been brought about by the way in which the City operated. The City had thus acted as a practical constraint forcing the Minister to react to new circumstances.

(iii) The third constraint with which a government has to deal is the independence of the firm. This subject has arisen at several points especially in Chapters 3 and 7. It was stressed that industrialists cannot be forced to respond to measures of encouragement and to advisory services, and in large part to financial inducements. Whether a firm will respond or not will depend on how the policy measure looks from the level of the firm in the context of its day-to-day problems, and its longer-term corporate strategy. It has been argued that for the most part industrial policy has been based on the principle of consent. The independence of the firm forced the IRC to concentrate on what was practical. This entailed dropping what it saw as desirable policy aims because agreement could not be reached with the firms concerned, as for example in special steels. Often the inability of the government or its agent to get agreement between the firm or firms concerned arises from differences between personalities. One documented example concerns the BLMC merger. Turner's account shows that one of the topics in pre-merger discussions between BMH and Leyland concerned the problem of finding the BMH executive Edwards a position in the new combine.[7]

The independence of the firm is not always a constraint. In the first place there are many instances where the firm in fact agrees with government that a particular course of action will be to the benefit of the firm. This was the case on those occasions when the IRC acted as a catalyst bringing together willing partners. The second instance when the independence of the firm is not a constraint arises on both those occasions when the government is prepared to override the wishes of the firm, and intervene directly to implement a policy which it judges to be of critical importance. In the case of the aviation mergers in 1959-60, of steel nationalisation in 1967, and of the GEC/AEI, Kent/Cambridge and RHP mergers, Conservative and Labour Governments were prepared to impose their will. It must be stressed that although a government is sometimes prepared to use its powers to achieve what it sees as a desirable end, such a strategy is exceptional. For the most part a government proceeds on the principle of consent. Thus the IRC's suggestions for the paper and board industry, and the Labour Government's acceptance in principle after the Plowden Report of the need for a merger between Hawker Siddeley and the British Aircraft Corporation were not enforced. The reason why a government is not often prepared to impose its will on resisting companies is not just the political storm that is liable to be unleashed. Rather it is that the process of doing so would endanger its working relationship with the private sector because such action would alienate firms and industrial interest groups far removed from the particular sector involved. Although a government is liable to be prepared to make some exceptions, the independence of the firm, with the implication that industrial policy is largely based on consent, is a significant practical constraint on the government's ability to implement all the policies it sees as desirable. The independence of the firm is of particular importance in the follow-up situation where the government or its agent thinks that a project is getting out of control. It may accept the need for acting, but find the firm's independence an obstacle.

(iv) The next problem facing policy-makers is the fact that industry is constantly evolving. Firms are responding to changing market conditions, to changes in industrial structure, to new technologies and so on. This becomes in effect a constraint for two reasons. First a change in circumstances can mean that a policy becomes outdated because it has been impossible to foresee changes that have taken place. Greater efforts would probably have been made for example to rationalise BLMC in the late 1960s and early 1970s if policy-makers had been able to foresee the impact on the car market of the oil crisis, following the Middle East War of October 1973.

The second way in which the evolution of industry acts as a constraint concerns the fact that industrial policy has constantly to be made in the context of previous policies. When a new government is approached by industries or firms that have previously received assistance, that government does not necessarily have a free hand. Thus Labour policy towards the aerospace industry in the 1960s was limited by the contracts and the relationships that the industry had established with the preceding Conservative Administrations. Similarly under Heath, the Conservatives found it very hard to look afresh at problems like ICL, Rolls Royce, and UCS, which had been receiving government financial support under Labour. The influence of previous policy was partly responsible for the extension of industrial training policies in the mid- and late 1960s and early 1970s; and for the introduction of the 1972 Industry Act. The self-generating nature of intervention thus becomes a constraint because it is extremely difficult to clear the decks and formulate policies from first principles. This is especially the case when considerable sums have already been invested. There is always the temptation to put more money in to recoup what has been invested, instead of writing it off as a loss. On the other hand with industries which have received little or no government assistance in the past, government is much more readily able to formulate policies from first principles. A typical example was the scheme announced in the summer of 1973 to make up to £15 million available in a variety of ways to the wool textile industry for investment and re-equipment. This followed extensive talks with the industry and represented an attempt to construct policy on the basis of the industry's real needs. The facts that very little money had previously been invested in the industry by government, and no precedents had been set, made the IDE's task much simpler as it had no established interest or position to defend.

(v) The highly politicised nature of high unemployment was underlined towards the end of the last chapter. This is also true in a localised context. The fear of being seen to be responsible for large-scale redundancies is a fifth constraining factor on a government's freedom to implement the industrial policies that make the most commercial sense. This is a problem that can arise in the context of a potential bankruptcy like UCS, or a post-merger rationalisation programme of the type mentioned towards the end of Chapter 10. Often protests about redundancies in the private sector which were the result of government action are in fact directed at the company and the government does not find it difficult to stand its ground and avoid becoming involved, except over redeployment. This was the case for example over GEC and RHP. On the other hand, it was fear of redundancies that led MinTech to agree to give UCS further assistance in 1969 even though the SIB had refused the company a loan.[8] It should not be thought, however, that this is mainly a problem for a Labour Government. In 1973-74 Chataway made repeated efforts to save the BSA plant at Meriden, near Coventry, which the management of the new company wanted to close. The fact that this occured in the West Midlands which has one of the lowest rates of unemployment in Britain needs to be underlined to illustrate the reality of this constraint. This is an even more difficult problem in the public sector. In the case of BSC, for example, successive governments counselled delay over establishing and implementing a rationalisation and development programme between 1967 and 1975.

(vi) The next constraint facing a government is the domestic political one which can take several forms. A government can for example be saddled with the consequences of a pledge or attitude established while in opposition. This happened to the Labour Government in 1967 over the Rootes case. Labour spokesmen had opposed the Conservative decision to allow Chrysler to buy into Rootes in 1963. As a result they could not let Chrysler take Rootes over completely four years later and had no option but to put government money into Rootes in one form or another. The Conservative Government found the 'disengagement' policy developed in opposition politically embarrassing in the early 1970s, when they discovered they could not avoid intervening in individual cases, and when they subsequently passed the 1972 Industry Act. Backbenchers can act as a constraint on a government as well. Labour benchbenchers expressed disquiet about redundancies following mergers, as for example in the GEC case. In the early 1970s the Conservative Government had to work in the context of its backbenchers indignation about the injection of public funds into apparently floundering companies like UCS and BSA. The Parliamentary timetable is a further example of the domestic political constraint. Within any government individual ministers want Parliamentary time to bring forward their own bills, but their demands have to be fitted into the government's overall priorities. Wedgwood Benn announced his intention to establish Nuclear Fuels Ltd. in the nuclear power field, but this had to wait until the next government could find the Parliamentary time for the necessary legislation.[9] Even where there is a clear priority, as with the IRC Bill and the 1972 Industry Bill, it took respectively a year and six months before the Acts were on the statute book and the organisations were beginning to be fully operational. Finally an interest group can act as a constraint on a government's ability to introduce the measure it wants to. Often groups influence the shape of policy, as the CBI did with the Heath Government's Stage Two proposals. However, there are other important occasions when the firm opposition of an organisation actually prevents the government from following the line it wants to. The Machine Tool Trades Association for example seems to have been able, through its opposition, to get MinTech to shelve permanently its scheme to introduce a Machine Tool Industry Board under the Industrial Expansion Act.[10]

In the 1960s and early 1970s it seems that the extent to which Parliament, especially the House of Commons, has acted as a constraint on the executive has been limited. Throughout this period there has been pressure for more effective Parliamentary control over the government's role in the appraisal and monitoring of individual projects, and greater accountability to Parliament over the spending of large sums of money. Obviously Parliament influences the government indirectly in that policy is formed partly on a basis of likely criticism, especially from a government's own backbenchers. However the extent to which the industrial departments have been more accountable to Parliament than independent organisations like the IRC has been limited. In practice there has been little difference between the sponsoring Minister answering questions about an independent outside body like the IRC and giving little away, and the Minister answering questions on matters like Concorde for which he is directly responsible and revealing no more information than he chooses to. In the case of the latter though it is true that in the last resort a Minister can be questioned closely on the floor of the House on a matter for which he is directly responsible, as Chataway was over BSA in March 1973. In such cases Parliament will expect an explanation, but a minister is free to give only a limited one if he so chooses because he can refuse to divulge information on the grounds that it would be revealing commercial secrets. This has enabled a minister to give brief answers in the Commons and to conduct what amounts to a stonewalling operation. There have been very few instances of the House of Commons changing a government's stated attitude. The amendments to the 1972 Industry Bill provide a rare example. The Government accepted an amendment so that projects costing more than £5 million could only be supported if a Parliamentary resolution was passed; the IDAB was put on a statutory basis; and it was written into the Bill that if the minister acted contrary to the Board's advice, the Board's view of the matter could if it so desired be published.[11] It remains to be seen whether these clauses or similar ones in future legislation will lead to greater accountability and increased influence on Whitehall.

The whole question of accountability turns on the extent to which an organisation like the IRC or an individual minister publishes the information on which their decisions relating to project appraisal and monitoring have been based. During the 1960s and early 1970s, Whitehall revealed only limited information of this kind often sheltering behind the cloak of 'commercial secrecy'.[12] In these circumstances the increased activity of Parliamentary committees during this period has been directed not just at influencing policy, but at increasing the amount of information that has actually been published. The Trade and Industry Sub-Committee of the Expenditure Committee, the Select Committee on Science and Technology, and the Public Accounts Committee (PAC) especially have made important contributions in these areas. However, it has to be pointed out that even here government departments have been able to frustrate attempts to dig out details they have not wanted to reveal and that "the possession of information is not to be equated with the ability to influence policy." One exception was the influence of the PAC on the changes in the tax concessions to oil companies in the North Sea, introduced in the Budgets after 1973.[13] For the most part however these committees have been enquiring into what happened retrospectively. When they have made recommendations governments have usually acted by stalling or rejecting them.[14] The growing technical and commercial complexity of many of the decisions governments take in these fields, and the growth of day-to-day contacts between government and industry have together further undermined Parliament's influence.

(vii) The final constraint arises from the fact that governments are limited by international agreements that they enter into. Some of these have a great deal of impact on policy-making. One of the ministers concerned with the aluminium smelter project in the late 1960s has written:

> Far greater control was exercised by our EFTA partners breathing down our necks and watching every move, than was exercised by Parliament in whom nominally the chief duty of oversight lay. Indeed, the evidence of this particular episode is that governments have to work much harder to justify their interventions in industry to their partners in international communities than they are ever likely to have to do to win the support of Parliament.[15]

Other measures have a more limited impact. It was for example possible for Britain to offend her EFTA partners by imposing a temporary import surcharge in 1964, but international pressure led to its being withdrawn within two years.[16] On other occasions the government can stand firm and effectively not react to foreign complaints that it is breaking international agreements. The Heath administration strenuously argued its case that the 1972 Industry Act did not contravene EEC regulations, and made no concessions over its content and administration.[17] Sometimes governments face conflicting demands from different international organisations and agreements. Britain was a founder member of the International Sugar Agreement, governing such issues as exports to the developed countries from the Third World. Britain was left in an ambiguous position when the EEC refused to become a party to this agreement after the enlargement of the Community in 1973.[18]

National sovereignty is also being eroded in more indirect ways. The preceding chapter (p.179) discussed the international dimension of the self-generating nature of intervention. A government's policy options are limited by the existence of international contracts like the RB211 one. In industries like aerospace and computers the research costs are such that huge resources are needed and individual national companies may lack these. These and other factors have prompted high-level talks of possible links between British and American companies, as with ICL and Burroughs, and BAC and Boeing. Links between ICL, BAC and Hawker Siddeley, and European companies have also been discussed both before and after Britain formally signed the Rome Treaty. Membership of the Common Market has given the process an added dimension, because the Commission has begun to try and formulate EEC wide-policies in industries like computers, aerospace, energy and shipbuilding. Although this is a long-term programme that may never be implemented, it is yet one more way in which British policy-makers have to think through the international consequences of a particular policy before implementing it. A desirable line of action may be precluded because of the complications of international politics. A merger between BAC and Boeing, when the French Government wanted a merger between BAC and Sud Aviation, the French company, for example, would have enormous repercussions for the relationship between the British and French governments and effect the EEC itself.

The Impact of Constraints On Policy

It can therefore be seen that governments face a wide variety of constraints on their ability to formulate and implement industrial policies that, from a strictly commercial standpoint, appear to make the most sense. It also needs to be underlined that the extent to which these constraints are within the government's control is limited. It can for example do nothing about the fourth constraint, whereby industrial policy has to be made in the context of previous policy. On the other hand the extent which it allows both the fear of instigating redundancies and the domestic political constraints to influence policy-making is totally within its control.

The remaining constraints fall in between these two extremes, being partly within a government's control and partly outside it. To a certain extent a government can do nothing about the first constraint. Its lack of knowledge about means of running the economy and the unpredictable way in which industrialists react limits its ability to have an impact. On the other hand the outcome of industrial policy for a particular sector will depend on the accuracy of the forecasts of future markets, technologies, and other world-wide developments. This in turn will depend on the quality of the information available at the time, and the extent to which out-of-date statistics can be fully updated by questionnaires. However, two important developments have taken place here which should benefit governments. Big firms have begun to supply industrial departments and agencies on a regular basis with up-to-date information that previously they saw fit not to divulge. In addition there has been a series of initiatives on the subject within Whitehall. The Central Statistics Office has been strengthened, a Business Statistics Office has been established, and a new system of collating industrial statistics has been inaugurated.[19]

Information is also important with regard to the second constraint – the real world in which industry operates. Governments can do nothing for example about the time lag between the provision of funds for investment in new plant, and the start of production. However, it can be ready for swiftly moving events that bring on a crisis. If a company approaches the government because it faces bankruptcy, that government will be in a stronger position if it already has detailed knowledge about the future of the industry concerned, into which it can 'plug' the crisis, and decide whether it is worth assisting the firm. Otherwise it may give temporary support while it investigates, and subsequently find it is very difficult to withdraw. The lesson is clear. *The more up-to-date the information the greater the likelihood of forecasts being correct and future capacity being able accurately to meet demand.* The IRC found that the only way to approach this problem was by extensive field work, even though it was difficult in sectors with many small and medium-sized firms. Yet even then there are problems, as a firm may be unable to answer questions. The Booz Allen Report, for example, commented that the shipbuilding industry has "insufficient information on the market in which it is operating".[20] Detailed field work has an added advantage in that there is more chance to assess individual managers.

The independence of the firm and the international constraints are also factors that are partly within the government's control. With both these factors situations arise in which government sees the national interest as being so compelling that it is prepared to override the wishes of the firm and to risk offending other governments. The creation of RHP is an example. Not only did the IRC override the wishes of Pollard, but the Government was ready to take no notice of the Swedish complaints about the possible breaking of Article 16 of the EFTA Convention.[21]

Thus a picture emerges whereby a government is handicapped by a wide variety of constraints. It is important to stress the impact on policy of those over which it does have some control. In the process of formulating and implementing detailed, often interventionist industrial policies, governments allow *uneconomic* considerations to creep into their handling of the constraints within their control. This means that it is often not the optimum commercial solution that is translated from the drawing board into the harsh realities of the industrial world. A government lacks detailed up-to-date information which enables it both to initiate policies with confidence and to respond to the unexpected. It is usually unwilling to override the independence of the firm, and to assert the national interest, even if it means offending other governments. It often seeks to appease its backbenchers. Finally fear of redundancies prevents a government from announcing that after a cold theoretical examination of a contracting industry, it will seek to reduce the number of firms, install modern equipment and thus reduce the number of employees. The same problem can arise in expanding sectors where developing technologies can demand, solely from an economic standpoint, fewer, larger sites. The importance of the fear of redundancies is that it directly contradicts the aim of introducing new practices and modernising industry. From a strictly commercial standpoint financing a bankrupt company or allowing continued overmanning means that the maximum use is not made of their assets. In such circumstances social considerations override economic ones.

It is important to realise that the extent to which a government has freedom of manoeuvre in policy-making and can control even the constraints within its control is *limited.* The government's task is further complicated by the fact that it has to consider wider dimensions to any industrial problem, including for example the social factors. However the other side of the coin must be stressed. *The impact of the constraints within the government's control on the outcome of industrial policy is to limit the extent to which that policy will have an impact on the problem to which it is related.* It should thus be realised that governments tend to handicap themselves because they undermine the extent to which intervention can solve problems.

The constraints that have been discussed are also partly responsible for the way in which governments adopt a piecemeal, *ad hoc* approach to individual problems as they arise. Governments are reluctant to plan the future of whole sectors. This is the case whether a government is taking the initiative or is reacting to applications, or to the unexpected. In practical terms this means that for the most part decisions about support for industry are loosely related to the anticipated future development of whole sectors. The existence of constraints forces governments to search for practical solutions. The *ad hoc* approach is encouraged by the self-generating nature of intervention and by the fact that governments intervene and dispense aid according to unknown or loosely defined criteria. *The overall result is that governments seem unable to avoid detailed interventionist and industrial policies becoming a series of ad hoc, largely uncoordinated responses to individual cases.* This is one of the main reasons why British governments have become involved in such a wide variety of spheres, instead of concentrating their efforts and national resources on fewer industrial sectors.

CHAPTER 17 THE CONTINUOUS SEARCH FOR INFLUENCE AT THE LEVEL OF THE FIRM

The contribution of the detailed, often interventionist, policies described in this book towards the solution of the basic economic problems outlined at the start of Chapter 15 has been erratic. These policies have had a direct impact in that certain events have taken place as a result of government activity which almost certainly would not otherwise have happened. Examples include the building of the aluminium smelters, the continued existence of UCS, and the emergence of such companies as Kent, RHP, and probably ICL. On the other hand the provision of state aid to companies like Rolls Royce led quite unexpectedly to bankruptcy. The impact of other policies has been disappointing. For all the stress on industrial training in the 1960s, shortages of skilled manpower still emerged as the economy expanded rapidly in 1973. Despite all government efforts Britain's share of world exports of manufactured goods has steadily declined from 15 per cent in 1964 to 11.4 per cent in 1969 and 9.6 per cent in 1973.[1] Still others produced unexpected side effects. One unforeseen result of the merger boom of the late 1960s was that the rationalisation process led to many second-hand machine tools coming on to the market which in turn contributed to the very depressed order books the industry faced in the early 1970s.

As explained in the Preface a full examination of the twin problems of the extent of the impact of intervention on the economy, and whether the impact has benefited industrial development, do not fall within the scope of this book. Both are intractable problems. When measuring the impact of intervention it is usually next to impossible to separate the extent to which prevailing market conditions have influenced executives at the firm level from the extent to which they have taken decisions because of government intervention. It is impossible to say for example, how far industrialists installing new machinery under the Pre-production Order Scheme are doing so because they consider it to be the best available machinery, or because of the incentives made available to them by the government. Another example is the discussion in Chapter 8 of Newbould's analysis of the reasons behind the merger boom in 1967-68. Similar kinds of unanswered questions arise when attempts are made to assess how beneficial intervention has been. It is impossible to say for example whether an IRC-backed merger provided net benefit to the economy, because nobody knows what would have happened if those companies had stayed apart or merged with others. Similarly it cannot be said that Rolls would have been better off without the RB211 contract, or whether in fact that would have meant, as the company argued at the time, opting out of a major British presence in the world aeroengines industry. These kinds of factors make it extremely difficult either to list the achievements of organisations like the IRC, MinTech, the EDCs or IDU, especially where they have vaguely defined aims, or to assess the value of their contribution. However the whole subject of the impact of, and the benefit of detailed industrial policies needs to be touched on, in order to explain further the problems that governments face, especially over the need to forge direct links with firms. (see Chapter 3).

The erratic impact of detailed, often interventionist policies leads governments into reappraisals of their approach. The continued existence of fundamental economic and industrial problems makes them question whether their interventionist strategy is inherently wrong. Yet governments have not been able to devise alternative strategies that they have been prepared to carry on implementing whatever the consequences. The 'disengagement' experiment was dropped because of its lack of impact on the basic economic problems. The Conservative Government's response in this situation took the form of an interventionist strategy. This illustrated that for all the drawbacks of a more interventionist approach governments have not been able to find a viable alternative. It could be objected at this point that 'disengagement' was an alternative, but that it had been practised in the wrong way with insufficient determination. If, for example, it had been implemented as capital investment was rising and unemployment declining, its chances of success probably would have been greatly increased. However, the discussion in this, as in other chapters, concentrates on the situation as governments have seen it and not on the accuracy of their analysis.

A major reappraisal of policy occurs basically on two types of occasion. This can be when a government voluntarily examines its attitudes towards the private sector, as in the winters of 1966-67 and of 1971-72. The second occasion is when a firm like Rootes or Beagle or Rolls or Herbert Ingersoll runs into a crisis and takes its problems to the government. *A basic reappraisal always raises two fundamental issues.*

The first of these is whether the government should nationalise the particular firm or industry. Chapter 14 showed that governments have been reluctant to extend nationalisation during the 1960s and early 1970s. The public sector can be extended by nationalising a series of firms so that, as with BSC in 1967, a whole industry is effectively nationalised. Alternatively a government can aim not to nationalise specific industries, but major firms in a range of industries. The latter approach was favoured by the Labour Party Study Group that in 1972 produced the so called '25 companies' proposal.[2] *Successive governments have tended to reject nationalisation because they have argued that far from solving anything, it tends to create further, often more intractable problems.* They have seen from their experience of dealing with existing nationalised industries how nationalisation destroys the commercial independence that is the driving force behind a firm's operations; and how it creates an inflexible slow-moving organisation. More recently, governments have seen how the history of BSC has shown that the process of planning and implementing a development programme is an extremely long drawn out process because of the huge cost, and because of the political pressures and constraints that arise when phased redundancies are announced. Governments have concluded that there is more chance of getting results *quickly* by taking the private sector as it stands and seeking to bring influence to bear on it so that its performance is more in accordance with the aims of the government.

Quite apart from the disadvantage and the slow speed of working through the public sector, there has been another reason why governments have taken this approach. It has been argued that one of the main reasons why governments intervene is to promote industrial productivity and increase exports. From the firm's point of view this can *potentially* mean expansion and increased post-tax profits, and dividends. Although the firm has to bring other considerations to bear – see pages 207-8 – it is the case that the government's aims are in large part also the firm's aims. The rejection of nationalisation leaves the government no option but to work through the private sector.

The second fundamental issue that lies at the heart of a reappraisal of industrial policy is how interventionist the government is prepared to be when working in the context of the private sector. All governments aim to provide macro-economic conditions that are conducive to soundly based economic expansion. Beyond that a government aims to solve the problem that was discussed in the second half of Chapter 3. A situation whereby a bottleneck develops between the government and its agents on the one hand, and the firm on the other, repeatedly emerges. Governments aim to bypass this by forging a link with individual firms in order that decision-making at the firm level better reflects government aims. Successive governments have sought to make the link a creative one by making the advisory services as useful as possible to industry, and by offering a widening variety of financial inducements. The second fundamental issue that arises is *just how far is the government prepared to intervene and impose its will on the firm?* This does not just concern economic and legal controls. It also applies to government attempts to try to make firms react positively to the advisory services and financial inducements that are made available.

Usually a government's real, as opposed to its stated, attitude to the question as to how far it is prepared to intervene is cloaked in secrecy. It only reveals itself as its programme unfolds, and as it responds to changing circumstances, and to crises as they arise. It then becomes possible to discuss how far, and in what ways, a government is interventionist. A government's attitude on the two fundamental questions as to whether it is prepared to nationalise, and how far it is prepared to intervene in the private sector, profoundly affects the nature of its industrial policy and its relationship with industry. During the period that has been examined, and indeed during the wider period from the late 1950s to the election in February 1974, successive governments have shown that they have not been interested in ownership and control. They have aimed to further their ends by seeking to influence private sector decision-making, occasionally by direct intervention.

The case studies throughout this book have shown that the injection of public funds into a private company solves nothing by itself. *Whitehall has gradually come to appreciate the importance of monitoring during the life of a project.* It has been very much the case of learning from experience.[3] Several methods of monitoring have been devised and each has its advantages and disadvantages.[4] The first possibility is that the organisation responsible for the appraisal of the individual project – be it a government department or a para-government agency like the IRC or SIB – receives regular progress reports from the company concerned. The second is the appointment of a government director to the board of the company. The third is an equity holding in the company which is often associated with the appointment of a government director. This must be distinguished from nationalisation of an individual company. When the government has holdings, varying between 10.5 per cent of the equity in ICL and (up to 1975) 48.6 per cent in British Petroleum, the model remains that of a private sector company which is much more independent of Whitehall than a wholly nationalised company like Rolls Royce. The fourth means of monitoring projects is a combination of these, and often in the case of a major government involvement includes the development of informal links between Whitehall and the chief executive of the firm. The situation is made more difficult by the inadequacy of a firm's internal financial control mechanisms, as the Rolls case showed, and by the delay, and perhaps secrecy over the passing of information to Whitehall, as seemed to occur at the end of 1970 in the UCS case. The test of any method of monitoring is whether it can uncover unpromising developments, but even that is of no consequence unless the government or its agent is prepared to take remedial action of the kind described in Chapter 7. In the last resort the success of selective financial intervention is dependent on a readiness on the part of government to act if things go wrong.

Experience of the period that has been studied has shown that in this context not only is the machinery for project appraisal of vital importance, but the *machinery for monitoring and follow-up* is of even greater importance. Chapter 14 argued that there has been a growing reliance on recruiting outsiders to help handle these problems from the government's side. Project appraisal can be done within a department, in which case there is greater accountability to Parliament, but there is the danger that those constraints within a government's control will bring uncommercial ingredients into the situation. This is less likely to happen if the project appraisal is done by an independent agency like the IRC. This was shown for example in the case of UCS where MinTech made finance available to the company after the SIB had refused it. The disadvantages of the outside agency, however, are that the independence which is essential if it is to operate commercially means that it is less accountable to Parliament, and that there are problems of co-ordinating such a body into the wider framework of Whitehall and government policy as a whole. An outside agency is much more likely to be independent if it is financially independent. The IRC case-study also showed how Whitehall took advantage of the fact that an independent agency could operate, as in the Cammell Laird case at greater speed than a department, while retaining its commercial approach. On the basis of the limited evidence of the case studies it seems, despite the IRC's mixed record in this field, that an outside agency is better placed than a department when it comes to conducting a follow-up operation, and being prepared to take remedial action. Broadly speaking, the choice seems to lie between the greater accountability of a government department and the more commercial approach of an independent outside agency.

Whatever form of organisation is chosen to handle the tasks it seems clear that the usefulness of an *ad hoc* committee is limited. Lord Plowden, who chaired the committee enquiring into the aircraft industry in 1965-66 has underlined the factors that handicap such an approach.

> I should now like to touch on the whole question of how problems such as the one put to our Committee should be dealt with. I do not think that an *ad hoc* Committee such as ours is the right way. The members of our Committee were largely ignorant of the industry when we were appointed. This was deliberate. We were chosen as a 'Jury' – a body of men without preconceptions or already fixed positions on the subjects we were investigating. We were extremely short of time and pressed against our better judgement to report in less than a year after we were appointed.

> This meant that most of our time was absorbed by taking evidence and learning the basic facts. Even two more months would probably have doubled our "thinking" time, and the paradox is that, just as we were reaching some understanding of the problems of the industry, we finished our report and the Committee disbanded. The expertise, so painstakingly and expensively acquired, is unlikely ever to be used again.[5]

This emphasises one of the great advantages of an independent organisation or a specialist unit within a department. Such bodies accumulate experience as they go along, and will take advantage of the lessons they learn.

A variety of suggestions as to the best form of machinery for project appraisal and monitoring have been put forward.[6] Possibly the most important is that monitoring should be conducted by a different organisation from that which was responsible for the project which has been appraised.[7] The attraction of this suggestion is that the whole area of monitoring projects has emerged as being the key to the successful use of public funds in the private sector. However effective the project appraisal is, this is useless if things subsequently go wrong and this is not spotted. Because it is an emerging problem, Whitehall's experience of dealing with it is obviously limited. The great advantage of a specialist unit to handle all, or at least most, monitoring of projects would be that it would quickly accumulate experience in a difficult area, as the IRC did, and bring this to bear across the whole range of the firms with which it was dealing. It has been suggested that it should be located in the Treasury.[8] However, as an organisation handling this problem would need to have a strictly commercial approach, its effectiveness might well be the greater if it was removed from Whitehall and established as a fully independent agency. Then there would be no chance of any political interference, and no possibility of any of the constraints that are within the government's control allowing un-commercial influences to be brought to bear. If ministers subsequently wanted to introduce non-economic criteria as for example with the social reasons for supporting shipbuilding, then this could be made quite clear as a separate issue and not incorporated into the actual monitoring process. In the past nobody has really known whether to expect that such a company will need to be subsidised continually or will actually become self-supporting.

The only other really outstanding factor in the field of the machinery for project appraisal and monitoring is that it is as yet unclear from empirical evidence whether an independent agency, subject like a nationalised corporation to ministerial directive, could in practice win the trust of industry, adopt a strictly commercial approach, and because it was closer to the Minister be seen to be accountable to Parliament.

Analysis of the period that has been examined has shown how government's attempts to get firms to behave in new ways has led them to become involved with the affairs of a firm *on a continuing basis.* This has happened when the search for influence has led to a government or its agent becoming financially involved. It has been shown how the IRC came to appreciate that there was no point putting money into firms and leaving them to their own devices. If maximum use was to be made of public funds, monitoring procedures had to be developed, and the Corporation realised that if necessary it had to be ready to act to safeguard its funds. It had to be prepared, as in the Kent case, to use the influence gained through being financially involved, to take strategic decisions, and if necessary, to change the management. The case-studies of Rolls and UCS show how weak the monitoring of the use of public funds was. Weaknesses within the companies which subsequently contributed to the crisis were allowed to develop without any action – as opposed to analysis – being initiated by Whitehall. It has been pointed out that the monitoring of its financial involvement becomes much more complicated for government in those industries where it is not just providing financial and other support, but is also purchasing some or all of the end product.[9] This is the case for example when the government or public sector organisations purchase civilian and defence aircraft, ships for the Royal Navy, computers, machine tools, and power stations.

Analysis of the period that has been studied clearly shows that monitoring and follow-up are vital to the success of the use of public funds in the private sector. It has become clear that when government becomes involved financially in the private sector in practice it does so on an ongoing basis in a developing situation. Relying on being only passively involved does not guarantee that the project will be successful. During the decade following the establishment of MinTech, Whitehall departments became steadily more ready to intervene in industry, and to discriminate between firms within industry. The basic outlook of the DTI was far removed from that of the Board of Trade in the early 1960s. Yet Whitehall has been slow to come to terms with the implications of intervening on a discriminatory basis. It has found it hard to accept that the act of intervention could never be an end in itself, that *in the last resort intervening took it into the whole area of internal management of a company.* This is because if things go wrong with the project, government has to be prepared to accept the consequences of its involvement and *to take remedial action,* if necessary over-ruling the independence of the firm.

Yet this runs completely counter to one of the fundamental features of the mixed economy as it has developed in Britain during the period that has been studied. Chapter 14 showed how the expansion of the nationalised industries has been limited, and how successive governments have sought to work within the context of a mixed economy based mainly on a large private sector within a system of state-supported capitalism. The basic unit of this system has been the individual firm which has been independent of government and, for the most part, has not been owned wholly, or in part, by governments. The aim of government policy has been to strengthen the performance of individual firms so that they would be able to compete in international markets and make a contribution towards the solution of the basic economic and industrial problems facing the country. To be successful in the government's eyes firms have had to compete with others, and to do this they have had to be commercially independent. *The policies of successive governments have thus been based not just on maintaining the commercial independence of the individual firm, but on exploiting it,* because a strong independent firm run along commercial lines will have more chance of standing up to world competition and exploiting market forces to its own advantage for the benefit of itself and the British economy. Sir Richard Clarke has described "the company's independence and ability to carry out its business with other customers at home and abroad" as "the decisive characteristic which justifies supporting the company as a long-term national asset."[10] Another Permanent Secretary has argued that monitoring arrangements:

> Must not be such as to remove the prime responsibility and main focus of initiative from the board of the company. That may sometimes be quite a difficult balance to hold, but it is very important that it should be held.[11]

It seems that there has been a fundamental conflict of objectives underlying the industrial policy of successive governments. On the one hand governments base their policies on the commercial independence of the firm. On the other, however, they have found that the systems of project appraisal that have been developed do not by themselves lead to the successful conclusion of a scheme in which the government is financially involved. Governments have found that their involvement is continuous and that they cannot avoid the need to be ready to intervene in the internal affairs of an individual company, thus breaking down its commercial independence. Governments thus face an appalling dilemma. *They rely on the commercial and managerial independence of the firm to help achieve their broad ends. yet bitter experience has shown independent private sector firms cannot be relied on to complete projects partly sponsored by the government.* The situation is made more difficult by the fact that in the case of some companies the process of extracting finance from government becomes an end in itself, and this undermines the commercial and managerial independence of the firm.

> Once the company begins to determine its policy by what it has to do in order to continue to get money from government, its national value in the widest sense is already beginning to disappear . . . There are companies at various stages in this insidious process.[12]

Apart from the need to be ready to be active in a follow-up situation, there is a second problem area which Whitehall has been reluctant to come to terms with during the 1960s and early 1970s. The discussion just above has referred to Whitehall having to be concerned with the management of the firms with which it has become financially involved. However governments cannot avoid being concerned with the performance of management on a wider scale. If major manufacturing companies are being run inefficiently, then there will be a misuse of resources and a wasteful use of assets. This will mean that the companies concerned will be undermining the government's industrial and economic strategy and industry's capacity to help solve the basic underlying problems that have been discussed. The way in which the IRC sought to rescue firms from their own inefficient managers has been outlined in Chapter 4. This has been a preoccupation of successive governments, but they have been unwilling to act themselves. After the abolition of the IRC, Davies sought to persuade the institutional shareholders in the City to become more actively involved with monitoring the performance of management in companies in which they had large holdings, with a view to being ready to take remedial action, by for example changing the management.[13] Institutional shareholders are in a special position in that their large holdings make it impossible for them to sell the shares of the company of which they have come to disapprove because they cannot sell out. If they did the market price would fall so quickly that their losses would be intolerable. The Governor of the Bank of England sought to establish a 'ginger group' of institutional shareholders as a first step towards this end. It was originally intended to establish a strong formal organisation with its own secretariat, but opposition within the City ensured that the Institutional Shareholders Committee that emerged in April 1973 was much weaker than had been originally envisaged.[14] If this organisation is judged by Whitehall to be ineffective then it may be that a future government will accept responsibility for this area and seek to act itself in the way that the IRC did.

The very real independence of the firm is at the root of these problems, making government's task even more difficult. It has been argued in this chapter that governments have sought to encourage the commercial and managerial independence of the firm, and to base their policies on it. However it is important to draw out at this point the separate but related theme of the ability of the private sector firm to retain its autonomy over its strategic decision-making and to take no notice of government's attempts to persuade it to act in new ways. This theme has recurred throughout this book. Chapter 3 for example showed how the individual firm has no need to react to measures of encouragement, and how it is completely free to ignore all the advisory services and financial inducements provided by government in an attempt to stimulate it into behaving in new ways. It was argued in Chapter 16 that the independence of the firm was a very real constraint on the ability of government to implement the policies it wanted to. Chapter 7 illustrated this in the context of the IRC's work.

It is important to note again at this stage the *few* occasions when the firm's autonomy is broken down. It has been shown how only on very rare occasions has the government been prepared to go to the extent of overriding the wishes of the firm and forcing it to act against its will. In a case like RHP or Kent, where the national interest was seen to be so overriding, the IRC was prepared to take the consequences of acting decisively. On the other hand it took the view that while it was important for Simon Engineering to merge with another big firm, it was not of such critical importance that it was ready to override Simon's opposition to the whole idea.[15] The firm's autonomy is also eroded when a liquidity crisis removes, as in the UCS, Cammell Laird, and Rolls Royce cases, a firm's ability to be financially self-sufficient, and effectively the basis of its remaining independence. In addition there can be a partial loss of autonomy as in the case for example of some IRC 'catalyst' mergers and many development contracts. In such a case the firm is often ready to accept through the monitoring process a limited loss of autonomy because it can treat intervention as a resource which, through the opening of new opportunities expands its freedom of action.. *Yet the overall result of the ability of most firms to maintain their independence is that they can frustrate the achievement of the aims of government industrial policy.*

Governments have thus based industrial policy on the concept of the private enterprise firm that was basically financially and managerially independent. Governments have sought to work through the private sector because the aims of the firm and of the government were thought to coincide. They have argued that their aims of increased productivity and exports meant expansion and more profits for the firm. However, this problem has to be examined from the firm's rather than from the government's standpoint as well. While it may appear to the government that re-equipment means increased productivity, to the firm it means extra expenditure. Similarly, exporting can be a hazardous venture into the unknown especially if it means ceasing to rely on tried and safe markets. From the firm's point of view the danger of expanding production is that there will be too much overcapacity to carry when orders fall off as the economic cycle dips. It is often 'safer' for the firm to turn down orders when demand is high letting them go to other firms or be fulfilled through imports. When demand falls again the more limited orders will mean that a factory can tick over at perhaps 80 per cent of its productive capacity. However expanding the factory when demand is high can mean being faced with substantial losses when orders fall off, because perhaps as little as 60 per cent of capacity will then be fully utilised. Firms also tend to be suspicious of taking a course of action urged on them by government. They fear that once government has begun to influence their decision-making and got a foot in the door it will seek, as the IRC in fact did, to use the influence gained within the firm itself. In 1973 for example Peter Walker, the Secretary of State for Trade and Industry, attempted to persuade heavy engineering firms to expand their capacity in order to deal with the increased orders for steel plant that were available as a result of the BSC expansion programme. The government was anxious lest these orders would go abroad and thus lead to increased imports. However the firms

> were wary of accepting special help offered under the Industry Act, even though they need new machine tools and the like, in order not to be vulnerable to government-prodded rationalisation schemes.[16]

Thus a situation has emerged in which government seeks to work through the private sector because it sees its aims and the firm's aims as being similar, *but in practice there are many instances where the two are poles apart.* This means that basing industrial policy and the relationship between government and industry on the principle of consent, and relying mainly on persuasion and cajolery will not always achieve the government's end, because the independence and autonomy of the firm enables it to resist government's attempts to influence its decision-making. The reluctance that governments show to overrule the wishes of the firm, as for example in a takeover or follow-up situation, means that basic economic problems continue to exist because the independence of the firm frustrates the implementation of policy and its impact on the basic problems. It is *the search for means of bringing government influence to bear on the firm that do not involve the firm losing its commercial independence,* that has been at the heart of British industrial policy between the late 1950s and the election in February 1974.

This analysis of the evolution of British industrial policy has uncovered a *circular process*. Since the late 1950s, and increasingly thereafter, successive governments have faced an amalgam of complex pressures on the economic and industrial fronts. Each successive government has found these pressures to be irresistible, and the results have been that each has developed a steadily widening variety of detailed, often interventionist, policies designed to help solve the basic problems facing the economy. However, when acting, successive governments have encountered a series of practical problems and constraints on their ability to implement the policies, that from a strictly commercial standpoint make the most sense. The result has been that the impact of industrial policy has been erratic. A by-product of these more detailed policies has been, as described in Chapter 14, greater uncertainty for individual firms. This has also contributed to the erratic impact of economic and industrial policy, and to the continued existence of the basic problems. The wheel thus comes full circle. Facing the continued existence of fundamental economic and industrial problems leads governments to ask whether intervention is inherently wrong and damaging. However, the ongoing need to solve pressing problems, and the lack of proven alternative strategies, has led them to conclude their policy reappraisal by arguing not that detailed, often interventionist policies are wrong, but that they have been practised in the wrong way. The result is increasingly detailed policy-making and a new search for means of bringing the public interest, as represented by the government, to bear on decision-making at the firm level.

Breaking out of this circle will depend on a new answer being found to either of the two fundamental questions that arise during a policy reappraisal. Will a way be found to nationalise in such a manner as to maintain the advantages of flexibility, managerial independence, and so on, that governments have argued make it advantageous to work through the private sector? It was this search that led the Labour Party to examine European, and particularly Italian experience whilst in opposition in the early 1970s. The argument that developed[17] was that the performance of the private sector and the limited impact of bodies like the IRC showed clearly that the private sector could not be relied on to further government aims. It was argued that the issue was not ownership as an end in itself, but finding a means of bringing government influence to bear on the firm. In the last resort this could only be done if the government was effectively in control because attempts at persuasion and cajolery had failed. It was thus argued that the only certain means of bringing the public interest, as represented by government, to bear on the decision-making of private firms was to bring them under greater control.

Alternatively will the government find more effective ways of intervening in the private sector, of bringing its influence to bear on decision-making at the firm level in the context of the mixed economy as it has developed? In particular will a way be found around the dilemma of increasing government influence within the firm, especially during the process of conducting monitoring operations and taking remedial action, while at the same time maintaining the commercial independence of the firm on which policy has been based? If governments are to adopt this approach it is only by solving this problem that detailed, often interventionist, policies will be able to make a substantial impact on the basic underlying economic and industrial problems that intervention seeks to reduce if not remove.

NOTES

Chapter 1

1. For a useful survey of the growth of intervention see A. Skuse, *Government Intervention and Industrial Policy,* 2nd edition, Heinemann, London, 1972. Seven of the nine chapters deal with the development of intervention to 1962. For the earliest developments see Sir John Clapham, *A Concise Economic History of Britain,* Cambridge University Press, 1957, Chapters I and II; and M.W. Thomas (ed.), *A Survey of English Economic History,* 2nd edition, Blackie and Sons, London, 1960, Part I.
2. Skuse, ibid., p.10.
3. P. Deane, *The First Industrial Revolution,* Cambridge University Press, 1965, p.219. See also A. Redford, *The Economic History of England 1760-1860,* 2nd edition, Longmans, London, 1960.
4. Skuse, op. cit., p.17.
5. Ibid.
6. See for example J.W. Grove, *Government and Industry in Britain,* Longmans, London, 1962, Chapters 1 and 2; and Skuse, op. cit., Chapters 3 and 4.
7. Skuse, op. cit., p.32.
8. Grove, op. cit., p.61. For other books on the period 1939-51 see Grove's bibliography.
9. See M. Sanderson, *Universities and British Industry 1850-1970,* Routledge & Kegan Paul, London, 1972, Chapters 8 and 12.
10. Grove, op. cit., Chapters 6-9.
11. Ibid., Chapters 11 and pp.248-50; and G. McCrone, *Regional Policy in Britain,* Allen and Unwin, London, 1969, Chapter 4.
12. Grove, ibid., p.257. See also pp.245-59, and 307-19; and K. Hartley, 'UK Military Aircraft Market' *Yorkshire Bulletin of Economic and Social Research,* May 1967, pp.15-36.
13. See for example A. Shonfield, *Modern Capitalism,* Oxford University Press, 1965, pp.102-12 and 171-5; and G. Denton, M. Forsyth, and M. MacLennan, *Economic Planning and Policies in Britain, France and Germany,* Allen & Unwin, London, 1968, pp.108-17.
14. *The North-East: A Programme for Development and Growth,* Cmnd 2206, 1963; *Central Scotland: A Programme for Development and Growth,* Cmnd 2188, 1963; and *The South-East Study 1961-81,* HMSO, 1964.
15. See *The Economist,* 14 December 1963, pp.1187-8; the DSIR Annual Reports, Cmnd 2027 and 2394; and 1963 Report of the National Physical Laboratory, pp.66 and 77; and the 1964 Report, pp.84 ff; and the 1963 Warren Spring Laboratory Report, pp.24-5. See also 699, HC Debs. cols 260-2 (WA).
16. S. Brittain, *Steering The Economy,* 2nd edition, Penguin, Harmondsworth, 1971, p.290.

17. See *Board of Trade Journal,* 24 April 1964, p.893. The Mitchell Report was *The Machine Tool Industry – A Report by the Sub-Committee of the Machine Tool Advisory Council appointed to consider Professor Melman's Report to the European Productivity Agency,* HMSO, 1960.

Chapter 2

1. See Chapter 15.
2. The problem of defining 'the firm' is a complex one. For a useful discussion see A. Beacham and W.J. Cunningham, *Economics of Industrial Organisation,* 5th edition, Pitman, London, 1970, pp.2ff. Throughout this book when the phrase occurs the main consideration has been the location of decision-making authority on strategic as opposed to day-to-day issues. The phrase thus basically refers to what Beacham and Cunningham call the 'economic firm'.
3. See for example M. Posner, 'Policy towards nationalised industries', in W. Beckerman (ed.), *The Labour Government's Economic Record: 1964-70,* Duckworth, London, 1972.
4. See for example *New Technology,* April 1969, pp.1-2.
5. Sir Richard Clarke, 'MinTech in Retrospect', *Omega,* Vol. 1, No. 2, p.147. Part I is in Vol. 1, No. 1, pp.25-38, and Part II in Vol. 1, No. 2, pp.137-63.
6. *Production Engineer,* July 1969, pp.289-90.
7. See letter from NEL's Director in *The Economist,* 3 August 1968. NC has been an important development. On a conventional tool 85% of the time it takes to complete each machining operation is taken up with adjusting the machine and positioning the workpiece. With NC machines detailed instructions are put on magnetic tape by a computer. Once connected an NC machine follows the instructions on the tape.
8. R. Bailey, *Managing the British Economy,* Hutchinson, London, 1968, has a complete list of EDCs, including dates of formation, in Appendix III. For details of these reports see *Neddy in Print,* published quarterly by NEDO.
9. *Market – The World,* NEDO 1968. See also editorial in *The Times* (Business Section), 5 August 1968.
10. Distributive Trades EDC. See its General Report 1969-70, NEDO, 1970, pp.5 and 10.
11. For a brief résumé see the *EDC Activity Reports* published spasmodically by NEDO from 1966.
12. *Action on Banwell,* Building EDC, May 1967; and *Contracting in Civil Engineering since Banwell,* Civil Engineering EDC, November 1968. The Conference was held in London by the Civil Engineering EDC and the Institute of Municipal Engineers on 25 June 1969.
13. These are subsequently often referred to below as "advisory services".
14. See respectively *New Technology,* March 1968, pp.5-6, and March 1969, pp.4-5. On government research establishments and research associations see *The Report of the Committee of Enquiry*

into the Research Associations (Bessborough Report), published by the Conference of Industrial Research Associations, April 1973. In addition see *The Ministry of Technology, 1964-9,* published by MinTech (Blue Book) paras.68-112.

15. *New Technology,* March 1969, pp.3 and 6.
16. Ibid., February 1969, p.3.
17. Ibid., March 1969, p.5.
18. Ibid., January 1967, p.3; and October 1970, pp.1-2.
19. Ibid., August 1969, pp.1-2.
20. Ibid., May 1967, pp.1-2.
21. Ibid., March 1967, pp.1-2.
22. Ibid., November 1969, p.3.
23. To fully appreciate the range of technical information and other services available from government organisations by the time the Labour Government had left office see *Technical Services for Industry,* DTI, 1970.
24. About seventy were established. See *New Technology,* November 1968, pp.2-3.
25. For a summary see E. Lubbock, 'Government Support for the Hardware Industry, in E. Moonman (ed.), *British Computers and Industrial Innovation,* Allen & Unwin, London, 1971, pp.1-14.
26. Report of the Committee of Inquiry into the Aircraft Industry, Cmnd 2853, December 1965. For an assessment of its impact on the relationship between the Government and the industry see A. Reed, *Britain's Aircraft Industry,* Dent, London, 1973, Chapter 5.
27. *Report of the Committee of Inquiry into the Shipbuilding Industry,* Cmnd 2937, 1966. Details of the SIB's work are to be found in its annual reports.
28. Op. cit., MinTech Blue Book, paras.26-7 and 83.
29. See *The Economist,* 16 December 1967 and 11 May 1968; and *Production Engineer,* June 1969, pp.241-2.
30. See for example W. Plowden, 'MinTech Moves On', *New Society,* 12 January 1967; and articles by Sir Richard Clarke: 'The Structure of MinTech', *New Technology,* February 1968; 'The Shape of the New MinTech', *Financial Times,* 17 November 1969; and op. cit., *Omega.*
31. Ibid., *Omega,* p.144.
32. Quoted by G. Turner, *Business in Britain,* 2nd edition, Penguin, Harmondsworth, 1971, p.70.
33. See *The Economist,* 16 December 1967, p.1169.

Chapter 3

1. See Chapter 7, note 9.
2. Op. cit., W. Beckerman (ed.), p.182.
3. H. Wilson, *Purpose in Power,* Weidenfeld and Nicolson, London, 1966, p.52.
4. H. Wilson, *The Labour Government 1964-70,* Weidenfeld and Nicolson and Michael Joseph, London, 1971, p.712.
5. See J. Bray, *Decision in Government,* Gollancz, London, 1970, pp.155-62.

6. See Chapter 2.
7. *New Technology,* July 1967, pp.1-3.
8. S. Brittan, op. cit., p.186 (first edition).
9. M. Shanks, 'The Irregular in Whitehall', pp.244-62, in P. Streeten (ed.), *Unfashionable Economics: Essays in Honour of Lord Balogh,* Weidenfeld & Nicolson, London, 1970, pp.251-2.
10. The Industrial Reorganisation Corporation, Cmnd 2889, 1966, para.2.
11. Quoted by Sir K. Joseph, 765, HC Debs. col. 1595.
12. See Chapter 9.

Chapter 4

1. IRC Act, Section 2(1).
2. Op. cit., Cmnd 2889, para.3. See also The 1965 National Plan, Cmnd 2764, Chapter 1, para.17, and Chapter 4, para.21; and the speech on the Second Reading of the IRC Bill by the Secretary of State for Economic Affairs, Michael Stewart, 734 HC Debs. cols. 218-30.
3. IRC White Paper, para.2.
4. IRC Act, section 2(2).
5. M.E. Beesley and G.M. White, 'The Industrial Reorganisation Corporation: A Study in Choice of Public Management', *Public Administration,* Vol. 51, Spring 1973, pp.69-70.
6. IRC Act, Section 2(3).
7. See for example Expenditure Committee, 6th Report from the Trade and Industry Sub-Committee, *Public Money in the Private Sector,* HC 347 of 1971-2, the evidence of Grierson and Roll (e.g. Qs 1251, 1252, 1261, and 1262); and Wedgwood Benn 757 HC Debs. col. 1581. Beesley's and White's own researches have led them to a similar conclusion – Beesley and White, op. cit., p.68.
8. Industrial Reorganisation Corporation Report and Accounts for the year ended 31 March 1969, HC 286 of 1968-9, p.7. (This Report is subsequently referred to as IRC Report for 1968-9.)
9. To assist the reader a Diary of the Main IRC Projects has been included as an Appendix. In order to facilitate the tracing of references, the principal ones dealing with each project have been included in the Diary, and not scattered through the text in footnotes.
10. Industrial Reorganisation Corporation, Report and Accounts (December 1966 – March 1968), HC 252 of 1967-8, p.5. (This Report is subsequently referred to as IRC Report for 1967-8.) See also *Guardian,* 25 October 1966, and 5 January 1967.
11. IRC Report for 1967-8, p.5.
12. William Davis, *Three Years Hard Labour,* Andre Deutsch, London, 1968, pp.53-4.
13. Sir Joseph Latham, *Takeover,* Iliffe, London, 1969, pp.59-61; and R. Jones and O. Marriott, *Anatomy of a Merger,* Jonathan Cape, London, 1970, pp.268-9.
14. See footnote 9 above with regard to references on this project.
15. See the first section of Chapter 9.
16. HC 347 of 1971-2, op. cit., note, p.262.

17. Ibid., Q 1261. With regard to Grierson's resignation see also *The Times*, 28 October 1967, 29 January 1968 and 28 October 1968; *Guardian*, 28 October 1967, and 30 October 1967, *London Evening News*, 30 January 1968; and R. Grierson, 'The Curse of Gimmickry', *Spectator*, 10 November 1967, p.566.
18. IRC Report for 1967-8, pp.10-11.
19. Ibid. The Nuclear Enterprises merger is an example.
20. IRC Report for 1968-9, p.9.
21. See *The Times*, 3 November 1967.
22. IRC Report for 1968-9, p.6.
23. British United Trawlers and Plessey Numerical Control appear clear examples.
24. Respective examples would be Rowntree/Mackintosh, and Clarke Chapman/John Thompson.
25. Respective examples would be Studebaker-Worthington/ Worthington-Simpson; and the creation of the International Compressed Air Corporation.
26. See the second section of Chapter 9.
27. See the second section of Chapter 6.
28. W.G. McClelland, *The Industrial Reorganisation Corporation 1966/71; An Experimental Prod*, pamphlet published by The Manchester Statistical Society, 1972, p.3. This was also published as an article in *Three Banks Review*, June 1972, pp.32-42. Beesley and White, op.cit., have succinctly summed this up: 'The Corporation attempted to rescue companies from their inefficient management,' p.80.
29. Industrial Reorganisation Corporation, Report and Accounts for the year ended 31 March 1970, HC 310 of 1969-70, p.6. (This Report is subsequently referred to as IRC Report for 1969-70.)
30. Ibid., p.7.
31. Alistair Morton, 'IRC: In Memoriam', *Crossbow*, January-March 1971, p.36.
32. See IRC Report for 1969-70, pp.6-7. See also *Sunday Times*, 24 May 1970.
33. IRC Report for 1968-9, p.9.
34. IRC Report for 1967-8, p.11.
35. A.K. Panni, 'Friend, Foe – or Catalyst?', *Business Management*, April 1969, pp.36-9.
36. HC 347 of 1971-2, op. cit., "It became apparent that the restructuring role was becoming largely completed." Villiers Q1807.
37. See IRC Report for 1967-8, pp.17-21; IRC Report for 1968-9, pp.23-30, IRC Report for 1969-70, pp.23-32; and Industrial Reorganisation Corporation, Report and Accounts covering the period 1 April 1970 to 30 April 1971, HC 443 of 1970-1, pp.18-24. (The last mentioned report is subsequently referred to as IRC Report for 1970-1.)
38. E.g. company law reform, and the ways in which taxation inhibits investment. See IRC Report for 1970-1, pp.9-10.
39. IRC Report for 1970-1, pp.14, and 37-8, and Roger Williams, *European Technology*, Croom Helm, London, 1973, pp.28-9.

40. Peter Wilsher, *Sunday Times*, 23 June 1968.
41. Alistair Morton, op. cit.

Chapter 5

1. 723 HC Debs. col 55. See also George Brown, *In My Way*, Penguin Books, Harmondsworth, 1972, p.94.
2. *The Times*, 5 May 1966.
3. McClelland, op.cit., p.13. This was his self-description.
4. *The Economist*, 7 May 1966, p.615.
5. Brown, op. cit., p.96.
6. See *Sunday Times*, 23 June 1968.
7. See *The Times*, 1 February 1968.
8. See *Guardian*, 30 October 1967; *The Times*, 21 December 1967 and 1 February 1968.
9. IRC Report for 1969-70, p.15.
10. See IRC Report for 1968-9, pp.15-16; *The Times*, 21 December 1968 and 25 January 1969. The 'exclusion' point is discussed towards the end of this chapter.
11. For details of Wheeler's resignation see *The Times* and *Guardian*, 28 October 1967, and R. Jones and O. Marriott, op. cit., pp.274, 276 and 279.
12. *The Times*, 29 April 1969.
13. See for example *Sunday Times*, 23 June 1968.
14. Quoted in *Sunday Times*, 16 February 1969.
15. See IRC Reports for 1967-8, p.16; 1968-9, p.21; 1969-70, p.20; and 1970-1, p.14.
16. There are details on the executives in *Guardian*, 25 October 1966; *Financial Times*, 16 November 1967; *Sunday Times*, 23 June 1968 and 16 February 1969; and in *The Times* (Business News Diary section), 9 June, 27 August, 8 September, and 7 and 28 October 1970, and 28 March 1972.
17. Quoted by G. Turner, op. cit., p.76.
18. See for example McClelland, op. cit., p.13.
19. Article by Villiers in *The Times*, 22 May 1970 (Finance for Industry Supplement).
20. A. Sampson, *The New Anatomy of Britain*, Hodder and Stoughton, London, 1971, pp.573-6. For example, "Villiers was convinced that Britain's economic situation was desperate, and something had to be done about it very quickly. He liked to bring industrialists into the lunch room and lecture them briskly about the appalling state of their industry." See also IRC Reports for 1968-9, pp.7, and 16-17; for 1969-70, pp.5 and 15-16. Finally see B.R. Cant, 'The Role of the IRC in Promoting Structural Change' in B.W. Denning (ed.), *Corporate Long Range Planning*, Longmans, London, 1969, pp.41-3.
21. For the details in this section see IRC Reports for 1967-8, pp.13-16; 1968-9, pp.18-22; 1969-70, pp.18-22; and 1970-1, pp.12-17. McClelland, op.cit., pp.17-18, has assembled two summary tables from IRC's accounts.
22. This excludes a figure of £185,000 which the IRC paid "in

connection with a disputed valuation of a business and with a merger that was not implemented" (IRC Report for 1970-1, p.14, note 5.) Although it has been excluded here to show IRC's normal running costs, the possibility of similar non-recurring items escalating the costs remained.

23. Cf. A. Fels, *The British Prices and Incomes Board,* Cambridge University Press, 1972, p.59.
24. IRC Reports for 1969-70 and 1970-1, pp.31 and 24 respectively.
25. Beesley and White, op. cit., p.74.
26. McClelland, op. cit., p.6.
27. IRC Report for 1968-9, p.8.
28. McClelland, op. cit., p.6.
29. Ibid.
30. Beesley and White, op. cit., p.79.
31. Ibid., p.78.
32. IRC Report for 1968-9, p.8. On the role of the Board and executives generally see also *Sunday Times,* 23 June 1968, and 16 February 1969; McClelland, op. cit., p.13; Beesley and White, op. cit., pp.78-80; and D. Smith, 'What the IRC wrought', *Management Today,* October 1969, p.90.
33. IRC Report for 1968-9, p.8.
34. McClelland, op. cit., p.13.
35. *Sunday Times,* 16 February 1969.
36. Ibid.
37. McClelland, op. cit., p.13.
38. Quoted in G. Turner, op. cit., p.76.
39. D. Smith, op. cit.
40. IRC Report for 1967-8, p.17.
41. G. Turner, op. cit., p.77.
42. See IRC Reports for 1967-8, p.16; 1968-9, p.22; 1969-70, p.20; and 1970-1, p.14.
43. 786 HC Debs. col 43, and 787, HC Debs. col 1509; and IRC Report for 1970-1, pp.9-10.
44. See R. Jones and O. Marriott, op. cit., p.268; and G. Turner, *The Leyland Papers,* Eyre and Spottiswoode, London, 1971, pp.114-5.
45. Cant, op. cit., p.148.
46. McClelland, op. cit., pp.13-14.
47. Beesley and White, op. cit., p.76.
48. *Sunday Times,* 16 February 1969.

Chapter 6

1. Almost everything that was written by (or about) the IRC discusses the criteria it sought to use. See for example IRC Reports for 1967-8, pp.6-7; for 1968-9, pp.7-9; and 1969-70, pp.5-7.
2. IRC Report for 1969-70, p.6.
3. Sir Leon Bagritt, Chairman of Elliot Automation (in the context of the EE/EA merger), quoted in *Observer,* 25 June 1967.
4. McClelland, op. cit., p.16.
5. IRC Report for 1969-70, p.11.

6. *Guardian,* 31 March 1971, Supplement on ballbearings.
7. IRC Report for 1969-70, p.7.
8. G. Turner, op. cit., *Business in Britain,* p.77.
9. See respectively pp.7, 8, and see also 810, HC Debs. cols 368-9.
10. IRC Report for 1967-8, p.8.
11. *Observer,* 25 June 1967.
12. *The Economist,* 24 June 1967, p.1376.
13. IRC Report for 1967-8, p.8.
14. Ibid.
15. *Sunday Times,* 1 October 1967. Reyrolle and Parsons merged in May 1968, and even before Plessey's bid for EE precipitated the GEC/EE merger, these two companies had discussed the possibility of an eventual link. Reyrolle Parsons merged with Bruce Peebles in March 1969.
16. *The Times,* 21 October 1967.
17. *Sunday Times,* 1 October 1967.
18. *Financial Times,* 10 May 1968.
19. IRC Report for 1968-9, p.8.
20. See for example Section 2(3) of the IRC Act.
21. On IRC finance see McClelland, op. cit., and Villiers in *The Times,* 22 May 1970. The information in this section basically comes from IRC Reports as follows: 1967-8, pp.17-23; 1968-9, pp.20-21, 23-30 and 39; 1969-70, pp.17, 21-32 and 39; and 1970-1, pp.11, 15-16, and 18-26.
22. McClelland, op. cit., pp.9-10.
23. G. Turner, op. cit., *The Leyland Papers,* p.197.
24. McClelland, op. cit., p.10.
25. HC 347 of 1971-2, op. cit., Q.976.
26. Rootes, Reed, Dixon, Samuel Osborn, and Herbert Ingersoll. The 2(1)(b) Clause was also used in the case of Rolls Royce and Kearney and Trecker which are described below.
27. IRC Report for 1970-1, p.20.
28. IRC Report for 1969-70, p.9.
29. See IRC Report for 1968-9, p.9.
30. The link between the Brown Bayley and RHP cases is described in the IRC Report for 1969-70, pp.21 and 24.
31. IRC Report for 1969-70, p.8.
32. Cmnd 2889, op. cit., para.9.
33. McClelland, op. cit., pp.2-3.
34. IRC Report for 1967-8, p.7.
35. IRC Report for 1969-70, p.7.
36. Ibid., p.7.
37. IRC Report for 1968-9, p.9.
38. E.g. IRC Report for 1967-8, p.7.
39. Ibid., p.8.
40. On the IRI see S. Holland (ed.), *The State as Entrepreneur,* Weidenfeld and Nicolson, London, 1972. The IRC represented a fusion of several ideas of which the IRI was one.
41. IRC Report for 1968-9, p.9.
42. IRC Report for 1969-70, p.14.
43. McClelland, op. cit., p.2.

Chapter 7

1. McClelland, op. cit., p.8. The next three paragraphs draw heavily from pp.8-12, with some variations.
2. Ibid.
3. IRC Report for 1967-8, p.12
4. McClelland, op.cit., p.10. With regard to loans and minority equity holdings see Chapter 6.
5. *The Times,* 6 November 1967
6. McClelland, op. cit., p.9.
7. Ibid., p.11.
8. IRC Report for 1968-9, p.33.
9. G. Turner, op. cit., *The Leyland Papers,* pp.83-7, 117, 120-2, 141, and 143.
10. See IRC Report for 1968-9, p.9, where a similar phrase is used.
11. McClelland, op. cit., p.9.
12. IRC Report for 1968-9, p.11.
13. See IRC Reports for 1967-8, p.9; and for 1968-9, p.13.
14. IRC Report for 1969-70, p.12.
15. IRC Report for 1968-9, p.15.
16. IRC Report for 1969-70, p.15.
17. IRC Report for 1968-9, p.15.
18. Ibid.
19. IRC Report for 1969-70, p.13.
20. Ibid. For Villiers' view of BLMC, see *Banker's Magazine,* June 1975, p.19.
21. It may be this that Professor McClelland hints at in his reference (p.12) to the usefulness to the IRC of shareholders when working through the stimulation of third parties.
22. Others include C.A. Parsons/A. Reyrolle; BICC; Lucas; Nuclear Enterprises; and Kent.
23. Op. cit., HC 347 of 1971-2, Q 1194. Kent, RHP, Cammell Laird and Brown Bayley are all examples of companies where IRC was instrumental in the appointment of a new chief executive.
24. Examples include Kent, Rolls Royce, and Cammell Laird.
25. IRC Report for 1969-70, p.6.
26. See pp.15 and 12 respectively.
27. p.10.
28. IRC Report for 1969-70, p.13.
29. HC 347 of 1971-2, op. cit., Q 1741.
30. "Not until 1970 did the IRC decide to use its 25% of the Kent equity to insist on new management, and brought in Lutyens . . . At the same time the IRC withdrew the ban which it had imposed to prevent Kent from interfering with the Cambridge management." Keith Richardson, *Sunday Times,* 18 April 1971.
31. IRC Report for 1968-9, p.8.
32. IRC Report for 1967-8, p.5.
33. W. Davis, *Three Years Hard Labour,* p.52. Davis recalled this later: 810, HC Debs. col 348.
34. *The Times,* 10 November 1967, and *Financial Times,* 30 November 1967.
35. McClelland, op. cit., p.9.
36. 13 December 1969, p.64. See also *The Times,* 11 & 12 December 1969; *Guardian,* 27 June 1970; *Sunday Times,* 26 February & 12 March 1967.

Chapter 8

1. HC 347 of 1971-2, op. cit., Qs 974-6 and 1285.
2. The three firms were Clarke Chapman (CC), John Thompson (JT) and International Construction (IC). See IRC Reporf of 1968-9, p.12 and *Guardian,* 5 February 1974. In the meantime CC and JT had merged their engineering interests under IRC auspices (IRC Report of 1970-1, p.21.).
3. G. D. Newbould, *Management and Merger Activity,* Guthstead, Liverpool, 1971, see pp.122-46.
4. See for example *Management Today,* September 1967, p.88.
5. For different views see for example C.F. Pratten, 'Merger Boom in Manufacturing Industry,' *Lloyds Bank Review,* October 1968, pp.39-55; and *Financial Times,* 28 January 1970. This subject has spawned a vast literature – see Bibliography.
6. McClelland, op. cit., p.3.
7. IRC Report for 1969-70, p.6.
8. *The Times,* 18 January 1968. This idea failed: see p.210.
9. These two articles deal with the issues of monopolies and restrictive practices. There was also doubt about Article 67 which requires that all capital movements be free – see *Guardian,* 11 November 1969.
10. G. Turner, op. cit., *Business in Britain,* p.77.
11. IRC Report for 1968-9, p.8.
12. See for example R.E. Caves and Associates, *Britain's Economic Prospects,* George Allen and Unwin, London, 1968, p.321. (This book is widely quoted as the 'Brookings Report'.)
13. *Financial Times,* 19 February and *Guardian* 3 September 1974.
14. Article by Villiers in *The Times,* 22 May 1970.
15. D. Smith, op. cit., p.90. At that time John Davies was Director General of the CBI. He subsequently became Secretary of State for Trade and Industry in the Heath Government, 1970-2.
16. R. Spiegelberg, *The City: Power without Accountability,* Blond and Briggs, London, 1973, pp.55-68.
17. See *Guardian,* 23 October 1970.
18. This is HC 347 of 1971-2: The Sixth Report From The Expenditure Committee by its Trade and Industry Subcommittee. There is a report and two volumes of evidence from a wide range of people involved with the formulation and implementation of industrial policy in the late 1960s either from inside Whitehall, or at the level of the individual firm. It is probably the single most valuable document on the whole subject. The evidence up to 21 July 1971 was also published as HC 546 of 1970-1.

Chapter 9

1. 740, HC Debs. col 653. See also 739, HC Debs. cols 34-47 and G. Turner, op. cit., *The Leyland Papers,* pp.83-7.
2. *The Times,* 2 October 1967.
3. *The Economist,* 1 July 1967, p.41.
4. Quoted in *The Times,* 21 June 1967.
5. Ministerial changes were announced in the press on 29 August 1967.

6. Quoted in *Financial Times*, 19 July 1967. See 750, HC Debs. col 1716.
7. W. Davis, *Three Years Hard Labour*, p.54, and 753, HC Debs. col 1238.
8. See for example, *Financial Times*, 13 and 20 July 1967, and *The Times*, 29 January 1968.
9. See Lejeune, 'IRC: Friend or Foe', *The Director*, October 1967. See also *Sunday Times*, 23 June 1968.
10. G. Turner, op. cit., *Business in Britain*, p.78.
11. *The Times*, 21 June 1967.
12. IRC Report for 1968-9, p.9.
13. See *The Economist*, 14 February 1970, pp.61-2.
14. E.g. G. Turner, op. cit., *Business in Britain*, p.74.
15. 777, HC Debs. col 1299.
16. HC 347 of 1971-2, op. cit., Q413.
17. IRC Report for 1970-1, p.20.
18. Ibid.
19. This is made up of £80,472,000 worth of investments at 31 March 1970 (IRC Report for 1969-70, p.19.), £6,190,000 commitments at 31 March 1970 (IRC Report for 1969-70, p.32.); and the sums committed to Miles Roman (£211,000), Rolls Royce (£20 million); and Herbert Ingersoll (£2½ million). These were all known at the start of May.
20. Beesley and White, op. cit., p.84.
21. G. Brown, op. cit., p.94.
22. G. Turner, op. cit., *Leyland Papers*, p.112.
23. IRC Report for 1967-8, p.6.
24. IRC Report for 1969-70, p.12.
25. IRC Report for 1968-9, p.11.
26. HC 347, op. cit., Q 1740.
27. HC 347, op. cit., Q 1871.
28. *Financial Times*, 6 January 1969 (Finance for Industry Supplement).
29. IRC Report for 1968-9, pp.33-6; and *The Times*, 6 May 1970, and *Observer*, 18 October 1970.
30. IRC Report for 1968-9, p.8.
31. IRC Report for 1969-70, p.11.
32. IRC Report for 1968-9, p.32.
33. McClelland, op. cit., p.7.
34. IRC Report for 1968-9, p.13.
35. IRC Report for 1969-70, pp.11 and 25.
36. IRC Report for 1968-9, p.8.
37. Ibid., p.11.
38. IRC Reports for 1967-8, p.7, and for 1968-9, p.14.
39. IRC Report for 1968-9, pp.25 and 36.
40. HC 19 and 216 of 1969-70.
41. IRC Reports for 1968-9, pp.8 and 23, and for 1969-70, p.33.
42. IRC Report for 1967-8, p.18.
43. IRC Report for 1967-8, p.9.
44. IRC Report for 1968-9, p.33.
45. McClelland, op. cit., p.11.
46. IRC Report for 1968-9, pp.33-4.
47. IRC Report for 1967-8, p.9.

48. Ibid., p.11. See also *The Times,* 5 October 1968.
49. *The Times,* 6 March 1969.
50. IRC Report 1967-8, p.6.
51. IRC Report 1969-70, pp.11, 33 and 35.
52. See for example G.S. Minto, *Investment Analyst,* December 1969, pp.34-7 (a review article); and 'Should We Believe in Giants?', *The Economist,* 10 January 1970, p.13.
53. *The Times,* 1 August 1969.
54. W. Davis in *Merger Mania,* Constable, London, 1970, p.147.
55. S. Brittan, *The Price of Economic Freedom,* Macmillan, London, 1970, p.25.
56. *The Control of Monopoly,* Industrial Policy Group Paper No. 8, 1971.
57. See *Sunday Times,* 16 March 1969; *The Times,* 3 April 1969; and HC 42 of 1966-7 (The Monopolies Commission report on Ross/AF). By 1969 Crosland seemed to agree with the Commission's dissenting note, and with what the White Fish Authority had said about the advantages of a bigger fleet in 1966.
58. Cant, op. cit., p.45. See also Mergers, A Guide to Board of Trade Practice, paras. 65-6.
59. HC 347 of 1971-2, op. cit., Q 1705.

Chapter 10

1. *Sunday Times,* 16 February 1969.
2. See IRC Reports for 1969-70, p.14; and for 1970-1, pp.9-10.
3. IRC Report for 1969-70, p.13.
4. HC 347 of 1971-2, op. cit., Q 1807.
5. See for example 756, HC Debs. cols 472 and 1940; and 760, HC Debs. col 624.
6. See respectively, McClelland, op. cit., p.7; *The Times,* 24 April 1969 (Supplement on the QE2); and IRC Report for 1969-70, pp. 12 and 27.
7. IRC Report for 1969-70, p.13.
8. Beesley and White, op. cit., p.81, and IRC Report for 1968-9, p.8.
9. HC 347 of 1971-2, op.cit., Q 1741.
10. Ibid., Q 1742.
11. HC 347 of 1971-2, op. cit., Q 1807.
12. p.13.
13. Beesley and White, op. cit., p.81. They approach the problem of IRC's independence rather differently, laying greater stress for example on the importance of IRC's vaguely defined aims. Although they specifically deal with the basis of IRC's independence on pp.81-2, the subject is a recurring theme throughout their article.
14. *The Times,* 7 July 1970.
15. IRC Report for 1970-1, p.8. See Chapter 13.
16. E. Dell, *Political Responsibility and Industry,* Allen & Unwin, London, 1973, p.80.
17. See *Guardian,* 30 October 1967; *The Times,* 21 December 1968.
18. Beesley and White, op. cit., p.84.
19. See the first section of Chapter 9.
20. See IRC Report for 1968-9, p.26.

21. See *The Times,* 4 January 1969. In the end IRC did not have to give a view – IRC Report for 1969-70, p.13.
22. IRC Report for 1969-70, pp.13-14.
23. *The Times,* 2 February 1968, and 30 January 1969. See also W.W. Daniel, *Whatever happened to the workers at Woolwich?,* PEP Broadsheet, 537.
24. HC 347 of 1971-2, op. cit., Q 1271, "In the original remit by the Government to the IRC this whole problem of relations with labour, and of redundancies following rationalisation was very much stressed." (Grierson.)
25. *The Economist,* 25 March 1967, p.1170.
26. p.14.
27. *The Times,* 5 and 30 September 1968, 810, HC Debs. col 369.
28. *The Times,* 11 November 1967.
29. IRC Report for 1968-9, p.8.
30. IRC Report for 1968-9, p.14. See also IRC Report for 1969-70, p.13, and HC 347 of 1971-2, op. cit., Q 1271 (Mr. Duffy, one of the Sheffield MPs.)
31. IRC Reports for 1968-9, p.14; and for 1969-70, p.13. The DEA was involved too. See also *Report of 101st Annual Trades Union Congress,* September 1969, published by the TUC, pp.415-6, 418-9, 460-2.
32. See *The Times,* 12 February 1968, and *Sunday Times,* 1 June 1969.
33. 740, HC Debs. cols 629-61 (Rootes); and 768, HC Debs. cols 61-122 (Kent).

Chapter 11

1. Sir Keith Joseph, Opposition Spokesman on Technology in a speech at the Greater London Area Trade Union Advisory Committee Meeting, at Conservative Central Office, 24 January 1970.
2. Quoted by Iain MacLeod in *A Fresh Approach,* Conservative Political Centre (CPC), No. 327, p.80.
3. Sir Edward Boyle, *Conservatives and Economic Planning,* CPC, 1966, No. 335, p.11. See also John Pinder's contribution to *A Fresh Approach,* ibid.
4. Rt. Hon. Edward du Cann, *A Fresh Approach,* ibid., p.12.
5. R. Lewis, *A Bonfire of Restrictions,* CPC, 1965, No. 324.
6. *Government Expenditure and the Nationalised Industries,* CPC, 1967, No. 360, p.4.
7. *The Reform of the Civil Service,* CPC, 1968, No. 356, p.5.
8. Report of the Royal Commission on the Civil Service 1966-8, Cmnd 3658, 1968, Vol. I, para. 7.
9. Ibid., para. 147
10. Ibid., para. 190.
11. D. Howell, *A New Style of Government,* CPC, 1970, No. 463.
12. Ibid., p.26.
13. See *Denationalisation,* CPC, 1968, No. 423.
14. *A Better Tomorrow,* 1970 Conservative Election Manifesto, p.14.
15. Sir Keith Joseph, addressing The Young Conservatives National Advisory Committee, 7 March 1970.

16. *Fostering Enterprise*, CPC, 1968, No. 422.
17. Sir Keith Joseph, 7 March 1970, op. cit.
18. Ibid.
19. Ibid.
20. See for example *Guardian*, 26 January 1970.

Chapter 12

1. The Reorganisation of Central Government, Cmnd 4506, 1970.
2. D. Howell, op. cit.
3. For articles on the CPRS see *The Times*, 31 January 1972; and *Observer*, 18 July 1971. Pollitt, C., 'The Central Policy Review Staff' *Public Administration*, Winter 1974, pp.375-92.
4. Cmnd 4506, op. cit., para. 21.
5. Government Organisation for Defence Procurement, Cmnd 4641.
6. Joe Rogaly in the *Financial Times*, 16 October 1970.
7. Published 17 December 1971.
8. Sir Richard Clarke, *New Trends in Government*, Civil Service College Studies, HMSO, 1971, p.2.
9. The Chancellor's Mansion House speech, October 1970.
10. A distinction should be drawn between the NBPI set up by Labour and the Consumer Council established earlier by the Conservatives.
11. The Public Trustee Office, Cmnd 4913, 1972.
12. Cmnd 4564, 1971.
13. Quoted in the *Guardian*, 19 January 1971.
14. The hornets' nest of the customer/contractor principle in government R&D was raised by Lord Rothschild, leader of the CPRS, in 'The Organisation and Management of Government R&D'. See Cmnd 4814, 1971. See also R. Williams, 'Independence and Accountability after Rothschild', *R&D Management*, June 1972. MinTech had been moving in the same direction – op. cit., Clarke, *Omega*, pp.140-1.
15. D. McKie and C. Cook (ed.), *The Decade of Disillusion*, Macmillan, London, 1972, p.146.
16. See minutes of evidence of the sub-committees of the Select Committee on Science and Technology during the summer of 1972.
17. See McClelland, op. cit., p.16 (note 2); Beesley and White, op. cit., p.89; and speeches by Davies and Ridley – 810, HC Debs. cols 347-57 and 447-58 respectively.
18. See *The Times*, Diary section, 10 July 1972.
19. Cmnd 4942. For a fuller discussion see S.C. Young, 'How is the Industry Act Working Out?', *New Society*, 30 August 1973, pp.510-12.
20. See Chapter 16, note 11.
21. Cmnd 5178, Table 2.7 and paras 4-14.
22. Cmnd 4234.
23. See Cmnd 4578 and 4829 respectively.
24. *A New Style of Government*, op. cit., and *A Better Tomorrow*.
25. The National Federation of Builders and Plumbers Merchants

called for the NCB to sell T.H. Sankey, the builders' merchants, back to the private sector on the grounds that it represented unfair competition.

26. Lord Melchett, the then BSC Chairman, greeted it as "a good, sane, logical industrial solution to the problems that the steel industry has to face." *Financial Times,* 29 June 1971.
27. The *Guardian,* 29 June 1971.
28. Civil Aviation Policy Guidance, Cmnd 4899, 1972.
29. M. Barratt Brown and R. Pryke, *Stop Messing Them About,* Public Enterprise Group, 1971, p.16.
30. See for example C. Foster, *Public Enterprise,* Fabian Research Series No. 300, 1972; and his book, *Politics, Finance and the Role of Economics,* Allen and Unwin, London, 1972.
31. Nicholas Faith in the *Sunday Times,* 2 April 1972.
32. David Watt in the *Financial Times,* 4 December 1970.
33. See the *Sunday Times,* 20 January 1974.

Chapter 13

1. Quoted in *The Times,* 9 October 1970.
2. Nicholas Ridley, Under-Secretary of State at the DTI writing in the *Sunday Times,* 20 January 1974.
3. *Guardian,* 5 February 1971.
4. Third Report from the Public Accounts Committee, HC 447 of 1971-2, para 18 and references. There is no doubt that R-R believed it needed the contract. See also the evidence of Sir Denning Pearson, the then chief executive, in HC 347 of 1971-2, op. cit., Q 2035. The Ministry accepted R-R's own judgment on this, and therefore agreed to provide launching aid.
5. HC 347 of 1971-2, op. cit. Memorandum from Sir Denning Pearson and Sir David Huddie about the contract, pp.471-482. See also Q 2021ff. The two rival engines were General Electric's CF6 (being used in the McDonnel Douglas DC10), and Pratt and Whitney's JT9D (being used in Boeing's 747).
6. Ibid., Q 2042.
7. Ibid., Q 1899.
8. Quoted by Geoffrey Owen in *Financial Times,* 21 August 1973.
9. Geoffrey Owen, ibid. See also *Financial Times,* 22 August 1973.
10. HC 347 of 1971-2, op. cit., para. 74. See also Qs 2486 and 2488.
11. Ibid., Qs 1740-98. This covers the IRC's relations with Rolls.
12. See article by Geoffrey Owen in *Financial Times,* 22 August 1973. See also ibid., Qs 1204 and 1742.
13. HC 347 of 1971-2, op. cit., Qs 2667ff.
14. 807, HC Debs. cols 50-61.
15. See *The Times,* 26 October 1970 and 12 November 1970; and *Financial Times,* 12 November 1970.
16. HC 347 of 1971-2, op. cit., Q 2684.
17. Despite the publication of the White Paper, Rolls Royce Ltd., and the RB211 Aero-Engine, Cmnd 4860, January 1972.
18. HC 347 of 1971-2, op. cit., Q 2684.
19. 811, HC Debs. col 58.
20. Ibid.

21. 811, HC Debs. cols 100, and 998.
22. Price (Parliamentary Secretary) 811, HC Debs. 1041. See also 811, HC Debs. col 57 (Barber) and 812, HC Debs. col 1094 (Corfield).
23. See *Guardian,* 5 February 1971, for these three quotations.
24. Quoted in *Financial Times,* 5 February 1971.
25. See *Financial Times,* 3 August 1971.
26. See Cmnd 4860, op. cit., and HC 347 of 1971-2, op. cit., para 58.
27. The first plane was delivered to Eastern Airlines on 6 April 1972.
28. See Geoffrey Owen's two articles, op. cit.
29. Report of the Shipbuilding Inquiry Committee, 1965-6, Cmnd 2937.
30. HC 347 of 1971-2, op. cit., paras. 106-9.
31. Ibid., Qs 2163 and 2167.
32. Ibid., Q 2132.
33. *Guardian,* 29 December 1970.
34. HC 397 of 1968-9, pp.250-1.
35. HC 347, op. cit., Q 2314.
36. Ibid., para. 111.
37. Ibid., Qs 2110-2114.
38. 811, HC Debs. cols 808-13.
39. HC 447 of 1971-2, op. cit., published the DTI and Treasury advice in Appendix 2, pp. 415ff.
40 Agreement on this point had been reached in principle with the Labour Government.
41. 29 December 1970.
42. HC 347, op. cit., paras. 113-4 and footnotes.
43. The Report of the Advisory Group on Shipbuilding was published by HMSO in July 1971.
44. A copy of this was printed in A. Buchan, *A Right to Work,* Calder Boyars, London, 1972.
45. Clydebank, formerly John Browns, was the oldest and most outdated of the yards; and Scotstoun, formerly Connells, was the smallest of the yards.
46. The members of this committee were Professor Roy Illsley of Aberdeen University, Frank Cousins and Mr. G. Perry of General Motors.
47. See *Financial Times,* 26 August 1971.
48. Shipbuilding on the Upper Clyde, Report by Hill, Samuel and Co., Cmnd 4918.
49. See particularly the evidence of Mr. Hepper, Chairman of UCS, before the Committee, in HC 347 of 1971-2, op. cit., and the evidence of Mr. Douglas, Managing Director, before the Scottish TUC Committee of Enquiry. The latter's interim report was publsihed on 29 September 1971.
50. Evidence of Mr. L. Pliatsky, Under-Secretary at the Treasury, HC 347 of 1971-2, op. cit., Q 256. See also Q 257.
51. See *Guardian,* 14 June 1971, and *Observer,* 13 June 1971 respectively.
52. See HC 347 of 1971-2, op. cit., para. 101 and footnotes.
53. Speech to the Conservative Local Government Conference, 4 March 1972.
54. 832, HC Debs. col 52.

55. HC 347 of 1971-2, op. cit., para. 123.
56. HC 447 of 1971-2, op. cit., para. 8.
57. See especially *Guardian* and *Financial Times,* 7 July 1971.
58. 27 October 1971.
59. *The Times,* 5 May 1972.
60. R. Williams, op. cit., p.63.
61. *British Economy Survey,* Autumn 1971, p.11.
62. Ridley, op. cit.
63. See *The Times,* 19 August 1972; and *Guardian,* 26 August 1971, and 19 August 1972.
64. Industry Act 1972, Annual Report 1972-3, HC 429 of 1972-3, pp.8 & 11.
65. See *Trade and Industry,* 31 March 1971, p.685 for example. See also *Financial Times,* 17 September 1973 Supplement on the Machine Tool Industry: much of what is described was also taking place during the 'disengagement' period.
66. See the Public Expenditure White Papers published in Janury 1971 (Cmnd 4578), and in December 1972 (Cmnd 5178). The figures are arrived at by adding up the assistance to the private sector given in each case in Table 2.7. The January 1971 figure has the assistance to the coal industry deducted, and with the December 1972 figure the assistance to the nationalised industries has been removed.

Chapter 14

1. M. Rees, *The Public Sector in The Mixed Economy,* Batsford, London, 1973, includes in Chapter 5 government equity holdings in private enterprise firms, as being in the public sector. Strictly speaking this is of course correct, but it is argued in Chapter 17 below that such a company is in the private sector because that company bears little relationship in practice to a nationalised corporation. BP for example in which the government has a 48.6% holding is regarded as a major firm in the private sector, and not a nationalised firm: see press 24 January and 21 May 1975.
2. Public Expenditure in 1963-4 and 1967-8, Cmnd 2235, 1963. Para. 24 says that of the £665 million for assistance to industry, transport and agriculture, £495 million is for purposes outside the private sector of industry. The research councils, Northern Ireland and the nationalised industries have been excluded from these and the following figures.
3. Public Expenditure, Planning and Control, Cmnd 2915, 1966. See Table 1 and para. 28.
4. Public Expenditure to 1978-9, Cmnd. 5879, 1975. Table 2.4 Trade, Industry and Employment, with the exclusion of compensation to the nationalised industries for price restraint, and expenditure under the Coal Industry Act.
5. Ibid., Table 2.4 with nationalised industries assistance excluded.
6. Ibid. (see Table 3.1) and Cmnd. 2235 op. cit.
7. Strictly speaking this gave a new organisational structure to companies that were already publicly owned.
8. Annual Report of the National Institute for Economic and Social

Research quoted in *Financial Times,* 16 February 1973.
9. See Chapter 15.
10. The Financial and Economic Obligations of the Nationalised Industries, Cmnd 1337, 1961; and The Nationalised Industries: A Review of Economic and Financial Objectives, Cmnd 3437, 1967.
11. Lord Hirshfield conducted an enquiry into this subject in the autumn of 1972. See Press, 7 and 8 December 1972, and *Financial Times,* 30 November 1972.
12. *The Machine Tool Industry, Report of the Machine Tool Expert Committee* under the chairmanship of Sir Richard Way, DTI, 1970, p.94.
13. S. Blank, *Industry and Government in Britain,* D.C. Heath Ltd., Farnborough, 1973, p.233.
14. Clarke, *New Trends in Government,* p.7.
15. *New Statesman,* 24 July 1970. See also *New Technology,* April 1968, pp.1-2.
16. Clarke, *New Trends in Government,* pp.26-7.
17. Dr. P.E. Sherriff, 'Outsiders in a closed career', *Public Administration,* Winter 1972, pp.398 and 403.
18. See Fulton, op. cit., Vol. 1, Chapter 2, para. 36; and Brittan, *Steering the Economy,* p.39.
19. Dell, op. cit., p.75.
20. R. Boardman and A.J.R. Groom (eds.) *Britain's External Relationships,* Macmillan, London, 1972, p.182.
21. David Watt, Political Correspondent in *Financial Times,* 27 October 1972.
22. Quoted in *Engineer,* 24 August 1972, p.31.

Chapter 15

1. It is easy to think that inflation only became a problem in the early 1970s. However one commentator wrote in the mid-1960s: "The problems of inflation have plagued many economies besides the British over the past twenty years, but for us they have been particularly acute." H. Collins in R. Malik (ed.), *Penguin Survey of Business and Industry 1966,* Penguin, Harmondsworth, 1966, p.118.
2. The limit up to the early 1970s is shown by the largest sum ever raised in the City. This was £370 million raised by British Petroleum for North Sea oil development. It was then the largest wholly private bank loan raised anywhere in the world. See *The Times,* 31 October 1973, Supplement on Offshore Supply.
3. See *The Economist,* 3 June 1972, p.81, and 846, HC Debs. cols 831-2, and correction at col 1714.
4. See *Financial Times,* 17 September 1973, Supplement on the machine tool industry; Way Committee Report, pp.33, 45 and 116. See also HC 347 of 1971-2, op. cit., p.699.
5. Quoted by H. Stephenson, *The Coming Clash,* Weidenfeld and Nicolson, London, 1972, p.49.
6. Way Committee Report, p.iii. See also p.2.
7. Report of the Committee of Enquiry on Small Firms (Bolton Report), Cmnd 4811. See also *British Economy Survey,*

Spring 1972, pp.8-10.
8. Way Committee Report, pp.44-7. Cf. 833, HC Debs. col 1366.
9. See 845, HC Debs. col 2 (WA), and 847, HC Debs. col 283 (WA)
10. See *The Times,* 23 July 1971, and 29 December 1972; and Press, 22 December 1972.
11. R. Williams, op. cit., p.73.
12. Beesley and White, op. cit. This is suggested throughout their article.
13. E. Boyle, and A. Crosland, *The Politics of Education,* Penguin, Harmondsworth, 1971, p.179.
14. See N. Ridley, *Industry and the Civil Service,* Aims of Industry, 1973.

Chapter 16

1. B. Edwards, *Sources of Economic and Business Statistics,* Heinemann, London, 1972, p.91.
2. Ibid., p.265.
3. *British Shipbuilding 1972,* A Report to the DTI by Booz Allen and Hamilton International, HMSO, 1973.
4. Clarke, *Omega,* p.139.
5. Ibid., pp.138-44.
6. Press, 14 & 16 March 1972, and *Guardian,* 17 March 1972.
7. G. Turner, *The Leyland Papers,* pp.133-5 and 142-7.
8. Clarke, *Omega,* p.157.
9. Ibid., pp.159-60.
10. *The Economist,* 20 July and 12 October 1968, pp.60 & 86 respectively.
11. Sections 8(8), the inclusion of Section 9 (added at the Committee stage), and Section 9(4) respectively. On the CBI and backbench pressure see *The Times,* 16 June, 12 & 14 July 1972, and *Guardian,* 21 July 1972.
12. See for example Cmnd 5186, December 1972, p.7. This was the DTI reply to op. cit., HC 347 of 1971-2.
13. D.R. Shell, 'Specialist Select Committees', *Parliamentary Affairs,* Autumn 1970, p.404. See also HC 122 of 1972-3.
14. Cmnd 5186, op. cit., and Ibid., pp.396-400.
15. Dell, op. cit., p.120.
16. Ibid., pp.103-4.
17. See *The Economist,* 22 July 1972, p.80; and 21 October 1972, pp.70-1; and Press, 18 July 1972.
18. *Financial Times,* 18 and 21 September 1973.
19. Edwards, op. cit., pp.22-6, 82-3 and 101-2.
20. Booz Allen, op. cit., p.6.
21. Dell, op. cit., pp.104-5.

Chapter 17

1. *The Economist,* 23 February 1974, p.81.
2. *The National Enterprise Board, Labour's State Holding Company,* Report of a Labour Party Study Group, published by the Labour Party, London 1973.
3. See for example the evidence of Sir Anthony Part, Permanent Secretary at the DTI, in March 1972: HC 447 of 1971-2, op. cit., Q 1548. See HC 303 of 1974, para 44 for Whitehall's late position.

4. See for example op. cit., HC 347 of 1971-2 Paras 228 and 256-9 and footnotes.
5. Quoted in H.E.R. Catherwood, *Britain With The Brakes Off,* Hodder and Stoughton, London 1966, p.158.
6. See for example HC 347 of 1971-2, op. cit., Chapters 7-9; Dell, op. cit., pp.214-20; Beesley and White, op. cit., pp.86-9; and W. Friedmann and J.F. Garner, *Government Enterprise,* Stevens, London, 1970.
7. Clarke, op. cit., *Omega,* p.152.
8. Ibid.
9. Ibid., p.151.
10. Ibid.
11. HC 447 of 1971-2, op. cit., Q 1548, sub-para 9.
12. Clarke, *Omega,* p.151.
13. Press, 6 November 1970.
14. Press, 16 March 1972, 20 October 1972, 19 December 1972 and 17 April 1973. See also *Sunday Times,* 17 December 1972.
15. D.F. Channon, *The Strategy and Structure of British Enterprise,* Macmillan, London, 1973.
16. *The Economist,* 10 March 1973, p.82.
17. See footnote 2 above; Chapter 6, footnote 40; article in the *Guardian,* 24 May 1973 by Stuart Holland, a member of the Study Group; and HC 347 of 1971-2, op. cit., Vol. II, Appendices 22 and 23.

APPENDIX A DIARY OF THE MAIN IRC PROJECTS

1967

During 1967 the IRC conducted a number of enquiries for various government departments. These included telecommunications, steel, the financial condition of Cunard, and proposals to build aluminium smelters. See the IRC Report and Accounts (December 1966–March 1968), HC 252 of 1967-8, pp.10-11 and 17. (This Report is subsequently referred to as the IRC Report for 1967-8.) On telecommunications see also the Press for 6 January 1967 and 27 July 1968: *The Economist,* 14 January 1967, p.152 and 13 January 1968, p.57; and *The Times,* 12 October 1967; on steel see the *Sunday Times,* 26 February and 12 March 1967; on Cunard see *The Times,* 29 April 1969 (Supplement on QE2); and on the aluminium smelters see *The Times,* 3 May 1968, and Dell, op. cit., pp.109-17.

January — *Rootes Motors.* The Government agreed to allow Chrysler to extend its minority holding in Rootes on certain conditions. One of these was that at least 15% of Rootes' equity capital was to be held by shareholders other than Chrysler. The IRC took up a holding of this size investing £1,662,228 in the company. See the IRC Report for 1967-8, pp.17 and 22; and the IRC Report and Accounts for the year ended 31 March 1969, HC 286 of 1968-9, p.30. (This Report is subsequently referred to as the IRC Report for 1968-9.) See also 699 HC Debs., cols 36-41, and 739 HC Debs, cols 34-47; 740 HC Debs, cols 629-61; interview with Wedgwood Benn in the *Sunday Times,* 22 January 1967; *The Economist,* 21 January 1967, p.239; and G. Turner, op. cit., *The Leyland Papers,* pp.83-7. Chrysler subsequently bought this holding: see the Press, 5 and 7 December 1972.

June — *English Electric/Elliott Automation.* The IRC supported a merger between two companies that were mainly involved in electronics and provided a loan of £15 million. See Chapter 6, footnotes 10-13. In addition see the IRC Report for 1967-8, pp.17-18; *The Times,* 23 June 1967, and 10 July 1967; the *Sunday Times,* 25 June 1967; and *The Economist,* 24 June 1967, p.1376. See also the IRC Report and Accounts for the year ended 31 March 1970, HC 310 of 1969-70, p.31. (This Report is subsequently referred to as the IRC Report 1969-70); and the IRC Report and Accounts for the period from 1 April 1970 to 30 April 1971, HC 443 of 1970-71, p.24. (This Report is subsequently referred to as the IRC Report for 1970-71.)

September — *GEC/AEI.* The IRC had tried to bring about an agreed merger between these two in the spring of 1967. The scheme was dropped because of AEI's opposition, but GEC reopened the possibility of a link in September 1967 by making an outright takeover bid for AEI. This move was supported by the IRC Board. Despite the opposition of the AEI Board, GEC's bid was ultimately successful. See Chapter 6, footnotes 14-18. See also the IRC Report for 1967-8, p.18; R. Jones and O. Marriott, op. cit., especially Chapter 15; Sir Joseph Latham, op. cit.; and *The Times,* 13 October 1967.

October — *Dunford and Elliott/Hadfields.* The IRC supported Dunford's bid for another special steels company. See IRC Report for 1967-8, pp.10 and 18.

December — *Nuclear Enterprises.* The IRC supported the acquisition by Nuclear Enterprises of three companies in the scientific instruments field, and provided a loan of £600,000. See *The Times,* 6 December 1967; and the IRC Reports for 1967-8, pp.10 and 18-19; and for 1968-9, p.30.

1968

January — *BLMC.* The IRC supported an agreed merger between British Motor Holdings and Leyland Motors, and provided a loan of £25 million. See the IRC Reports for 1967-8, pp.19-20; and for 1968-9, pp.26-7. See also W. Davis, op. cit., *Merger Mania,* Chapter 7; G. Turner, *The Leyland Papers,* op. cit. especially Chapters 7 and 8; Press, 18 January 1968; and the *Sunday Times* and *Observer,* 21 January 1968.

January — *British Oxygen.* The IRC supported British Oxygen's successful offer for Edwards High Vacuum, and subsequently made a loan of £2½ million to the company. See the IRC Reports for 1967-8, pp.10 and 19; and 1968-9, p.23.

February — *Reed Paper Group.* The IRC made a loan of £1½ million to Reed to help finance two plants to de-ink and reconstitute printed paper. See *The Times,* 1 February 1968; and the IRC Reports for 1967-8, pp.20 and 23; for 1968-9, p.23; and for the 1969-70, p.31. More generally on paper and board see the IRC Report for 1968-9, p.13 and the *Guardian,* 13 March 1970.

April — *The International Compressed Air Corporation.* The IRC supported a merger between Broom and Wade, and Holman in the compressed air industry. See the IRC Report for 1968-9, pp.13 and 23; and for 1969-70, p.29.

June — *George Kent/Cambridge Instruments.* Rank made a bid for Cambridge Instruments and Kent put in a counter bid. Rank topped this. The IRC supported a second bid from Kent, and when Rank topped this again, the IRC purchased Cambridge and Kent equity in the market. Kent's last offer was successful and the Corporation ended up with 24.9% of the Kent equity. See the IRC Report for 1968-9, pp.10-11, 23 and 31; and W. Davis, op. cit, *Merger Mania,* pp.136-9. See also the *Sunday Times,*

1 November 1970 and 18 April 1971; and the *Financial Times,* 4 May 1973.

June — The IRC investigated the functions of the Army Kinema Corporation and the Royal Air Force Cinema Corporation for the Ministry of Defence, and recommended their amalgamation. See IRC Report for 1968-9, p.21.

July — *Peter Dixon.* The IRC made a loan of £350,000 to help finance a plant to de-ink and reconstitute paper. See IRC Report for 1968-9, pp.24 and 39.

July — *Nuclear Power Construction.* The Minister of Technology asked the IRC to implement its report on the structure of this industry. Accordingly the IRC helped established TNPG and BNDC. See IRC Report for 1968-9, pp.11-12 and 24; for 1969-70, p.32; and for 1970-71, pp.23-4. See also the Fourth Report of the Select Committee on Science and Technology, HC 401 of 1968-9, which deals with the IRC's involvement with this industry.

September — *GEC/EE.* Plessey announced a takeover bid for EE in August and sparked off a chain of events in which the IRC was prominently involved, leading ultimately to a merger between GEC and EE. See the IRC Report for 1968-9, pp.10, 25 and 32-6; and R. Jones and O. Marriott, op. cit., Chapter 16.

1969

January — *Studebaker-Worthington/Worthington-Simpson.* The IRC supported a merger between these two companies in the pump industry. See the IRC Report of 1968-9, pp.13 and 26; and *The Times,* 4 January 1969. This was one of several mergers in pumps. See the IRC Reports for 1968-9, p.25; and for 1970-71, p.18. More generally see article by A.K. Panni (Chapter 4, footnote 35).

January — *Brown Bayley Ltd.* The IRC made a successful offer for this company at a cost of approximately £5,818,000. The importance of Brown Bayley Ltd. was that it had a controlling interest in both a special steels company (Brown Bayley Steels), and in a ball-bearing company (Hoffmann Manufacturing). See the IRC Reports for 1968-9, pp.11, 27, and 37-8; and for 1969-70, p.22.

February — *Clarke Chapman.* The IRC supported a series of acquisitions by this company in the crane industry and provided a loan of £2 million. See the IRC Reports for 1968-9, p.28; and for 1969-70, pp.26-7.

March — *Dobson-Park.* The IRC played a prominent part in the merger between two companies manufacturing mining machinery – Dobson Hardwick and William Park. See the IRC Report for 1968-9, pp.13 and 29. For other mergers in this sector see the IRC Reports for 1969-70, pp.9, 25 and 29; and for 1970-71, p.6. See also *The Times,* 3 February 1969.

March — *Bacon Curing Industry.* The IRC undertook a study of this sector for the Ministry of Agriculture, Fisheries and Food. See IRC Reports for 1968-9, p.29; and for 1969-70, pp.12 and 27. See also *The Times,* 22 July 1969.

April *Rowentree/Mackintosh.* The Corporation supported a merger between these two companies, after General Foods, a multinational, had put in a bid for Rowntrees. See the IRC Report for 1969-70, pp.12 and 23; and *The Times,* 10 January 1969.

April *Allied Textiles/H.F. Hartley.* The IRC supported a merger between these two companies and made a loan of £1 million. See the IRC Reports for 1969-70, pp.11 and 23. On this sector see also the IRC Reports for 1967-8, pp.9-10 and 19; and for 1968-9, p.17. See also the *Observer,* 15 December 1968, and *The Times,* 17 December 1968.

May *RHP.* In the autumn of 1968 the IRC decided to aim at creating a major British-owned ball-bearings company made up of Ransome and Marles, Hoffman, and Pollard. The Corporation subsequently managed to block a bid for Ransome and Marles from Skefko (the British subsidiary of the Swedish multinational SKF). Attempts to bring Skefko into the IRC's discussions on the future of the industry floundered over the issue of control. The IRC's successful takeover of Brown Bayley (see above) put it in a stronger position, because it was then able to control Hoffmann. However, Pollard announced in April 1969 that Skefko, was to take a 15.6% interest in Pollard. The IRC reacted by supporting a bid for Pollard from Ransome and Marles, and a revised bid was in fact successful. The Corporation spent just under £9½ million to secure the creation of Ransome/Hoffmann/Pollard. In November 1970 it also provided standby credit of £1 million. See the IRC Reports for 1969-70, pp.8, 23-4 and 33-6; and for 1970-71, p.24. See also *The Times,* 31 January, 13 May and 14 October 1969; the *Sunday Times,* 9 February, 18 May and 8 June 1969; and the supplements on ball-bearings in the *Guardian,* 31 March 1971, and in the *Financial Times,* 30 October 1972. Finally see the Press, 20 May 1972.

July *British United Trawlers.* The fishing fleets of the Ross Group and Associated Fisheries were brought under joint management with the creation of this firm. The land-based interests of these two firms remained quite separate. See the IRC Reports for 1968-9, pp.12 and 29; and 1969-70, pp.11 and 24-5; and Chapter 9, footnote 57. See also *The Times,* 1 October 1968, and 3 April and 13 May 1969; and the *Sunday Times,* 16 April 1969.

July *Davy Ashmore.* A City consortium made £5 million available to Davy. £1,200,000 of this rescue operation came from the IRC: it was repaid within twelve months. The need for this finance arose from unexpected delay and losses on the contract to build a refinery at Immingham. See the IRC Reports for 1969-70, p.26 and for 1970-71, p.24; *The Times,* 30 July 1969, and 28 January 1970; the Press, 11 August 1970; the *Observer,* 3 August 1969; and the *Sunday Times,*

15 February and 25 October 1970. The IRC was involved with Davy on other occasions: see IRC Reports for 1967-68, p.21; for 1968-69, p.24; and for 1970-71, p.12.

September *BTR/Leyland Birmingham.* The IRC supported an agreed merger between two companies which manufactured general rubber goods. See IRC Report for 1969-70, pp.11 and 27.

December *Plessey Numerical Controls.* The Corporation played an important role in building up this company in the NC sector of machine tools. Plessey first acquired Airmec-AEI from Racal Electronics and then bought Ferranti's NC interests. A loan of £3 million was made to Plessey. See the IRC Report for 1969-70, pp.9 and 28-9. See also C. Layton, *Ten Innovations,* Allen and Unwin, London, 1972, Chapter 12.

1970

January *Reed/IPC.* The Corporation's role in this merger was to help the DEP by holding talks with Reed, IPC, and Bowater, Bowater being Reed's principal competitor in the supply of newsprint to IPC. Guidelines were established by which IPC was not to discriminate in favour of Reed when purchasing newsprint. See *The Times,* 31 January 1970; and the Press, 25 February 1970.

January *Klinger/Qualitex.* The IRC supported a merger between Klinger and Qualitex in the yarn bulking industry. Ernest Scragg acquired Klinger's machinery assets, and it was basically the Qualitex management that was left in charge of the new group. The IRC made a £2 million loan to Qualitex. See IRC Report for 1969-70, pp.11 and 29-30; *The Times,* 6 February 1970; and the *Guardian,* 9 and 24 March 1970.

February *Samuel Osborn.* The IRC announced that it was providing this special steels company with a loan of £1,750,000 to help finance the building of a new plant at Ecclesfield, near Sheffield. See the IRC Report for 1969-70, pp.30 and 39; *The Times,* 12 February 1970; and the *Guardian,* 8 July 1970. On the IRC and special steels more generally, see *The Times,* 7 February, 11 August and 12 December 1969; the *Guardian,* 27 June and 11 December 1969; and the *Sunday Times,* 2 November 1969, and 6 June 1971.

March *Marwin.* The Corporation agreed to provide this machine tool firm with up to £1½ million to assist with expansion. See IRC Reports for 1969-70, pp.30-31, and for 1970-71, p.24.

May *Miles Roman.* The Corporation agreed to provide this computer software firm with a loan of up to £211,000. See the IRC Report for 1970-71, pp.7 and 18.

May *Rolls Royce.* Following the completion of its report for the Minister of Technology, the IRC was asked to implement its proposals with regard to Rolls Royce. A loan of

£10 million was made to the company. See the IRC Report for 1970-71, pp.8, 19, and 25-6; and Chapter 13.

May *Herbert/Ingersoll.* A loan of £1 million, with standby credit amounting to an additional £1½ million was made available to these two machine tool firms for a joint project. See the IRC Report for 1970-71, pp.6, 19 and 26.

June *BLMC.* Quite separately from its other loan to BLMC, the IRC lent the company £10 million as a revolving loan to purchase machine tools. See Chapter 6, footnote 28; and *The Times,* 1 June 1970.

June *Cammell Laird.* The IRC was asked to help the Government implement the report it had completed on the problems of this shipbuilding and engineering firm. Arrangements costing just over £6 million were put in hand to bridge a liquidity crisis, and a longer-term programme was drawn up. See the IRC Reports for 1969-70, p.12; and for 1970-71, pp.8-9 and 20. See also the Press, 8 May 1970; the *Guardian,* 5 June 1970; the *Observer,* 18 October 1970; and *Financial Times,* 12 December 1972.

June *Clarke Chapman/John Thompson.* The Corporation supported a merger of these two heavy engineering companies, and made a loan of £5 million available the following January. See the IRC Report for 1970-71, pp.6 and 21.

Autumn *Textile Re-equipment Scheme.* This was designed to encourage investment amongst smaller and medium-sized companies in this industry. Four loans totalling £2,300,000 were made to Harwood Cash, Perseverance Mill, Highams, and Ventona/Hartley. See the IRC Report for 1970/71, pp.8 and 22-3; and *The Times,* 5 November 1970.

December *Kearney and Trecker.* £300,000 was made available for expansion to this machine tool firm, the amount being matched by another loan from the Midland Bank. See the IRC Report for 1970-71, pp.6, 23 and 26.

1971/2

On abolishing the IRC, the Conservative Government aimed to dispose of the IRC's investments. Progress up to April 1973 is outlined in the following Written Answers: 819, HC Debs. cols 13-16; 826, HC Debs cols 27-30; 836, HC Debs. cols 463-6; 847, HC Debs. cols 233-6; and 858, HC Debs. cols 111-2.

ABBREVIATIONS

AEA	Atomic Energy Authority
AEI	Associated Electrical Industries
AF	Associated Fisheries
BAC	British Aircraft Corporation
BEA	British European Airways
BLMC	British Leyland Motor Corporation
BMH	British Motor Holdings
BNDC	British Nuclear Design and Construction
BOAC	British Overseas Airways Corporation
BOTAC	Board of Trade Advisory Committee
BSA	Birmingham Small Arms
BSC	British Steel Corporation
CBI	Confederation of British Industry
CEGB	Central Electricity Generating Board
CIR	Commission on Industrial Relations
COI	Central Office of Information
CPC	Conservative Political Centre
CPRS	Central Policy Review Staff
CSEU	Confederation of Shipbuilding and Engineering Unions
DEA	Department of Economic Affairs
DoE	Department of the Environment
DSIR	Department of Scientific and Industrial Research
DTI	Department of Trade and Industry
EA	Elliott Automation
EDCs	Economic Development Committees
EE	English Electric
EFTA	European Free Trade Area
EMI	Electrical and Musical Industries
GEC	General Electric Company
H & W	Harland and Wolff
ICL	International Computers Ltd.
IDAB	Industrial Development Advisory Board
IDCs	Industrial Development Certificates
IDE	Industrial Development Executive
IDU	Industrial Development Unit
IRC	Industrial Reorganisation Corporation
IRI	Institute for Industrial Reconstruction (an Italian organisation – see Chapter, 6 footnote 40)
ITBs	Industrial Training Boards
LEAFAC	Local Employment Act Finance Advisory Committee
MC	Monopolies Commission
MDHB	Mersey Docks and Harbours Board
MinTech	Ministry of Technology
NBPI	National Board for Prices and Incomes
NC	Numerical Control (for machine tools – see Chapter 2, footnote 7)

NCB	National Coal Board
NCC	National Computing Centre
NEDC	National Economic Development Council
NEDO/ NED Office	National Economic Development Office
NEL	National Engineering Laboratory
NPL	National Physical Laboratory
NRDC	National Research Development Corporation
PAC	Public Accounts Committee
PERA	Production Engineering Research Association
RAs	Research Associations
R&D	Research and Development
REP	Regional Employment Premium
RHP	Ransome Hoffmann Pollard
RR	Rolls Royce
SCST	Select Committee on Science and Technology
SET	Selective Employment Tax
SIB	Shipbuilding Industry Board
TNPG	The Nuclear Power Group
TUC	Trades Union Congress
UCS	Upper Clyde Shipbuilders
VTOL	Vertical Takeoff and Landing

SELECT BIBLIOGRAPHY

1. Government, Industry, and Industrial Policy in Britain

(a) Books

Abraham, N., *Big Business and Government: The New Disorder*, Macmillan, London, 1974.

Alexander, K.J.W., and Jenkins, C.L., *Fairfields*, Penguin, London, 1970.

Allen, G.C., *Monopolies and Restrictive Practices*, Allen and Unwin, London, 1968.

Allen, G.C., *The Structure of Industry in Britain*, Longmans, London, 3rd edition, 1970.

Bailey, R., *Managing the British Economy*, Hutchinson, London, 1968.

Barbash, J., *Trade Unions and National Economic Policy*, John Hopkins Press, London, 1972.

Beacham, A., and Cunningham, N.J., *Economics of Industrial Organisation*, Pitman Publishing, London, 5th edition, 1970 (Bibliography).

Beckerman, W. (ed.), *The Labour Government's Economic Record 1964-70*, Duckworth, London, 1972.

Bray, J., *Decision in Government*, Gollancz, London, 1970 (Bibliography).

Breckon, W., *The Drug Makers*, Eyre and Methuen, London, 1972.

Brittan, S., *Capitalism and the Permissive Society*, Macmillan, London, 1973.

Brittan, S., *Steering the Economy*, Penguin, Harmondsworth, revised edition, 1971.

Broadway, F.E., *State Intervention in British Industry 1964-8*, Kaye and Ward, London, 1969.

Brown, G., *In My Way*, Penguin, Harmondsworth, 1972.

Burgess, T. (ed.), *Matters of Principle: Labour's Last Chance*, Penguin, Harmondsworth, 1968.

Cairncross, Sir Alec (ed.), *Britain's Economic Prospects Reconsidered*, Allen and Unwin, London, 1971.

Cairncross, Sir Alec, *Essays in Economic Management*, Allen and Unwin, London, 1971.

Cairncross, F. and McRae, H., *Capital City*, London, Methuen, 1972.

Catherwood, H.F.R., *Britain with the Brakes Off*, Hodder and Stoughton, London, 1966.

Caves, R.E. (ed.), *Britain's Economic Prospects*, Allen and Unwin, London, 1968 (Brookings Report).

Channon, D.F., *The Strategy and Structure of British Enterprise*, Macmillan, London, 1973 (extensively footnoted on individual companies).

Channon, D.F., Stopford, J., and Norburn, D., *Business Policy in Britain*, Macmillan, forthcoming.

Clarke, Sir Richard, *New Trends in Government*, Civil Service College Studies, HMSO, 1971.

Confederation of British Industry, annual reports.

Confederation of British Industry with the Association of British Chambers of Commerce, Report of the Commission of Enquiry into Industrial and Commercial Representation (Devlin Report), 1972.
Conference of Industrial Research Associations, *Industrial Research and Development,* Report of the Committee of Enquiry into the Research Associations 1972-3 (Bessborough Report).
Costello, J., and Hughes, T., *Battle for Concorde,* Compton Press, Salisbury, 1971.
Davis, W., *Merger Mania,* Constable, London, 1970.
Davis, W., *Three Years Hard Labour,* Andre Deutsch, London, 1968
Dell, E., *Political Responsibility and Industry,* Allen and Unwin, London, 1973.
Denton, G., Forsyth, M., and MacLennan, M., *Economic Planning and Policies in Britain, France and Germany,* Allen and Unwin, London, 1968.
Dow, J.C.R., *The Management of the British Economy 1945-60,* Cambridge University Press, 1964.
Dunning, J.H., and Thomas, C.J., *British Industry,* Hutchinson, second edition, 1963.
Edwards, R., *Sources of Economics and Business Statistics,* Heineman, London, 1972.
Fairley, P., *Project X: The Exciting Story of British Invention,* Mayflower, London, 1970.
Fels, A., *The British Prices and Incomes Board,* Cambridge University Press, 1972.
Frank, W.F., *The Legal Aspects of Industry and Commerce,* Harrap, London, fourth edition, 1966.
Friedmann, W., and Garner, J.F., *Government Enterprise,* Stevens, London, 1970.
Grant, W.F., and Marsh, D., *The Confederation of British Industry,* Hodder and Stoughton, forthcoming.
Glyn, A., and Sutcliffe, B., *British Capitalism, Workers and the Profits Squeeze,* Penguin, Harmondsworth, 1972.
Grove, J.W., *Government and Industry in Britain,* Longmans, London, 1962.
Harris, N., *Competition and the Corporate Society: British Conservatives, the State and Industry, 1945-64,* Methuen, London, 1972.
Hays, S., *The Engineering Industries,* Heineman, London, 1972.
Hodges, M., *Multinational Corporations and National Government,* Saxon House, Farnborough, 1974.
Langrish, J., Gibbons, M., Evans, W.G., and Jevons, F.R., *Wealth from Knowledge,* Macmillan, London, 1972.
Lapping, B., *The Labour Government 1964-70,* Penguin, Harmondsworth, 1970.
Jones, R., and Marriott, O., *Anatomy of a Merger: A History of GEC, AEI, and English Electric,* Jonathan Cape, London, 1970
Knight, A., *Private Enterprise and Public Intervention,* Allen and Unwin, London, 1974 (paperback).
Malik, R., *What's Wrong with British Industry?,* Penguin, Harmondsworth, 1964.
McGill, J., *Crisis on the Clyde,* Davis-Poynter, London, 1973.
Meyer, F.V., Corner, D.C., and Parker, J.E.S., *Problems of a Mature Economy,* Macmillan, London, 1970
Miles, C., *Lancashire Textiles, a Case Study of Industrial Change,*

Cambridge University Press, 1968.
Mitchell, J., *The National Board for Prices and Incomes,* Secker and Warburg, London, 1972.
Moonman, E., *Reluctant Partnership,* Gollancz, London, 1971.
Newbould, G.D., *Management and Merger Activity,* Guthstead, Liverpool, 1971.
Prest, A.R. (ed.), *The UK Economy. A Manual of Applied Economics,* Weidenfield and Nicolson, London, 3rd edition, 1970.
Reed, A., *Britain's Aircraft Industry. What went Right? What Went Wrong?* J.M. Dent, London, 1973.
Rees, M., *The Public Sector in the Mixed Economy,* Batsford, London, 1973.
Samuels, J.E.S. (ed.), *Readings on Mergers and Takeovers,* Acton Society Trust, Elek, 1972.
Sanderson, M., *Universities and British Industry 1850-1970,* Routledge and Kegan Paul, London, 1972.
Seldon, A., *Rebirth of Britain,* Pan, in association with the Institute of Economic Affairs, London, 1964.
Servan-Schreiber, J-J, *The American Challenge,* Hamish Hamilton, London, 1968.
Skuse, A., *Government Intervention and Industrial Policy,* Heineman, London, 2nd edition, 1972.
Smith, B.L.R., and Hague, D.C., *The Dilemma of Accountability in Modern Government,* Macmillan, London, 1971.
Smith, R., and Brooks, D., *Mergers,* three volumes, The Acton Society Trust, London, 1963.
Smith, T., *Anti-Politics,* Charles Knight, London, 1972.
Society of Business Economists, *Changes in the Industrial Structure of the UK,* Unwin, 1970.
Society of Business Economists, T.M. Rybczynski (ed.), *A New Era in Competition,* Basil Blackwell, Oxford, 1973.
Spiegelberg, R., *The City: Power Without Accountability,* Blond and Briggs, London, 1973 (Bibliography).
Sutherland, A., *The Monopolies Commission in Action,* Cambridge University Press, 1969.
Trades Union Congress, Annual Reports.
Turner, G., *Business in Britain,* Penguin, Harmondsworth, revised edition, 1971.
Turner, G., *The Leyland Papers,* Eyre and Spottiswoode, London, 1971.
Turpin, C., *Government Contracts,* Penguin, Harmandsworth, 1972.
Taylor, C.T., and Silberston, Z.A., *The Economic Impact of the Patent System,* Cambridge University Press, 1973.
Vice, A., *The Strategy of Takeovers,* McGraw Hill, London, 1971.
Vig, N., *Science, Technology and British Politics,* Pergamon, Oxford, 1968.
Watts, B.K.R., *Industry and Finance,* McDonald and Evans, London, 1971.
Wiggs, R., *Concorde,* Pan, London, 1971.
Wilson, J.H., *The Labour Government 1964-70,* Weidenfeld and Nicolson and Michael Joseph, London, 1971.

(b) Pamphlets and Articles

Adamson, C., 'The Role of the Industrial Adviser', *Public Administration,* Summer 1968, pp.185-190.
Allen, G.C., 'State Intervention: The Economic Dilemma', *Economic*

Age, vol. 1, pp.13-17.
Balogh, T., *Labour and Inflation,* Fabian Tract No. 403.
Balogh, Lord, 'Governments and the North Sea', *Banker,* 1974, pp.1065-7.
Beesley, M.E., and White, G.M., 'The Industrial Reorganisation Corporation: A Study in Choice of Public Sector Management', *Public Administration,* Spring 1973, pp.61-89.
Branton, R., 'Reconstructing British Industry', *Banker,* October 1966, pp.699-707.
Boswell, J., *Can Labour Master the Private Sector?,* Fabian Research Series No. 271.
Cant, B.R., *Britain's Economic Problems in International Historical Perspective,* Centre for Business Research, Manchester Business School. See also a report on a seminar on this in the *Financial Times.* 23 January 1973.
Catherwood, Sir F., 'Why Neddy Survived', *Lloyds Bank Review,* April 1971, pp.3-16.
Caulkin, S., 'The Merger Aftermath', *Management Today,* February 1975, pp.58ff.
CBI, *Industry and Government,* 1974.
Channon, D.F., *Strategy and Structure of Management in Private and Public Industry,* Aims of Industry, 1974.
Chataway, C., *New Deal for Industry,* Conservative Political Centre, 1972.
Clarke, Sir R., 'Mintech in Retrospect', *Omega,* vol.I, 1973, pp.25-38 and 137-63.
Clarke, Sir R., *The Ministry of Technology and Industry,* published by the Foundation for Business Responsibilities (formerly the Industrial, Educational and Research Foundation), Seminar Paper.
Clarke, Sir R., 'The Structure of Mintech,' *New Technology,* February 1968.
Counter-Information Services, *Anti-Report on GEC,* 1972.
Davies, J., 'Industry and Government', *Three Banks Review,* June 1967, pp.16-28.
Dean, Sir M., 'The Ministry of Technology', *Public Administration,* Spring 1966, pp.43-60.
Edwards, C. and L., *Concorde: Ten Years and a Billion Pounds Later,* Pluto Press, London, 1972.
Fraser, T.C., 'Economic Development Committees – A New Dimension in Government-Industry Relationships', *Journal of Management Studies,* 1967, pp.154-67.
Foundation for Business Responsibilities, *Industry: Its Relationship with Government and Parliament,* a symposium.
Grant, W.P., and Marsh, D., 'The Confederation of British Industry', *Political Studies,* 1971, pp.403-15.
Grant, W.P., and Marsh, D., 'The Politics of the CBI: 1974 and After', *Government and Opposition,* Winter 1975, pp.90-104.
Hindley, B., *Industrial Mergers and Public Policy,* Institute of Economic Affairs, Hobart Paper No. 50.
Howell, D., 'The Rocky Road to Government Reform', *Management Today,* September 1974, p.58ff.
Industrial Policy Group, *The Structure and Efficiency of British Industry,* Paper No. 6.

Jewkes, J., *Government and High Technology,* Institute of Economic Affairs, Occasional Paper No. 37.
Johnson, P.S., 'The Development of the Hovercraft in the United Kingdom', *Three Banks Review,* December 1974, pp.28-45.
Lejeune, A., 'IRC: Friend or Foe', *Director,* October 1967, pp.99-101.
Lester, T., The Unmaking of Mintech' *Management Today,* November 1973, p.91ff.
McClelland, W.G., 'Government/Business Relations in the UK' in Beesley, M.E., and Hague, D.C. (eds.), *Britain in the Common Market: A New Business Opportunity,* Longmans, London, 1974, pp.149-66.
McClelland, W.G., 'The IRC 1966-71: 'An Experimental Prod', *Three Banks Review,* June 1972, pp.32-42. This was also published as a pamphlet by the Manchester Statistical Society in 1972.
Midgley, J., 'How Much Control do Shareholders Exercise?', *Lloyds Bank Review,* October 1974, pp.24-37.
Midland Bank Review, 'Special Arrangements for Financing Exports', unsigned article, August 1972, pp.3-10.
Owen, W., 'Competition and Industrial Structure', *Trade and Industry,* 22 March 1973, pp.586-8 (see in this connection *The Economist,* 31 March 1973, p.62).
Papps, I., *Government and Enterprise,* Institute of Economic Affairs, Hobart Paper No. 61, 1975.
Powell, Sir Richard, *Industry and Government,* Third Sir George Earle Memorial Lecture, published by the Foundation for Business Responsibilities, 1968.
Radice, G., and Ebsworth, R., 'Life Among the Little Neddies', *Management Today,* March 1966, p.107ff.
Roll, Sir E., 'The Department of Economic Affairs', *Public Administration,* Spring 1966, pp.1-12.
Roy, D., *State Holding Companies,* Young Fabian Pamphlet No.40, 1974.
Sandford, C.T., 'Is Planning Back in Fashion?', *Banker,* 1974, pp.33-6.
Shanks, M., 'The Irregulars in Whitehall', in Streeten, P. (ed.), *Unfashionable Economics: Essays in Honour of Lord Balogh,* Weidenfeld and Nicolson, London, 1970.
Shell, D.R., 'Specialist Select Committees', *Parliamentary Affairs,* Autumn 1970, pp.380-404.
Shone, Sir R., 'The National Economic Development Council', *Public Administration,* Spring 1966, pp.13-28.
Smith, D., 'What the IRC Wrought' *Management Today,* October 1969, p.91ff.
Sutherland, A., 'The Management of Mergers Policy', in Cairncross, Sir A. (ed.), *The Managed Economy,* Basil Blackwell, Oxford, 1970.
Utton, M.A., 'Future Prospects for Mergers Policy', *Bankers Magazine,* September 1970, pp.123-8.
Vaughan, G.D., 'Economic Development Committees', *Public Administration,* Winter 1971, pp.363-84.
Villiers, C., 'The IRC', *Investment Analyst,* December 1969, pp.3-7.
Williams, R., 'Independence and Acountability After Rothschild', *R & D Management,* vol. 2, No. 3, pp.131-5.
Wilsher, P., Articles on the IRC in the *Sunday Times (Business News),* 23 June 1968, and 16 February 1969.
Young, S.C., 'How is the Industry Act Working Out?', *New Society,* 30 August 1973, pp.510-12.
Young, S.C., 'Reshaping Industry: the IRC in Retrospect', *New Society,* 19 November 1970, pp.906-8.

See the press following the publication of Cmnd. 5710 on 15 August 1974; and the announcement about BLMC on 25 April 1975. In addition see the following feature articles in the *Financial Times:* 31 July 1974; and 6, 9, 14, and 29 January, 21 February, 7 March, 30 April, and 10 and 19 June 1975. See *The Times* (Business Section) features page for 17 May, 4 July, and 16 September 1974; and 13 13 January, 13 and 16 May, and 4 June 1975. The *Guardian* published relevant articles on 28 June, 25 October and 7 December 1974; and 28 April 1975; the *Sunday Times* (Business News) did so on 5 May 1974; and 2 and 23 February 1975; and the *Observer* did on 29 September 1974; and 19 January and 29 May 1975.

Branton, N., 'Regeneration by NEB?', *Banker,* January 1975, pp.13-5.

(c) Official Publications

Annual Reports. Many government organisations produce these, outlining their activities and patterns of expenditure. Examples include the Highlands and Islands Development Board, the various industrial research establishments like NEL, the IRC, the Industrial Training Boards, the Northern Ireland Finance Corporation, and the NRDC. Annual Reports are also published outlining the ways in which the powers granted to government departments in connection with specific Acts of Parliament have been used. Examples include the 1968 Industrial Expansion Act, the 1972 Industry Act, the 1965 Redundancy Payments Act, and the 1970 Sea Fisheries Act.

British Leyland: The Next Decade, HC 342 of 1974-5 (Ryder Report).

Committee on the Civil Service, Report, 5 vols. Cmnd. 3638, 1968 (Fulton Committee).

Committee of Enquiry into the Aircraft Industry, Report, Cmnd. 2853, 1965 (Plowden Committee).

Committee of Enquiry into the Machine Tool Industry, Report, DTI, HMSO, 1970 (Way Committee).

Committee of Enquiry into the Shipbuilding Industry, Report, Cmnd. 2937, 1966 (Geddes Committee).

British Shipbuilding 1972, A Report to the DTI by Booz-Allen and Hamilton International BV, HMSO, 1973 (Booz-Allen Report).

Committee of Enquiry into Small Firms, Report, Cmnd. 4811, 1971 (Bolton Committee).

Estimates Committee, *6th Report,* HC 365 of 1967-8.

Expenditure Committee, *6th Report,* Trade and Industry Sub-Committee, *Public Money in the Private Sector,* 3 vols., HC 347 of 1971-2.

Expenditure Committee, *2nd Report,* Trade and Industry Sub-Committee, *Regional Development Incentives,* 2 vols., HC 85 of 1973-4 (see also HC 327 of 1972-3 – Evidence).

Framework for Government Research and Development, Cmnd. 4814, 1971.

Framework for Government Research and Development, Cmnd. 5046, 1972.

Hansard.

Industrial Expansion, Cmnd. 3509, 1968.

Industrial and Regional Development, Cmnd. 4942, 1972.

Industrial Reorganisation Corporation, Cmnd. 2889, 1966.

International Conference on Monopolies, Mergers and Restrictive

Practices, Heath, J.B. (ed.), DTI, HMSO, 1971 (extensively footnoted on these subjects).
Mergers: A Guide to Board of Trade Practice, Board of Trade, HMSO, 1969.
Ministry of Technology (1967), Ministry of Technology.
Ministry of Technology (1969), Ministry of Technology.
Ministry of Technology (1970), Ministry of Technology.
Neddy in Print, NEDO (one easy means of tracing NEDO publications).
PAC, *Third Report*, HC 303 of 1974.
Public Accounts Committee, *2nd Report*, HC 273 of 1971-2.
Public Accounts Committee, *3rd Report*, HC 447 of 1971-2.
Public Money in the Private Sector: Government Observations on HC 347 of 1971-2, Cmnd. 5186, 1972.
Regeneration of British Industry, Cmnd. 5710, 1974.
Reorganisation of Central Government, Cmnd. 4506, 1970.
Research and Development 1972-3, DTI Report, HMSO, 1973.
Rolls Royce Ltd. and the RB211 Aero Engine Contract, Cmnd. 4860.
Select Committee for Science and Technology (SCST), *The UK Nuclear Power Industry*, HC 401 of 1968-9.
SCST, *The UK Computer Industry*, HC 137 and 272 of 1969-70.
SCST, *The Prospects for the UK Computer Industry in the 1970s*, HC 361 of 1970-71.
SCST, *UK Space Activities*, HC 629 of 1970-71.
SCST, *The Non-Reactor R&D Activities of the AEA*, HC 294 of 1971-2.
SCST, *Industrial Research Establishments of the DTI*, HC 302 of 1971-2.
SCST, *Offshore Engineering*, HC 313 of 1974-5.
Survey of Mergers 1958-68, DTI, HMSO, 1970.
Technical Services for Industry, DTI, various editions.

2. Broader Issues

Aaronvitch, S., and Sawyer, M.C., *Big Business*, Macmillan, London, 1975.
Allen, G.C., *Economic Fact and Fantasy*, Institute of Economic Affairs, Occasional Paper No. 14.
Archibald, G.C. (ed.), *The Theory of the Firm: Selected Readings*, Penguin, Harmondsworth, 1971.
Bannock, G., *The Juggernauts: The Age of the Big Corporation*, Penguin, Harmondsworth, revised edition 1973.
Bannock, G., 'Professor Galbraith and British Industry', *Business Economist*, Autumn 1974, pp.137-45.
Cohen, C.D., *British Economic Policy, 1960-69*, London, Butterworths, 1971.
Devine, P.J., Jones, R.M., Lee, N., Tyson, W.J., *Introduction to Industrial Economics*, Allen and Unwin, London, 1974.
Friedmann, W., (ed.), *Public and Private Enterprise in Mixed Economies*, Stevens, London, 1974.
Galbraith, J.K., *The New Industrial State*, Penguin, Harmondsworth, 1969.
Gilbert, M. (ed.), *The Modern Business Enterprise: Selected Readings*, Penguin, Harmondsworth, 1972 (extensive Bibliography).

Goodman, E., *The Impact of Size,* Acton Society Trust, 1969.
Hayward, J.E.S., and Watson, M., (eds.), *Planning, Politics and Public Policy: the British, French and Italian Experiences,* Cambridge University Press.
Heclo, H., and Wildavsky, A., *The Private Government of Public Money,* Macmillan, London, 1974.
Holland, S. (ed.), *The State as Entrepreneur,* Weidenfeld and Nicolson, London, 1972.
Unter, A. (ed.), *Monopoly and Competition: Selected Reading,* Penguin, Harmondsworth, 1969 (extensive Bibliography).
Industrial Policy Group, *Economic Growth, Profits and Investment,* Paper No. 10.
Kempner, T., Macmillan, K., and Hawkins, K., *Business and Society,* Allen Lane, London, 1974.
Kidron, M., *Western Capitalism Since the Way,* Weidenfeld and Nicolson, London, 1968.
Livingstone, J.M., *The British Economy in Theory and Practice,* Macmillan, London, 1974.
Lloyd, B., 'Invention, Innovation and Size', *Moorgate and Wall Street Journal,* Autumn 1970, pp.35-62.
Manchester Business School Library, *Bibliography No. 10, Mergers and Acquisitions.*
Mansfield, E. (ed.), *Monopoly Power and Economic Performance: The Problem of Industrial Concentration,* W.W. Norton, New York, revised edition, 1968.
Marris, R., and Wood, A., *The Corporate Society,* Macmillan, London, 1973.
Mishan, E.J., *Twenty-one Popular Economic Fallacies,* Penguin, Harmondsworth, 1973.
Newbould, G.D., and Jackson, A.S., *The Receeding Ideal,* Guthstead, Liverpool, 1972.
Ovenden, K., *The Politics of British Steel,* London, 1975.
Peter, L.J., and Hall, R., *The Peter Principle,* Pan Books, London, 1970.
Philips, L., *Effects of Industrial Concentration,* Amsterdam, North Holland, 1971.
Reid, S.R., *Mergers, Managers and the Economy,* McGraw Hill, New York, 1968.
Roberts, E., *Workers Control,* Allen and Unwin, London, 1973.
Sampson, A., *A New Anatomy of Britain,* Hodder and Stoughton, London, 1971.
Samuels, J., *Readings on Mergers and Takeovers,* Elek, London, 1972.
Shanks, M., *The Innovators,* Penguin, Harmondsworth, revised edition, 1971.
Sharpe, M.E., *John Kenneth Galbraith and the Lower Economics,* Macmillan, London, 1973.
Shonfield, A., *Modern Capitalism,* Oxford University Press, Oxford, 1965.
Smith, T., 'Politics, Economics, and Political Economy', *Government and Opposition,* Summer 1973, pp.263-79. (extensively footnoted).
Stephenson, H., *The Coming Clash: The Impact of the International Corporation on the Nation State,* Weidenfeld and Nicolson, London, 1970.
Tivey, L., *Nationalisation in British Industry,* Jonathan Cape, London, revised edition, 1973 (Bibliography).

Tugendhat, C., *The Multinationals*, Penguin, Harmondsworth, 1973 (Bibliography).
Turner, L., *Invisible Empires: Multinational Corporations in the Modern World*, Hamish Hamilton, 1970 (Bibliography).
Utton, M.A., *Industrial Concentration: Selected Readings*, Penguin, Harmondsworth, 1970 (extensive Bibliography).
Utton, M.A. 'Measuring the Effects of Industrial Mergers', *Scottish Journal of Political Economy*, February 1974, pp.13-28.
Vernon, R., *Sovereignty at Bay: the Multinational Spread of US Enterprises*, Longmans, London, 1970 (extensive Bibliography).
Williams, R., *European Technology*, Croom Helm, London, 1973.
Williams, R., *Politics and Technology*, Macmillan, London, 1971 (Bibliography).
Winch, D., *Economics and Policy: A Historical Survey*, Fontana, London, 1972.
Young Fabian Steel Group, *Crisis in Steel*, Young Fabian Pamphlet, No 38, 1974. See also pages 210, 238, and 239-46.

3. Digests, Abstracts and Other Reference Materials

The following are amongst the most useful means of keeping abreast both of what happens, and of what is written about it. Most of the following are published regularly through the year.

Anbar, Management Services Index, published in London by Anbar Publications Ltd.
British Economy Survey, published by the Oxford University Press.
British Technology Index, issued by the Library Association of London.
Business Periodicals Index, published in New York by H.W. Wilson Ltd.
Current Contents in Management, published by the Manchester Business School Library.
Economics and Management, published by the University of Aston's Social Sciences Library in Birmingham.
Fletcher, J. (ed.), *The Use of Economics Literature*, Butterworth, London, 1971.
Government Publications List. HMSO publishes an indexed annual list of all government publications to replace the various lists issued through the year.
Research Index, published by Business Surveys Ltd. of Wallingford, Surrey.
Trade and Industry, published weekly by HMSO, and subsequently indexed. It brings together government announcements on industrial policy, and is especially useful in that it enables one to avoid searching through unindexed parts of Hansard.

INDEX